P9-DXJ-616

I DON'T KNOW HOW TO BE A
WIDOW

MY JOURNAL OF FAITH AND HOPE

I DON'T KNOW HOW TO BE A
WIDOW

MY JOURNAL OF FAITH AND HOPE

BRENDA BROWN

21ST CENTURY
PRESS
CHRISTIAN PUBLISHING WITH A PURPOSE
WWW.21STCENTURYPRESS.COM

I Don't Know How to be a Widow

Copyright © 2003 *by Brenda Brown*
I can be contacted at brendabus@comcast.net

Published by 21st Century Press
Springfield, MO 65807

All rights reserved. No part of this book may be used or reproduced in any manner whatsoever or stored in any database or retrieval system without written permission except in the case of brief quotations used in critical articles and reviews. All scripture quotations are from The King James Version. Requests for permissions should be addressed to:

21st Century Press
2131 W. Republic Rd.
PMB 41
Springfield, MO 65807

ISBN 0-9717009-7-4

Cover: Chris Hartzler
Book Design: Lee Fredrickson and Terry White

Visit our web-site at: 21stcenturypress.com
                           and 21stcenturybooks.com

For childrens books visit: sonshippress.com
                           and sonshipbooks.com

21ST CENTURY
PRESS
CHRISTIAN PUBLISHING WITH A PURPOSE
WWW.21STCENTURYPRESS.COM

Dedication . . .

I would like to dedicate this book, first to **God, Jesus Christ, and the Holy Spirit:** Each of you, in your own way, have given me a reason to live, love, and keep on going – not just once but twice. May you be glorified in the pages of this book!

To two wonderful church bodies – **Capital Baptist Church** of Annandale, Virginia, and **New Life Baptist Church** of Fredericksburg, Virginia: Your pastors and your members have ministered to me in more ways than I can mention here. May God continue to bless and grow His churches for His glory.

To the **Washington Regional Transplant Consortium** (especially Lisa Colaianni, my donor family advocate), **Co. 8 Volunteer Fire Department and Rescue Station of Annandale, Virginia,** to the **Mary Washington Hospice Center** and the **Hospice Center of No. Virginia.** Each one of these organizations helped in so many ways. Thank you!

To my **Family and Friends!** I am so thankful to my two sons, (**Allen Fahey** and his wife, **Lisa**) and **Steve Fahey** (and his fiancée, **Lesley**). When God gave you to me, He gave me the best children in the whole world! You have been there for me from the night your father died. Your love and support held me up so many times. I am so proud of all of you! (And, Allen and Lisa, thanks for making me a grandma! **Justin** and **Tyler** are so incredible!) **Don** and **Judy**, thanks for being there for me. Don, you may not even know that I feel this way, but from the time we were growing up together, I always felt loved and protected by my older brother. Thank you for the stability that continued feeling brings. I love talking to you, Judy. You're always looking for the good in everything! Thank you!

To each of **Billy's family** and **friends!** When God brought Billy and I together, he brought me a whole new family! **Paula**, you are very special to me! (I waited for a sister for over fifty years!!!) **Jimmy** and **Kathleen, Mary Jane** and **Ralph, Frank** and **Nancy, Kenny** and **Diana, Billy** and **Sherry,** and **Victor** and **Glenda:** brothers, sisters, friends… you all have been so wonderful to accept me. Your children have blessed me beyond measure!

To **Chris Hartzler:** Chris, you took a title and an idea and turned it into an incredible cover! So many times, I've felt like running away. You captured the feelings from my very heart. Thank you!

And, I want to say a very special "Thank you!" to **Lee Frederickson, Terry White,** and **21st Century Press.** Lee, you believed in my journey through Grief…and, you accepted me as a client. You guys have played a very special part in getting this book of encouragement out to more than I could ever have managed. May God bless you and continue to grow your ministry!

Contents

Introduction 11

PART ONE I Don't Know How To Be A Widow 13

Chapter 1 - 3/20 - 4/19/1995
The Journey Begins 15

Chapter 2 - 4/20 - 5/19/1995
Who Am I? 25

Chapter 3 - 5/20 - 6/19/1995
Beginning To Move On 31

Chapter 4 - 6/20 - 7/19/1995
A New Happiness Begins To Set In 37

Chapter 5 - 7/20 - 8/19/1995
Real Loneliness Hits As I Look To The Future 45

Chapter 6 - 8/20 - 9/19/1995
Grief Becomes So Familiar 61

Chapter 7 - 9/20 - 10/19/1995
The Six-Month Mark – It's Over Now (Isn't It??) 77

Chapter 8 - 10/20 - 11/19/1995
Life Is Precious – Even Muff-Up's 93

Chapter 9 - 11/20 - 12/19/1995
It's Time To Give Thanks 105

Chapter 10 - 12/20/1995 - 1/19/1996
1995 Comes To An End 115

Chapter 11 - 1/20 - 2/19/1996
I'm Such A Yo-Yo! Up...Down...Up 123

Chapter 12 - 2/20 ~ 3/19/1996
    Every Emotion I've Felt So Far Is Revisited 135

Chapter 13 - 3/20/1996
    A Day of Celebration and A Few Letters 143

Chapter 14 - 3/21 ~ 5/19/1996
    The Black Hole 151

Chapter 15 - 5/20 ~ 7/19/1996
    It's That Yo-Yo Thing Again 155

Chapter 16 - 7/20 ~ 10/19/1996
    God's Waiting Room 161

Chapter 17 - 10/20/1996 ~ 1/19/1997
    Eagles Soar and So Can A Widow 167

Chapter 18 - 1/26 ~ 5/25/1997
    Year Two Comes To An End - Life Continues 181

PART TWO - Thanks For The Dance, Billy 193

Chapter 19
    Joy Unimaginable ~ An Update from 2001 195

Chapter 20 - 10/2~10/9/2001
    Ignorance is Bliss 203

Chapter 21 - 10/13~10/31/2001
    Our Lives Are Forever Changed 207

Chapter 22 – 11/1~11/30/2001
    I Am So Blessed To Be Here 215

Chapter 23 – 12/1~12/31/2001
    I Find A New Focus 219

Chapter 24 – 1/1~1/31/2002
It's 2002 and I Still Have My Billy! 227

Chapter 25 – 2/1~2/28/2002
Am I Ready To Lose Him? Yes...No 235

Chapter 26 – 3/1~3/19/2002
Memories of Billy 241

Chapter 27 – 3/20~3/26/2002
Billy's Home 251

Chapter 28 – 3/27~3/31/2002
A Heavy Sigh and Those First Few Steps 255

Chapter 29 – 4/1~4/30/2002
Starting Over - Again 259

Chapter 30 – 5/1~5/18/2002
They ask, 'Are You Okay?' I answer, 'Yes...No' 271

A Closing Note 275

Appendix 281

Introduction

HOW DO YOU SURVIVE THE LOSS OF THE ONE DEARER TO YOU THAN ANY OTHER ON EARTH?

"I Don't Know How To Be A Widow"
I kept saying these words the night Ron died.

I just couldn't imagine myself a widow. The night Ron died I began doing what came naturally - journaling. As time went on I began to share my journal with others; many suggested that I get it published.

Ron and I had a wonderful life together. Ron was a great husband and father AND he was a great confidant, friend, and protector for me. (Okay! Let go of my arm! He was human - he had some faults too!) Ron loved the Lord and we loved being in church together.

Go with me as I open the door that spring evening to find my life forever changed. Find out what day to day living is like without the one closest to me to share it. See the spiritual journey that Ron's death took me on and how I've won victories (and recovered from some losses) with the power of God shining through. You'll see how laughter was a part of my survival and how God had given me some very special blessings to help in the days that would follow March 20. Learn how I handled making decisions (big and small), how to budget, holidays, being followed by someone I didn't even know and so much more. You'll find more of a story of how I've survived than a "how you should do this" book. I'm still in school on the subject of how to be a widow. Please remember this is a journal and it's written as such. All the grammar and words may not be "correct" but to change everything would take away from the way the feelings and thoughts flowed.

I found a new appreciation for eagles in the second year. One of my favorite verses in the Bible is one that God showed me when Ron was out of work for several months before we moved to Indiana.

"But they that wait upon the LORD shall renew their strength; they shall mount up with wings as eagles; they shall run, and not be weary; and they shall walk, and not faint" (Isaiah 40:31).

I had heard a lot about the valleys and mountain tops but never heard anyone talk about soaring like the eagle. The freedom that comes from the passage of time and of the lessening of the deep, unrelenting Grief really helped me feel like a soaring Eagle. Things are clearer ~ easier to see from the vantage point of the Eagle. Eagles and Angels ~ they both fly. I think about the flight Ron took the night he died. I think about my journey as a flight ~ on the wings of an eagle!

I don't know how many angels came to our home that night. God, in His infinite wisdom looked down from Heaven and said, "Ron, my son ~ come home." There was no arguing (as he'd probably done with his earthly Father as a child). He didn't respond, "Oh, Dad, in just a minute." No, there was no hesitation or bargaining. He simply said, "Yes, Father," and went Home. That's when God must have held up His hand as the angels began to rise to carry Ron Home. As He instructed some to continue with Ron He knew what I was to face just a short time later. I'm convinced that He must have left angels behind to minister to me. Again, I don't know how many but there had to be more than one because I was cared for so gently, so lovingly ~ and so very completely.

I can't tell you that I saw the angels. I can't even tell you that I felt their presence, but isn't this the only thing that makes sense? How in the world could my focus at that moment be on heavenly things? I remembered praying for God to be glorified. A couple of years later, in a casual conversation my closest friend, Jan told me I had called her after calling the paramedics and asked for her to pray for me not to dishonor God in this but to bring Him glory. What I thought was a prayer had been a call ~ a reaching out to a friend I knew I could count on to pray for me. Scoff if you will, but I believe in angels!!! And, they continued to care for me into the second year.

Part One

I Don't Know How To Be A Widow

My Journal of Faith and Hope

It's the first day of spring ~ March 20, 1995. I'm going to the ladies' meeting at our new church tonight. Ron gets home before me so he's going to have the steaks going. But, as I enter the apartment, I realize immediately that something is wrong...

Chapter One

3/20 ~ 4/19/1995

The Journey Begins

Tuesday, 3/21/95 (1:30 a.m.)

I came home last night and found Ron in our bedroom. He apparently died about an hour before I got home.

I don't understand and I don't know how to be a widow. At forty-five, I'm certainly too young to fit the role.

So many emotions: a touch of uncertainty as I face the next few months without him. He was such a comfort when Mom and Dad died. *Who will hold me in the middle of the night now?*

I've donated his corneas, heart valves, and skin tonight. (It was too late for anything else.) I hate to think of them "harvesting" those things but what a blessing to think that through our loss, others may see.

Thursday Morning, 3/23/95

God's grace is sufficient! It's been hard these last two days. *(Can it only be two days?)* I've been to the pits of words like loneliness, denial, frustration, anger. I thought about the word fear. While I may have felt that emotion as I realized something was wrong with the picture as I opened the door Monday night, I can honestly say that I don't fear my tomorrow's. Oh — there's a tidal wave building and heading straight for me — I can see it but I refuse to run from it. I will stand with my God before me, on both sides of me, behind me, over me, under me, IN me. With such a total covering of protection

how could I ever be destroyed? God will not prevent the tidal wave
of pain from hitting me, but He has prepared me and He will let
this horrible pain through only as I can stand it. I know I must not
run from these feelings and emotions. I can only heal if I do so
from the inside out. God joined Ron and me together twenty-six
and a half years (to the day) before he left me.

Time stood still Monday night at 6:05 p.m. As I unlocked the
door, Muffin wasn't running to greet me — Ron wasn't on the sofa
smiling as I entered our home. What was immediately clear was
that to my left a light was on in our bedroom and to my right was
the sound of water running in the kitchen. You'd have to know Ron
to understand the instant confusion of this picture. He never in our
twenty-six and a half years left the light on in a room he left and
he never left a faucet running.

I called Muffin, knowing in my heart that she must be dead
and Ron was with her in the bedroom. She was given two weeks to
live a month and a half ago. Yet, as I called, I heard her whimper.
I went to the kitchen to find the gate still up (Ron always took her
out when he got home) and the hot water running in the sink. As
I reach down to open the gate for Muffin I stare at the running
water — *something's wrong*. I let her out and walk back in the living room. I call for Ron. I continue towards the light in the bedroom and, as I come into view of the bed, I see the drawer where
Ron keeps his exercise shorts opened. I look to my right — *the
computer/exercise room door is closed* — the light is out.

Then, time stood still, my heart stopped, and the deepest
denial possibly known to man entered my soul as I entered the
room and saw Ron kneeling on my side of the bed, his arms to the
side and his face deep into the waterbed. I see the empty milk glass
on top of the air filter. I hear the filter running. I feel the breeze
through the opened window. I hear the kids playing basketball. I
notice the bed I made an hour after Ron left for work this morning is unmade and, as I run to his side, calling his name, from the
depths of instant knowing — instant denying that with his face
buried in the bed there's no way he can be alive — I know that he's

dead. I've seen death before but I never realized what it really looked like. What the lack of any activity of the body breathing — the muscles contracting and expanding as all of those bodily functions of breathing, blood pumping, and the very Spirit of God living in us looked like. Death of the physical body is impossible to ever be acted effectively in my eyes again. Physical death is impossible to imagine. Our very soul is gone. The part of us that keeps all those bodily functions going leaves this shell we're in completely still. It also leaves the body very heavy. I now know the reality of the term "dead weight" as I try so hard to raise Ron from the bed. Just to lift his head and turn it to the side takes a tremendous effort. I try to raise his shoulders...I can't. I try to turn him over...I can't. I turn to call 911 (wondering why ~ yet, not knowing what else to do). *I wonder if I'll pass out.* I keep trying to waken Ron. I slap his face gently *(don't they always do this to wake people up?!!)* I cry from my heart, "Ron, wake up — please wake up! O, God, please let him wake up!" His back and shoulders are cold (he doesn't have a shirt on.) Yet, his face is still warm. It doesn't make sense. Surely those purple lips that have kissed me so passionately so many times will open and begin to breathe. Surely those eyes will open as he laughs and says, "Gotcha good this time!" *I'll kill him but I'll forgive him if only he will just wake up.* "Please, wake up, Ron!" I cry knowing it's hopeless.

911 is on their way. I've told them he's dead and now I'm trying to call the Pastor. I go to the living room to prop the door open so the paramedics can get in. *(Why aren't they here yet?!)* I go back to the bedroom to try once again to do the impossible — to wake him up before they come to take him from me.

The paramedics and the police come. The policeman comes to me — tells me how sorry he is, *(his care is so genuine — I know this can't be easy for him)* and, as they go into the bedroom, he guides me gently to the sofa and asks what happened. No — wait...I remember now — I go into the bedroom with the paramedics. I watch them check Ron and see the "TV" shake of the head and hear the most horrible words I could ever imagine - "I'm sorry." I'm in the living room with the officer explaining the procedures. He'll ask some questions, the criminal investigator will come, the ambulance will return to remove the body - do I want an autopsy? I tell him emphatically that I demand one. He tells me it's good I feel that way since one would probably be done "under the circumstances."

Several times while we're talking I just ignore the world and dial the phone. I get hold of Pastor Eagy. (Pastor Reynolds is out of town.) He's on his way. I asked if he'd take me to Ron's parents. *I wonder how I'll get to Steve and Allen.* I call Allen's and ask if Jerry's home. I want to tell him first so he can be prepared if Allen tries to leave. I ask Jerry to bring Allen to me. Steve and Angie are alone. I don't want them to be told alone, so I call Jay and June. They're not home so I leave a message to call me (not to call Angie) when they get in.

The detective shows up. They close the bedroom door. Flashbulbs are going off. *I'm so thankful that I've become a better housekeeper so I don't have to be embarrassed by a cluttered house.* (What a strange thing to think.) More flashes. I'm waiting for the "criminal" guy to ask me if I killed Ron. (*Why would they send a criminal investigator?* Don't they know I could never hurt the man I love so deeply?) I page Mike, cause I know I don't have the strength to go to College Park. Then, somewhere in the fog (in an order I can't remember now), I get hold of Jerry. I tell Allen that the father he loved so dearly — the father that was so proud of him is gone. Disbelief from him — concern for me — assurance that Jerry's bringing him to me.

Sometime in the fog, Pastor Eagy comes. I'm escorted to the kitchen because they don't think I should see Ron being taken out. *I remember Mom being wheeled out with her face covered up.* I listen to them cause they're the experts. If they say I don't need to see this, I'll trust them. *Is that when I turned the running water off?* June calls. I tell her what has happened and ask her and Jay to go to Angie and Steve and bring them to me. Disbelief from them — sorrow — and assurance they'll be here soon.

It's so late and Mom & Dad still aren't home. They're at a meeting at church. Mike is waiting for them. Karla is in shock – we all are. I don't like this…I don't know how to be a widow. I'm too young to be a widow! I don't understand. I keep saying that because I don't know what's happened.

Ron wasn't sick. I remember (and I'm thankful) that his wish was to go this way. How I wish I'd been with him, but God knows how much I can take. Apparently I wouldn't have been able to handle that or He would have arranged it.

I hated telling those Ron loved so much that he's gone.

Monday, 3/27/95

There have been SO many blessings in all of this. How my God's heart must have broken as He watched me turn the key in the lock last Monday night. I am so thankful for our faith. If I didn't have that, I would have a void left that couldn't be filled. I'd like to try to list all the blessings.

Ron died at home – not on the highway with others.

He didn't suffer. He passed out and died.

He didn't have to suffer horrible surgeries, etc.

There's no way (but one horrible test that they wouldn't have had any reason to do anyway) we could have found this problem so I don't have to be worried or mad at him for not having checkups.

I didn't call him that day as I usually did so he didn't tell me he wasn't feeling well. I would have been filled with guilt for not going home.

There's been some humor: a black wardrobe, Mike slapping me when I blacked out, "Where's the Spaceball?!"

I'll be out of debt.

We found Capital Baptist Church four weeks before Ron died.

All the people we visited recently or who visited us: Marilyn and Tony, Mike's birthday party, Pam and Howard's visit a couple of weeks ago, Brian and Linda's visit Friday night before he died, the Pastor and his family Saturday night.

He'd completed the taxes early this year.

He knew Christ!!!

During the last week of his life, we must have told each other a hundred times we loved each other. There's nothing to regret on what I "should" or "shouldn't" have said.

The Lord brought us back to this area so Steve and I aren't alone — away from family.

We're in a safe building. I don't "have" to move.

Before the paramedics ever got there I had turned everything over to God. When I went back into the room before the paramedics got there I remember standing by Ron, gently rubbing his shoulder and, through my tears, I asked God to be glorified through this — not to let me do anything that would bring Him dishonor. (I didn't remember this for a few weeks. I was praying one morning, thanking God for all the blessings, His grace, and His peace. I asked Him why He was blessing me so abundantly. It was then that I remembered these last few moments I'd had alone with "Ron" and God. It was as if God was telling me that because I'd put my faith and trust in Him from the very beginning He had picked me up and was carrying me.)

Wednesday, 3/29/95

So many people remind me of how young I am and how I'll remarry. Why do we, as a society see replacement of almost every living creature or person in our lives as the answer to grieving? Your dog dies — get another; your cat dies — get another; your child dies — have another; my husband dies so I'll just get another. For one thing, I don't have any intention of EVER feeling this kind of pain again. As deep as our love was, so is the pain of losing Ron. Our marriage was so perfect because we allowed each other to be imperfect and yet we stayed committed to our vows.

"My new life" — something I didn't ask for — something I could NEVER have imagined living. Yet, it's been forced upon me. Without God and His grace I couldn't have made it this far.

Friday, 3/31/95

Reality is setting in. Upon waking this morning I instantly thanked God for letting me finally wake up from the most horrible nightmare I've ever had *(it was SO real)*. I turned and reached to tell Ron..., but he wasn't there. It's not denial I've felt — just an empty hope that it's not real.

The thought of buying a home came to mind today. I found out that I can qualify. I called Debbie. We went to see several homes near work. I'll see Mom and Dad tomorrow and ask their opinion.

Monday Morning, 4/3/95

I returned to work this morning. There were cards and messages. Jeremy called me in and told me that he was amazed to see how, in the short time I've been at AMS, people were so touched by my loss and how dependent he'd become on me for all the little (and big) things I do for him. He wants me to know that I have nothing to fear about my job. He knows now, more than ever, how he's grown to depend on me. He told me to flex my time — that he'd work with me. The choir sang a song Sunday night about meeting again in the sweet by and by. I lost it and ran out. Renee was in the vestibule She held me and cried so hard herself. Then Debbie came out. We went into the bathroom and cried together. Everyone tells me what an inspiration I am.

Wednesday Evening, 4/12/95

Sunday is Easter. How thankful I am to our Lord who died for us. It's so much easier to bear my pain knowing that Ron is with the Lord. He's walking on those streets of gold tonight. People say that my pain, in the scope of time, is but a wink of the eye. So was Christ's. Yet, He cried sweat drops of blood, wanting to let His time pass another way. So, I carry on - one day (and night) at a time — shedding tears here and there along the way.

Thursday Morning, 4/13/95

I bought a condo Saturday. There's a feeling of walking out on Ron as I move towards buying a home. I haven't cried for two days – haven't felt like it.

It's raining today for the first time since Ron died. It reminds me of the trip we took in January to Luray Caverns. It had been raining for several days so there was a lot of water activity in the cave we hadn't seen before. We both agreed it was the best visit we'd ever had there. We've been doing things on the weekends. Ron had a sense of urgency on not "sitting" around wasting life. In February we went to Washington to site see. It was SO cold! We took the subway from Gallows Road — cost us $8.00 each! It had been years since we'd taken public transportation...we were so surprised at the cost!

People have been so wonderful to me! They call every night. One of the ladies brought me flowers last Wednesday night. Jeremy gave me a couple of very wonderful blessings yesterday. I stood in his office and almost cried. He's been so good to me.

When I think of a "widow," I imagine someone in their sixties or seventies — even older! But, here I am at forty-five, a widow, and God is fulfilling His Word about people caring for us! What a tremendous blessing!

We went to visit Ron's grave on Saturday. I really didn't feel anything as I looked at the mound of dirt. Ron is not in that grave. He's alive and doing well! I wouldn't wish him back to this earth for anything. Still, Mom and I cried. She had apologized last week for making me cry. I wish she really knew what a comfort it is for me to cry with her, of all people! She carried Ron in her body. I was the only person ever intimate with him. Of all the people in the world, I feel we knew him best. We need to cry together.

I don't believe I've given the coroner's findings in my journal yet. Ron died of a birth defect of his heart. The death certificate reads, "Ectopic origin right coronary artery (left Sinus of Valsalva)." It means that both arteries going into his heart went into the same chamber. When he died, his heart simply slowed until it stopped. As it slowed down, it caused the oxygen to his brain to be deprived, which explains the disorientation and confusion. There was no pain and no discomfort. What a blessing!! (It's a rare birth defect but, as far as they know, it's not inherited.)

Chapter Two

4/20 ~ 5/19/1995

Who Am I?

Friday, 4/20/95 (One month today)

I took Jamie home from church Sunday night. The car broke down. This totally scared me. I went home and called the guys. I called Debbie to see what impact buying a car would have on my loan. She reminded me of their mechanic in Fredericksburg which is 55 miles away. To make a long story short, the guys took me there Monday night.

The mechanic called yesterday to ask how far I'd driven the car since the light came on. I told him close to one hundred miles. He asked me what the red light said. We finally figured out that it was the engine light. He said he just didn't understand it cause there was not one drop of water in the radiator! I told him I could explain it — that I have a God who's watching over me.

Yesterday was the bombing of the Oklahoma City Federal building. How tragic. How my heart aches for all of those people. *So much sadness.*

Tuesday Evening, 4/25/95

I miss Ron so much tonight. There's an unreal permanency about this situation. I want for him to hold me so much. I want to go on a trip with him, to sit with his head in my lap just one more time *(ok — for the rest of my life)*. I just don't know how to cope. How do I go on without him?

Wednesday, 4/26/95 (lunch)

I realized this morning that the emotions I'm feeling are from finally beginning to actually "live" the fact that Ron is never coming back. I've been living with that fact, but, I believe I've been in shock until now. Except for the split second when I walked into the room and saw him, I have not experienced denial. Reality was complete in finding him.

Thursday, 4/27/95 (lunch)

I'm so glad I'm keeping this journal. It's good to see progress – and even to remember those first few moments, days, and weeks. It's still hard to believe this tragic thing has happened to me. Yet, why NOT me?! God never promised a life without pain. He promised to see me through whatever happens. He's kept that promise.

I'm reminded this week of another promise in God's Word that seems like He's let me down on. Ephesians 6:2-3 says, *"Honour thy father and mother; which is the first commandment with promise; That it may be well with thee, and thou mayest live long on the earth."* This scripture talks of respecting your parents and having a long life. Ron and I both had all our lives. As a matter of fact, I used this scripture to help the boys when a grandparent or someone else would die and they were concerned about Ron and I. I asked Pastor Reynolds about that and he admits he doesn't have a real good answer. *I'm glad he's honest!* Something to put in my "hum" box and study on. Maybe Ron did have a long life for someone with his birth defect. (I'll have to call the coroner.)

I do know that God has received a lot of glory through this. Why He chose me to glorify Him like this is beyond my comprehension, but I must say that it's only by His being with me that has brought Him glory. I'm reminded of what I wrote two days after Ron died about being surrounded by God's protection. Talk about the armor of God!!! Wow! I stand amazed...not at myself, but of

Him and His grace.

Monday, 5/1/95

Six weeks! When do I stop counting the weeks? When do I stop "noticing Mondays?!

Our Spring Jubilee began yesterday. Dr. Danny Lovett spoke. Last night he told us about losing his first wife and then a son from his second wife. He spoke of what I call the "TV shake of the head" and the, "I'm sorry." I literally poured my heart out at the altar. When I shook Dr. Lovett's hand, Debbie was there and told him I'd just lost my husband. He gave me a hug and told me he knows how I feel. We met before church tonight. I really felt the Holy Spirit assure me I'd turned a corner at the altar last night. I'm not sure what that means, but I'm glad I met with Dr. Lovett.

What a blessing! He's been through a lot and God has blessed him with the ability to share his pain – as well as the blessings. He tells me that time is the only thing that will heal this horrible pain. He encourages me to express my pain as I did at the altar last night. *So far that hasn't been a problem (although not to that extent in public).*

Yes, six weeks ago tonight my world took a drastic change, but I'm still standing — by the grace of God!

Wednesday, 5/3/95 (lunch)

I'm doing it again – holding back the tears. It's not that I feel like crying and don't, but I've even shut "feeling" down. I cried so hard at the altar Monday night. I can't explain how I know I should be crying. I just know.

A good way to explain my overall mood is to say I feel like I have about 600,000 pounds of pressure built up in this relatively small frame and there's no outlet for the still building pressure.

I begged God last night to let me dream of Ron being alive and with me. He chose not to answer that prayer so I must be unable to bear it. I don't understand that – and why can't I remember Ron as anything more than a distant memory as if I'd gone to high school with him? I spent twenty-six and one half (intimate) years with him and I cannot remember him. I don't understand this. I'm not asking to "feel his presence" (that's not possible). I only want to remember him. I know there's pain involved, but I can't stand being shut down – that's just not my style. Yet, I must quickly add that I know God's in control and He has His reasons for denying my wishes. *Maybe I would explode from the pressure.* In the mean time, I rest in His presence and tender loving care.

I called Dr. Byer this morning. I had a list of questions for him.

Allen's passing out was probably due to being upset and not eating. However, if he ever passes out while exercising, he should be tested. Ron's condition isn't something that's inherited.

Ron would go into a trance when driving sometimes. Was this a symptom? It may have been. It would be related to the proper flow of blood to the heart and therefore, oxygen to the brain.

Was his feeling sick the last day from this problem? No!

The autopsy mentioned a "slit" in the artery. What is the significance? When the origin of the blood vessel is not in the normal place it can be a slit (instead of round) and does not permit the influx of blood as a normal opening would.

What's the usual age of those who die from this (Dr. Byer sees one or two cases a year out of 600-800 autopsies) — younger or older than Ron? Varies, but usually younger.

Thursday Morning, 5/4/95

I was reminded while praying this morning of the times I'd wished I could stay home and be a housewife and Mom. Ron would tell me that, besides needing to work, I should work. He said if anything ever happened to him I'd need the income and the experience. I knew what he was saying was right, but he was going to be with me – growing older by my side...right?!! *Still don't understand, but I'm losing the need to.*

I'm reading Terry Rush's book, *God Will Make A Way*. He quotes from Charles Swindoll's book, *Encourage Me,* something that touched my heart. "As difficult as it may be for you to believe this today, the Master knows what He's doing. Your Savior knows your breaking point. The bruising and crushing and melting process is designed to reshape you, not ruin you. Your value is increasing the longer He lingers over you."

I sit and ask myself what I'm feeling, and – I'm not sure. I know I feel such loss. Ron gave my life direction. He guided me, protected me, and loved me. *I miss him.* Going to bed is a drag. He's not there to talk to – laugh with – make love with. This morning when the radio went off and wakened me, I lay there thinking how nice it would be to linger there with Ron by my side enjoying the still, quiet, cool breeze coming through the window. *That same cool breeze I felt the night I found him.*

"Sad" – I feel so sad. I never understood the meaning of this word. I'm not sure I can describe it. It's feeling bad – not bad enough to cry – just bad enough not to want to go on – yet knowing I will (not even "must" – *the emotions aren't that strong* – just "straight-lined"). It's knowing in my heart I'll never be happy again – yet knowing in my head I will be. And – it's not caring. Yet – I know deep inside – *yet near by* that I do care. It's wanting to go on to Heaven yet not wanting to leave here, and at the same time knowing that somewhere deep inside there's an excitement beginning to bubble up – AND – not wanting it to because I don't have the energy to deal with it. *I'm so tired.* Believe it or not, I'm not confused. It's possible to keep going with all these thoughts and feelings being processed all at the same time.

Tuesday, 5/9/95

Seven weeks. For some strange reason I now want time to slow down – stop, maybe. Time marches on and I'm so afraid people will forget Ron, and his death will become a "no big deal" thing. (I am so guilty of the same thing.) Friends and relatives who have died years ago have become a memory – the pain is gone. God knows I don't want this pain, but Ron was such a vital part of my life. If people forget the bond we've had through him then I'll be all alone.

The shock is wearing off and when I don't shut down and feel the pain, it's so deep that I feel I'll never find the end. It's as if I'm standing on the top of Cadillac Mountain and see the ocean so many miles below. It's so far away. Yet, it's not the end. The pain breaks the surface and goes deeper than I can see or imagine. (I don't know how deep the ocean is and I don't know how deep my pain goes.) Why can't I accept this and get beyond the pain? Why does this – the worst thing ever in my life, have to be the only thing I've been unable to "deal" with and get beyond?

Thursday, 5/11/95

Ron's grave marker came in Tuesday. I went to finish paying for it yesterday. I went to his grave. It's still a big mound of dirt. I got back in the car, looked up the hill and saw that mound of dirt. I sat there and got so happy as I realized that one of these days Ron's coming up out of that ground! He'll break through that casket, vault, and any dirt covering the grave. Oh, how I hope I'll grab his hand as he passes by and we can rise together. How wonderful it would be for him to introduce me to Jesus (not that introductions will be necessary, but it's a thought)! I can't begin to imagine what that day will be like – to realize it's finally the day Christ returns and we all go up into the Heavens. No more pain, sickness, or death! Why can't everyone see what we see?! It breaks my heart to see satan confuse and lie to so many.

Chapter Three

5/20 ~ 6/19/1995

Beginning To Move On

Saturday, 5/20/95

Another milestone — another day. Two months. I watched Dr. Quinn and Sully get married tonight and I cried — not as I would have anyway, but as I repeated our vows. I remember Ron got so nervous he said, "I do" twice. (I'm so glad that I can remember the fun things in the midst of this incredible pain.)

Monday Evening, 5/22/95 (nine weeks)

Today went really well. I guess that since I can remember Ron a little that my SUB-conscious mind doesn't have to "feel forced" to bring my conscious mind into the pain. _It's doing quite well on it's own now!_

I'm at the cemetery — it's 6:30. What a beautiful day. It's warm — the sun's shining and a cool breeze is blowing. The sounds of traffic passing by — birds singing — crows "crowing." Such peace amid such pain. I can't understand, but I can be thankful to a God who can orchestrate this entire scene so perfectly. _(Ron's marker still isn't in. I'll call tomorrow. I want it in for Memorial Day this week.)_

I'm not so sure time "heals." I think a more appropriate description of what Time does with our thoughts and memories is that it forgets them. "Healing" is a more gentle word then "forgetting." It's okay to say I'll "heal" and would be kind of cold to say

31

I'll "forget" Ron. Call it what you will, the end result is the same — life goes on and, the really neat thing is that I want it to. I don't like the pain right now, but I know I will get beyond it. I will live again. A part of me hopes to love again (some time in the far — far away future).

Ron's smile — his sucking his fat belly in and saying as he pats it, "See, it's slim and firm!" and me saying, "Yeah, now breathe!" As he lets out a big rush of air we both laugh! We've been getting "older" lately, determined never to get "old." But, a couple of times he'd say he was feeling old. Boy, satan could take my emotions right now and do some really heavy "what-iffin." But - greater is HE who is in me than he who is in the world!!! Period.

Friday, 5/26/95

Dear Ron,

I'm sitting on your grave wondering what to say to you. Your marker was installed yesterday so I wanted to come and put flowers on it for you (ok, for me).

It's so beautiful here. I never thought I'd find comfort in a cemetery — you know how we always felt about the body and soul, but, you know what, Hon? I find it's not so much that I feel near you, but it's awfully hard to suppress reality here. Six to eight feet below me is the shell of your life on this earth. Your name is in bronze that says you're no longer here. Reality is faced here at your grave, and there's rejoicing too. I am so glad you're a Christian, Ron. I'm so thankful for the last several years we had worshipping together. Remember how you used to tug on my hem if I stood during a song? I'd turn and you'd smile. O, how I miss you in church!

I hope I'm making you proud in how I'm handling things. I sure do love you! That love will never stop. The pain is pretty severe, but God's taking such good care of me. Steve and Allen are making you proud too, I'm sure. They've really come to my side from the night I found you.

I'm so glad that we did our "reverse retirement!" Who would

have thought your time on earth would be so short? Everyone who doubted our sanity then is glad now.

There's so much I'd like to say to you, but it's all so hard. I don't have any regrets. We've been so close this year since Mike and Angie separated. The last week of your life was SO special. I love you, Ron Fahey and I'm so glad you're with our Lord.

All my love!

Brenda

Wednesday, 5/31/95

I've put my grief on hold until I get moved in — there's been no time! Steve is coming tomorrow night to help me. I've been so paralyzed and unable to be motivated to get packed. *I wonder if maybe I've breezed on through the pain I've been dreading dealing with.* Maybe it's just not necessary to face it. After all, I've been doing okay the last few days. *(Haven't I?!!)*

Thursday Morning, 6/1/95

I found out that I'm not "breezing" through the pain. Things were "normal." Our Missions Convention started last night. When we started the invitation ("Trust and Obey"), I started thinking of Ron's absence from my side. The picture on his "Pace" card shows a bit of his orneriness. We were teasing each other as our pictures were taken. There's something about that picture that brings feelings out in me. I'd looked at it a couple of times near the end of the service. When we started singing, I felt the Lord telling me to trust and obey Him. I know He's dealing with me on my running from Him and the pain. I started crying softly. Cathy put her arm around me and we both began to cry. I sat down and the next thing I knew, I went down. It's so strange to experience this passing out thing. *I really must stop it!* I was aware of my surroundings, but was unable to respond. They poured water and ice all over my face. *I felt it, but it wasn't really cold.* Then someone pronounced me dead — couldn't get a pulse and said I wasn't breathing. I thought that was kind of neat! Although I didn't "feel" dead I was okay with the diagnosis and wondered where Ron was! Of course there was the "second opinion" that said I WAS breathing. I really wanted to go with the first lady, but what do I know?! They called 911. Someone decided to do the ole pain inducement to bring me around. They began the suppression between the thumb and first finger. I came around fighting. (I really can't take any more pain right now.) I clenched my fists to protect that part of my hand and started to try to get away. I still wasn't responsive. It was a while before I could answer questions. I really was afraid I'm losing my mind, although I know God's protecting me. I've got to stop suppressing these feelings. I just don't know how to do this thing — this grieving over losing my strength, my protection, and my best friend. God, of course, is first (and has been), but the loss of Ron is literally like tearing myself in half. *I still don't know how to be a widow!*

I've got a doctor's appointment. They did a blood sugar level last night, expecting it to be high since I had two cinnamon rolls and a glass of milk for supper. Instead, it was real low. I realized this morning that I dealt with the pain of spinal cord compression by suppressing it. Guess that's my method. Yet, I must be fair to myself. In that case, the doctors had told me my pain was in my head. They refused to believe there was a medical problem. So, I had no choice until they could "see" the evidence of it.

Friday, 6/2/95

I'm now a homeowner! Settlement went very smoothly. I got teary eyed a couple of times. Watching the sellers as he read everything before passing to her to sign brought back such memories. I didn't read much — relied on Debbie to advise me. I really am blessed with this house!

Thursday, 6/8/95

For the first time, I'm not sure I'm going to survive this grief. I want to — I want to be happy again. I want to serve God — to glorify Him, but I honestly feel like I'm going to die from a broken heart. Three people have told me today how much weight I've lost.

Weight is the least of my worries (even though I do care about my health). I'm doing everything I can to survive this. I'm crying again. (Boy, am I crying!!) I made an appointment with a Christian counselor through our employee assistance program. I'm trying to eat, but I can't do anything about my heart. I know I'm just beginning to feel the pain and I know millions have survived this kind of loss. I'm just not sure I'm strong enough. I keep thinking of Paul's statement about being strong in God when he was the weakest. If that's true for me then I'm going to come out a very strong person. I know God's with me, but I also know that no one (not even God) will take this pain away. His grace is sufficient, but it hurts so much.

Friday Morning, 6/9/95

I awoke several times last night, but I feel better today. Not really ecstatic — just accepting that life will go on (and, I want it to). I've got to slow down. It seems every minute is planned or scheduled.

God is so good. He's taking such good care of me. I'm not sure why I made the appointment with the counselor for tonight. I guess passing out last week kind of jogged my senses into thinking I may not be handling this so well!

I meet with a cardiologist today to discuss Ron's death. I really want to understand this defect and it's causes. I'm not doing a lot of "what-iffin," but I'd like to know how he may have been saved. I'm not second-guessing God. I still praise Him for all aspects of this situation. I want to be sure it's not something that is inherited.

Monday, 6/12/95 (12 weeks)

The cardiologist said people usually die much younger (even in childhood) from the condition Ron had. So he did live a long life! She's getting articles on his condition to be sure it's not inherited.

The counselor said I have an amazing coping mechanism and sees no reason to see me again. I just wanted to be sure I'm handling things as well as I think I am. It's so strange...I'm such a mess — but I'm an "ok" mess — a "normal" mess. (That probably should bring me some comfort, but it doesn't.) I don't care how many people I see — how many tears I cry — how much I scream or suppress, there's still only one way through this thing — through the center (the very core). I don't like that very much, but I don't really have a choice. Isn't it great that God's with me and is keeping me?

Wednesday, 6/14/95

I felt depressed today for the first time. It's because I feel like I'm letting people down. I'm just not as efficient as I normally am and that bothers me. I know the stress I've been under. It almost seems like the numbness is getting worse as the pain intensifies. Like so much else, those opposite feelings being felt at the same time don't make sense.

Also, dealing with my identity, I now fully feel I am not married — I am not "Mrs." Fahey. By our world's rules, when you marry you become "Mr. & Mrs." So, if I'm not married (since death ended that), then I'm also not "Mrs." Fahey any longer.

Monday, 6/19/95

People actually tell me they're glad to see me cry. I can understand (I guess). If they don't see me cry they must figure I never do. Why are we like that? How many times have I been guilty of the same thing?

Right now, I'm hanging onto my faith that God's going to get me through. (Sure don't feel like I'm going to make it.)

Chapter Four

6/20 ~ 7/19/1995

A New Happiness Begins To Set In

Tuesday, Marc——oops! June 20

Wonder what's on my mind?!! I was wondering this morning where the balance is in remembering Ron being so close (it causes such pain) and choosing not to let myself feel so sad. Seems like at some point it will become necessary to decide to quit hurting and concentrate on the joy of our relationship and be happy remembering him. Yet, I know that denial can figure into this equation (as can suppression). I've found out what suppression can do! I just want to be emotionally healthy.

I remember that two years ago at this time we were in New England. I remember wishing I could express the beauty of the mountains and trees and clouds. Now I wish I could express the pain, sadness, and loneliness. How come I have such a desire to express myself and such limited ability to do so?

God is so good! I want to serve Him so badly. It's hard to believe that living without Ron is being in God's perfect will, but I must trust that He knows what He's doing. I wonder how He decides things like Ron dying on March 20 at 5:05 p.m. Just how long was He preparing me to turn the key that night?

Tonight my heart is broken completely apart. I'm getting ready to do a devotion in a couple of weeks about hope. Tonight, I don't have any hope left. (I'm talking about the hope of ever seeing Ron again on this earth. There is no one who can give me any hope for that — not even my Lord.) Sure, I'm going to see him again in Heaven — and, yes — I know he's there now, but for me, for tonight, that doesn't mend my broken heart. I just want him to hold me tonight and let me cry in his arms. I want him to tell me it's going to be all right — that WE are going to get through this together. Pastor Reynolds says I'm the type of person who wants to fix things that aren't right and since I can't fix this, it hurts more. I guess he's right.

Yet, in the midst of all this indescribable pain, hope springs eternal — hope from God that He will get me to the other side of this deep, bottomless chasm called grief. He will accomplish what Ron can't (even couldn't have). God will mend my broken heart. He's also reminded me today that the Holy Spirit is so close to me (since He dwells in my heart) that I really do have someone close enough to hug. Sometimes He gives me a physical hug through a sister in Christ or a son or other family member. Even through my rebellious spirit tonight I find a light — I find hope. I'm rebellious because I can't have what I want so desperately. So I ask God for forgiveness. I cry my heart out and I'll go to bed now. God will give me a restful night's sleep that defies my very being at this moment. O, Abba Father - please don't ever leave me!

(By the way, to answer my own question this morning — no, I can't choose tonight not to feel this sadness. There's no negotiating or masking this.)

Monday, 6/26/95

O, Dear, God — PLEASE stop this pain! I can't handle it any longer. I cry "Uncle" to you today! Please get me beyond this or bring me on home. I can't bear it any longer. You know me and you know my pain. I'm not angry. I just don't understand how you can let me go on hurting so badly. You have the power to stop it and I can't understand why it has to go on. What purpose does it serve? I've felt the horrible pain of losing Ron. What good does it do me (or anyone) for me to keep revisiting it?

I know that, in the scheme of things, I don't need to under-stand your ways, but I also know I can come to you and ask, in the middle of my pain, "Why?!" Problem is, I also know you probably won't answer me in the near future. So, even in the middle of this — even though I don't want to accept your will right now — I know that I do because without trusting you, I have nothing left.

Please know Lord that the pain is getting worse. I have physical pain in my chest as I sit in my car and cry out to you. I haven't expe-rienced pain this severe before. Perhaps I should see my doctor, but I won't for two reasons. The first (and most practical) is because I know it's just the grief, but if I'm to be honest with myself, it's also because (right now — today) I really wouldn't care if I had a life threatening condition. I guess I've felt this way before (not the pain, but not "caring"), but I don't believe I've been willing to admit it. I sure don't feel very worthy today. It's good to know that even though I'm not worthy (forget about feelings), you still care and stay with me. Thank you Lord!

Tuesday, 6/27/95

I was thinking this morning that my life is something like standing on a diving board on top of a very high mountain. The platform's on fire and I can't go back (can't get Ron back), but the road ahead is so narrow and there's nothing to step out on — except (of course) faith. Faith is okay — it's a very solid entity, I believe. So, I step forward. Isn't it amazing that God's there to help and protect me?! Here I am, at forty-five still jumping off the edge into my Daddy's arms! Neat, huh?!

Wednesday Morning, 6/28/95

People say, "time heals." Before time heals — time hurts. The longer I live without Ron, the more real the separation and pain becomes. I don't want to do this (I don't know how to do it)! Where's the instruction book? I am so selfish! I've asked myself this morning if I'm doing self pity and I honestly don't believe so — I still don't envy other couples. Sometimes I have to hold myself back from running to couples and telling them to enjoy their time and appreciate each other! I'm still not looking for another relationship — so I don't think I'm full of self-pity.

I'm just so empty — so alone. *Is this what women who miscarry mean when they talk about feeling empty?* Right now, time is hurting me and I don't like it. However — I'm glad I'm not "getting over" Ron at the drop of a hat. I always thought I loved him with all my heart. Now I know I did.

Friday, June 30

I've shut down again. (I hate it when I do that!) I was wondering earlier if maybe God had eased my pain, but I don't think that's it. I don't think He's into suppression assistance and I'm sure I'm suppressing again. When I try to think of Ron I can almost see the curtain drop. I just don't want to deal with it again. I went to the Rescue Squad last night. I was curious about how long it took them to get there that night. I was sure it was fifteen minutes or so since I'd told them he was dead. I was shocked to find out it took them two minutes and five seconds to get to the building. Give them another two minutes to get upstairs. Guess time did stand still for a while! The ones who responded that night, and those who came to the church when I passed out were there. Wasn't long before there were ten paramedics in the room. I congratulated the expert in pain response techniques! *They also gave me a copy of the report. There was Ron's name again — in a context I just wouldn't have expected to see at this time in our lives - DOA.*

God blessed me with a wonderful dream about Ron a couple of nights ago. I walked up behind him and touched his shoulder. He turned and smiled at me. It was so real that it woke me up instantly. I was so happy and in so much pain (at the same time) that I smiled as I cried. I quickly thanked God and fell back to sleep. What a wonderful blessing!

Now, how bout if we eat a meal — or go to church — something that lasts longer than a touch and a smile?! (Oops — there I go slipping back into wanting more — in addition to being thankful for what God blessed me with. *Sorry!*)

Sunday Evening, 7/2/95

God needed a Coke, so I left church and went with Him. (Can't remember hookin church before!) Guess that's the norm lately — can't remember a lot of things like this cause I'm living a life of new experiences and feelings.

I have to wonder where my strength has been for the last several years. If you'd asked me (and Ron probably would have agreed), I'd have guessed I was the "strong" one. I thought I could survive anything. After all, I'd lived for over a year with spinal cord compression at the nerve root without aid of any medication. (I know — I didn't have a choice.) Yet, I came through by the grace of God and I know I'll come through this.

God, forgive me, but sometimes I feel like You're just not enough to get me through this. I know (in my head) that You are! And, I thank You for that, but God, my heart is broken. It's no longer "breaking" — it's destroyed. I'm so afraid I'll go so far that I won't be able to see You again! O, God, please don't let me go out of Your sight! Please keep Your hand on me. Send a pillar of fire to guide me. O, God, are You crying with me tonight? Please tell me how to stop this reaction.

I know You won't stop the pain, but I don't want to run away. I want to stand with You by my side. I asked You not to let me bring You dishonor and I pray that again. Seems it would be a lot simpler if You'd just take me out of here. If not, then help me to stand. Help me to see the blessings again. Please, put a Band-Aid on my heart and begin now to repair it. (Guess I'd better get back to church. Oh, and God, thanks for the Coke! You're awesome!)

This week's real busy at work. I realized yesterday that Ron had a calming effect on me (go figure). As I was feeling overwhelmed I'd think about getting home to him to relax, instantly knowing that's not possible and, therefore feeling even more overwhelmed.

I bought a car last night. I've done some shopping and found the facts of how women are treated are true, except at Saturn. There wasn't any sales pressure and they have a great product. The Grand Marquis needed another $600-$800 in repairs. I've already spent over $1,000 on it since Ron died.

Wednesday, 7/12/95

I picked my car up last night. It's really nice. A touch of sadness at walking away from my car (it's the last thing "we" had together — the RV, Spaceball, and the cars).

By the time I got home, my neck was hurting. I got a 5-speed and my foot is straight out operating the clutch. That puts a strain on my neck. I thought about trading it on an automatic, but don't really want to. I like the stick shift and would like to keep my $800! They'll be able to put an extension on the clutch pedal.

Then I got to thinking that maybe I should get an automatic because without Ron, if I ever break a leg I couldn't get to work. Then again — how many broken legs have I suffered in my life?!! None! *I really have to keep my imagination in check!*

Wednesday Evening

I was wondering tonight, as we were taking prayer requests in church, if Jesus ever asked, "Why me?!" Of the three in the Trinity, what would have happened if He'd felt sorry for Himself? Sure, He cried (he was human), but He didn't ask God, "why me and not someone else?" Guess I should be careful when I pray, "Why me?" To pray "why me?" is to pray, "Why not someone else?!" It's so easy to get caught up in self-pity sometimes. At least God hasn't allowed me to linger there for very long. He's so awesome! I'm so very blessed by my Father.

Thursday, 7/13/95

I don't pretend to understand this new life I'm living. It's a strange world I find myself in. I miss Ron so much. Yet, in some very strange way, I'm describing myself as "happy" more often. It just doesn't make sense that happiness can be experienced at the same time as such loneliness and pain.

It's funny to think that I normally would have been by myself at lunch. Ron would have been at work, or at lunch himself. Yet, I didn't "feel" alone. Just knowing he was alive was comforting and fulfilling. Now I feel like I'm alone in the world. Why don't Steve and Allen, or Mom and Dad (Ron's parents) fill that void?

Tuesday, 7/18/95

I finally bottomed out this week physically. I was so tired Sunday. I slept well the last two nights so I feel better. There are so many bugs, spiders, and ticks at home. And, I have to take care of these little pests myself. I hate bugs and I loathe spiders and ticks (the little blood suckers)! Most people have quit calling and coming over, which I think is fine. They were so faithful long after I'd have expected. It is great, isn't it, that God provided that companionship while I needed it? I guess He figures it's time to start winging it on my own more!

I keep seeing Ron's face as I lifted it out of the bed. He was so blue — so still — I just kept thinking, "This can't be — not my Ron!" I couldn't believe he was actually dead. It hurt so much, even then.

Ron and I seemed to thrive on changes in our lives. I wish I could find some excitement over this one! In some ways I do. Imagine, me being able to buy a home and a new car by myself (it is, of course, by God's provision). I wonder how many people judge me harshly for "going" on like I have. *I wonder why I wonder such a thing!*

Wednesday, 7/19/95 lunch

I was crying at my desk this morning — wondering where the "moments" (as I tell anyone who catches me crying) come from. I can be working on the computer and suddenly the sadness hits and it builds until I close my eyes and then feel the wetness behind my eyelids welling up until there's no choice — I'm smack in the middle of a "moment." I don't know what happens, but a thought of Ron, or a memory of the summer of '93 — or of last Christmas — or, whatever crosses my mind and I'm lost in the pain, in the helplessness of the "moment." Yet, as I cried this morning, I was reminded (I wonder by Who) of the many blessings I have been given. Let me analyze this for a minute...I'm out of debt (except for the car and house, and they don't count); I have a beautiful home, car, furniture — Muff-up's even still with me; I'm a member of a wonderful church; I have a great job and many friends; I have a loving, caring and supportive family. With Ron — we had an apartment; two old cars; were deeply in debt; still had the family, church, and friends, but, WE HAD EACH OTHER! In the scope of things on earth that was what was most important to us (after our relationship with God). Every time in our marriage when something bad happened we'd always come back to the fact that we still had each other. We'd say that we could get through anything as long as we had that. So, now what do I do? "Things" just can't buy the companionship I had with Ron (of course). So, I sit here in the middle of Burger King with the tears rolling down my face. I know I can survive this, but I sure don't want the pain.

Chapter Five

7/20 ~ 8/19/1995

Real Loneliness Hits As I Look To The Future

Thursday, 7/20/95

It's been a rough day. The tears came at the drop of a hat. Kendall shared her experience of losing her boyfriend at seventeen to a car accident. It helps to hear others' stories, but I keep hoping they'll say something magical that will end my pain. *When will I quit listening with those hopes? They only get dashed.* I met with Pastor Eagy last night. I knew he couldn't say anything either, but I still hoped he would.

Cecille called to let me know she was thinking about me. O, God, even though I know it's not true, it seems as though you've turned your back on me. I don't mean to go into a pity party here, but I feel so alone. I'm not asking you to bring Ron back, but why can't you bring me Home?! It would be so simple for you to do. I feel so abandoned. There's no one to hold me tonight. Your Spirit asks me if I'm willing to trust You — to believe that You know what You're doing. As much as it hurts, I answer, "Yes." But, God, You'll have to heal my hurts — okay?!

Friday, 7/21/95

It's happening again. I'm at my desk, working intently, suddenly Ron flashes across my mind and there goes the wet eyelids!

45

"Everlasting Love" is playing. Is it the songs? If it is, do I quit listening to music? I'll have to stay out of church — quit the choir and go stark raving mad! I love music — I love worshipping God through song. So, if it hurts to hear music it'll just have to hurt. I don't want this pain, but there's only so far I'm willing to go to avoid it — wait, did I just say what I think I said?! — to A-V-O-I-D the pain? Is that why I'm so exhausted?! If I'm avoiding it, then I need to stop. So, what do I do? Do I turn and bury my feet in concrete and say, "Okay, Pain, Time, hit me with all you've got?!" Naw — I'm too chicken! Besides, my feet are already planted firmly on the Rock of my salvation! He's protecting me. Besides, I really do love music. I couldn't begin to quit enjoying it. *It was just a thought!!*

I just realized something pretty horrible about myself. I believe I really do feel I should be beyond this horrible pain. After all, it has been four months! I can't believe I feel I should be doing something I've told people a hundred times not to expect from themselves or others! Who do I think I am?!! Some kind of Super Griever or something?!? I guess I've always been harder on myself than I should be. That can cause some stress in itself. I don't think I really expect myself to be "over" this so soon. I believe it's the fact that I've always been able to deal with things and get beyond the non-functionality of the situation. It's because I'm a chicken — I don't like pain! People have called me a "Survivor." Surviving sure can hurt sometimes.

Sunday Evening, 7/23/95

I really have to watch how I word things! Last night I hit bottom. I didn't want to live. There wasn't a cell of my body that held any hope for happiness. I shared my feelings in Sunday School this morning and asked for prayer.

A couple of people understood me to say that I was suicidal! I was taken completely by surprise! There's a big difference in saying, "I don't want to live" and "I wanted to do something about it!!"

Even last night, God picked me up again and carried me along the beach. He loves me and I love Him. I could never even think of ending my life! I know I don't have the gift of expression of my feelings. (Guess I have proof now, huh?!)

Tuesday, 7/25/95

I just about fell to sleep this afternoon. I went to the doctor. They did a blood test, an E K G, etc. Found out I'm dehydrated. Since I never drink water (leaves a bad taste in my mouth and makes me sick to my stomach) and I always drink Coke, and with the heat — it all got to me. I have to drink eight to ten, eight-oz. glasses of water a day. Don't see what the difference is in dehydrating from not drinking water and throwing said water up is, but, hey, I'm not a doctor! This is how all the people have died the last couple of weeks. It sneaks up on you. Guess it's good I realized my feelings weren't all emotional!

That's part of it. He said my body has caught up with the stress of grieving. Apparently that's taken a toll.

He's a fabulous doctor. They fit me in this afternoon and he spent a lot of time talking to me, but he fell into that (how do I say it) — what do I call it — "trap"(?) of hinting that it's time to start "expanding my circle of friends." He said a couple more things, so I knew what he was saying. Bless his heart, just like everyone else he means well. Who knows, maybe I misunderstood him. After all, I am dehydrated. (Maybe my brain's dry!) All I know is that I feel better knowing somethings physically wrong as well as the grief. First my thyroid hit — then Ron died — now I'm in menopause and I'm dehydrated. So, I sit here tonight thinking, "What next?!" knowing whatever it is that I'll be okay. All I have to do is keep looking up and remember I'm completely surrounded by God, Jesus and the Holy Spirit. *I like that!*

Wednesday Morning, 7/26/95

I really feel numb. I don't like it either! If I can't feel my feelings, then how can I deal with them?

I wanted some sodas, juice, etc. last night, but no one was there to go and get them for me. I certainly wasn't able to go.

I want to cry, but won't. Maybe I know intellectually that crying has helped me, but I sure don't see the results of its help. Right now I feel that if I give in to crying I'll never be able to stop. Maybe I'm feeling sorry for myself for the first time. I asked the doctor if I'm depressed (don't feel like I am). He said, "no" because I'm eating, sleeping, and working. If I'm just doing self pity, it's time to start counting the blessings again. Besides, I need to give me a break! I'm not physically well right now. I wish I was super spiritual and able to breeze on through this thing. Oh well, guess I'll just have to live with what I've got!!

Saturday Evening, 7/29/95

Lord, I don't understand something tonight. Ron lived to be forty-eight. Why didn't you let him live to be eighty-eight? When you joined us together, when I was only eighteen and Ron twenty-one, we never considered that "til death do us part" would come so young. God, I miss him so much. There is a void in my heart that only Ron can fill, so what do I do? "Til death do us part" means when we're eighty or ninety and use one of those horns to hear and we're gray and we walk with a cane and we sit in rocking chairs! How come my perception on that hasn't changed from the time I was eighteen?! O, Lord, I really don't mean to complain. I am so thankful for the time I had Ron. Is it wrong of me to want so much more? I want to sit with him again. I want to tell him I love him again. The pain is so severe, so ongoing, and so deep. God, if you ever decide to destroy mankind, and begin again, could I make a suggestion that would help us humans? One advantage I think Jesus had over us is that He had been in Heaven. He'd walked with, talked to and knew You personally and physically. I haven't seen You. It would be really helpful to have a way to physically see You and hear You. To have You physically sitting in my living room tonight would help so much. I guess that's where faith comes in though; faith that some day the pain won't be so severe; faith that, somehow, all this is going to work together for good.

Tuesday, 8/1/95

Yesterday was the best day I've had since Ron died. I was weak when I woke up and went to work, but the day was relaxed. There was a peace in my heart and soul — a peace that I know will some day be permanent as I remember Ron. I didn't have anything to do the last night or two. It was very relaxing!

I'm considering taking a course at church on Biblical studies. It'll be three hours on Monday night plus studying. Then, I'd like to teach Sunday School, but, a requirement is to do visitation once a week. That would mean four nights a week at church (plus studying). I'm not sure I'm up to that. Just as I was thinking last night that maybe I should slow down and enjoy more days like yesterday, a wave of loneliness hit me between the eyes. Will I ever get over missing Ron so much? I still don't fully comprehend the impact of his being gone.

Sometimes when I think of Ron, I get a rush of my Spirit wanting to run to him (like in those slow motion commercials running through the field) and hold him and have him hold me, but, as in the commercial on drunk driving, he suddenly disappears and leaves me looking around wondering what happened.

So, I crawl into bed and cry my heart out, wondering if maybe God took Ron away so I'd serve Him more (as I've done since he died), yet knowing that's not how my God operates.

Wednesday Evening, 8/2/95

Wow! The last three days have been good! I think they've been the best since Ron died. Yet, at the same time, I've gotten to know Loneliness much more than I ever imagined. Maybe I'm "Over the hump" of this thing called Grief. *What's this feeling of sadness as I say this?* O, God, suddenly I'm crying again. *I don't understand.* As I'm getting ready to say, "Maybe I'm over the worst part," W-H-A-M - up side my head, Grief hits again. I'm sitting in my car in front of the house (just came from church and it hits again). O, God, I really thought I'd made a breakthrough. I don't know how to do this! For the first time I don't want to go inside. I'll just go in, go to bed and get up tomorrow and do it all over again. So, I think I'll make some improvements! Sense of humor (seems like I used to have one). I'll see if I can find it tomorrow. My mission (should I decide to accept it), is to search for it until it's found. Now, go to bed, Brenda!

Thursday, 8/3/95

It is so good to be alive! For the first time I really know I'm going to survive this Grief. Intellectually, I've known all along, but now it's a feeling in my heart. *Why does that make me feel a little guilty?* Half of society tells me I can't be happy for a year — another part is telling me to go ahead and find a man. Any wonder our emotions go crazy?!

So I'll ignore these feelings of guilt. I know in my heart that I'm simply saying I'm feeling like living. God and I know that I'm not talking about remarriage. Even if I was, this is a subject that Ron and I had discussed. We agreed we'd want the other to go on — to find someone else to love. I can only speak for myself when I admit that I secretly (for a moment) wanted to scream, "Don't you dare! How could you?!!" Yet, in the next moment, I'd admit I'd really want Ron to be happy. When you truly love someone I think it's hard to be selfish.

Putting all that aside. Ron (in his present state) wants me happy. In his present state, he knows the depths of my suffering. He may even know my heart in a way never possible on earth.

Besides, I'm not sure how much all this matters. God is in control of all this — of my "new life." I trust Him completely! I stand amazed at His complete love and devotion to me, Brenda Fahey. Why me, God?! Why am I so blessed?

Friday, 8/4/95

I'm re-reading my journal and have a couple of notes to clarify. (I don't want to be a hundred and twenty years old and be confused over seeming contradictions or wonder what in the world "The Spaceball" was!!!) One of the earliest thoughts in writing this was to have something to pass on to my grandchildren or great grandchildren. I'd give anything if I had a journal from a former relative — to know what their day-to-day life was like. I've started so many "journals" of just that, but never kept them up.

On the entry for March 23, I mention feeling anger. Yet, I say later that's one emotion I haven't felt. The March 23 entry refers to anger at someone I love dearly (specifics aren't necessary); not at Ron for dying or at God for taking him. That's one thing I'm very thankful to Pastor Reynolds for. The first time he met with me after Ron died and the funeral was over, he said that the world tells me I have stages to go through and that I have to experience each one. He said he was there to tell me that is not true. He said that it's not unspiritual if I do feel any, or all of them, but that it's also not mandatory. I've been thankful for that. With my hospice training — feeling like the experts must be right — I probably would have felt it necessary to "get angry" if I wanted to heal properly. God's been so good. I can never forget how He'd set the scene those last few weeks and months to give me so many blessings. I praise him!

The Spaceball is an amusement ride. It's a flight simulator. You get strapped into a seat and get turned up side down and around and it's great! You can't get sick cause your stomach is in the center of gravity. Ron had been out of work after being laid off in Vincennes. We went to an entrepreneur convention in Indy and found the Spaceball. We planned on doing birthday parties and grand openings in the Indianapolis area. I came home from work one day and Ron asked what I thought about putting 90% of what we owned up for auction, buying an RV, and working our way across America for a year to see where the Lord wanted us.

I told him he was crazy and asked if we could leave the next day! Steve felt the same way, so we left within a week. We considered this our "reverse retirement." So many of our friends and relatives had gotten to the point of retirement and one of them would get sick or die. We had the money so we did it!

On March 27, I mentioned three points of humor in the list of blessings. The first one is kind of weird, but it was a blessing. On the day Ron died, I wore a black and white print blouse (mostly black), a black skirt, shoes, stockings, etc. to work. Gloria commented on how nice I looked. We talked about how we both like black. I thanked her, went into the ladies room and when I saw myself in the mirror, I said to myself, "One thing's for sure. If Ron ever drops dead, I won't have to buy clothes for the funeral!" Then, I laughed out loud and said, "Sure, but you'd never wear black cause you'd be rejoicing since you know where he'd be!!" The next day when I was feeling the sadness and remembered saying that, I laughed at the irony of saying such a thing and it actually coming true a few hours later. *Ron would have loved that!!!*

The second one is about Mike slapping me. When it was time to leave the funeral home for the last time, I passed out. I was aware of my surroundings, but was unable to respond. Mike, being a paramedic, was taking care of me. He gently slapped my face, calling my name. I'm laying there, laughing to myself, thinking, "It didn't work with Ron and it won't work with me!" I just wanted everyone to leave me alone and let me sleep in the same room with Ron's body one more night.

"Where's the Spaceball?" When Pam and Howard came to dinner a couple of nights before Ron died, the conversation turned to the Spaceball. In talking, Ron asked me if he'd told me where the Spaceball was (he had it stored at a co-worker's home). I said, "No, and I guess you should, cause if you ever drop dead, I won't know where to go to get my ball!"

At church the Sunday after he died, Howard came up to me and asked if Ron had told me where the ball was. I told him no -- but later, I found the address in his wallet and his co-worker, Dave had called me when he heard Ron had died.

Monday, 8/7/95

Maybe I'm off the wall, but I pray for the future sometimes. I often pray for the future spouses of my Pastors' kids (as well as mine)!

Recently I've begun to pray for the person God may have for me in the future. Whatever he's going to go through to put us at the same point is probably going to be painful. I pray today that God will spare him of that pain if at all possible, even if it means I spend the rest of my life alone. I wouldn't wish this pain on anyone else for anything.

I was wondering over the weekend what job God's got Ron doing. Since he was a controller, perhaps he's in charge of counting the tears. *Wonder if he's counting mine.* I've sure cried a lot today. I was thinking tonight (I think I think too much sometimes) about all the people I've seen and heard about who are healed from addictions like alcohol, drugs, adultery, etc. These people sometimes get up from the altar healed. Grief isn't an addiction, but it seems like at some point I could lay it on the altar and walk away. It would be easy to follow that with the question of why You tear us apart (or allow us to be), but I must quickly give credit where credit's due — good ole Sister Eve. She and Adam had it all. They had the chance to never be parted and she blew it, for herself, and for me. So, phooey on you, Eve! I sure don't like you much tonight!

Tuesday, 8/8/95

For some reason I'm thinking about the week Ron died. I haven't written much about it — or the funeral.

After the paramedics returned and removed Ron's body, things were set in place to unfold. Steve, Allen, and Trish spent the night. Jerry and Marilyn brought Trish and Allen over — Jay brought Steve and Angie. Angie and Jay stayed for a while and left. It was too late for Mom and Dad to come over. It was after 10:00 P.M. when they got home. They came the next morning.

Don came in Wednesday, I believe, and stayed until the weekend. It was such a comfort having him there. *He's okay for a big brother!!* He helped with advice on investments, cars, etc.

Aunt Barbara and Joyce came from Ohio. Ray came from

Louisville. (I'm glad he came for Steve.) Jane, Marie, Connie, Candy, and Adam came from New York. Lucille, Jim and Lucy were here too. Uncle Bob came from Indianapolis. So many others wanted to come, but couldn't.

Rita and Cassius came from West Virginia for the viewing, which meant a lot. She'd just had a slight heart attack a week or two before, but they wanted to come. They're such precious people.

Jeremy came to the funeral home. Kendall, Mary, Kristen, Weetie, and Stephnee (from work) came to the funeral. That meant so much to me!

Marilyn and Tony came too. Tony had to reschedule several meetings to make it. They went to the graveside service and then Marilyn went to the house while Tony attended one of his meetings. He had to drive all the back to Virginia from Baltimore to pick her up. People have been so wonderful!

The funeral was delayed until Friday, partly because of the autopsy, partly because of the transplants. It was hard not knowing for a week or two what Ron died from.

I was surprised when the cemetery wanted payment up front and the funeral home didn't. Seems backwards to me. At any rate, I didn't have the cash on hand so I was scrambling to find the credit cards. Ron always gave me one and put the rest "away." Two weeks before he died he hollered from the computer room to tell me where he was putting them. I couldn't hear him so I said, "Okay, Hon!" *I didn't need to know that stuff. That was his job!* It wasn't until I moved that I found them. That'll teach me to listen! I called Linda from Citizens in Vincennes and she (the bank) loaned me the money.

When we were choosing the grave marker, we could choose three symbols to put on it. When I saw the opened Bible with "Book of Life" on it, I knew that was it. I didn't want anything else on it. That said it all!

The funeral was beautiful. Pastor Reynolds really did a great job. I had the service taped. I'm so glad I did that. It's comforting to listen to it. The music was beautiful!

There's only one thing I'd change about the funeral if I could. The family went in together on a casket spray and standing basket. I wish I had thought of having an open Bible at John 14:1-6 with a single red rose lying across it. That's the scripture Pastor Eagy read to me the night Ron died. *He was so kind — his voice so soft and comforting.* He stayed with me when the police and ambulance left until the guys got there. None of us really had the money for flowers and Ron always thought that was a waste. I think they're a comfort.

Wednesday, 8/9/95

I was reminded of something I'd forgotten about finding Ron. The paramedics and Pastor Eagy were on their way. I remember thinking briefly that someone must have murdered Ron. I knew that "People" die suddenly, but that's "People" — not my Ron. He was so healthy! (I think I found my sense of humor cause saying that reminds me of something funny.)

Allen bought an iguana when he was seventeen. It died a few days later. The pet store gave him a hard time on the phone. They finally said to put it in the refrigerator and bring it in the next day. I went with him to the store. They took it to the back room to "examine" it. It was clear they were trying to build a case of neglect. They brought it back out front, laid the poor dead thing on the counter, looked at me and said, "There's only one thing wrong with this iguana." I, very skeptically said, "Yes, and what is that?" He answered, "It's dead." There was no apparent reason for its demise.

Same thing with Ron. He was healthy, ate right, and exercised, didn't smoke or drink. Yet, he was dead. Didn't seem logical.

Thursday, 8/10/95

Yesterday afternoon I had the feeling that I was waking up from a dream. The "dream" was my life — including Ron's death. It felt like I was waking up to reality — to my "real" life. It was interesting (almost a relief) like all the fighting against reality was dissolved and gone. There was such a peace.

Could this be called "Acceptance?" What ever it is, it felt good. Today I find a new excitement for the future in my heart. I even must admit (putting it in writing seems to help me "admit" to my feelings) that I'm excited about something else. I hesitate, even now to express it because others have read my journal and I would not want to hurt anyone. However, I must get back to the reason I'm keeping this journal — to help myself get through this pain. I must be honest.

Why am I finding it so hard to admit that I hope to love again — to find someone to hold — to be held by again? Could it be that old foe "Guilt?" Probably is, cause I really do feel guilty for having these feelings "so soon," but I've promised myself to be honest — completely honest with my feelings.

My marriage with Ron will always be a part of me, but it is a part of my past. Seems to me that when the feeling's right, it's time to start putting it in its place. Otherwise, you end up living in the past. I go back to my own heart and how I'd want Ron to react if I had died instead. No one but God and I know my heart. While I don't want to hurt anyone, it's He who knows the source of my lifted Spirit today. For some reason I feel the presence of the Holy Spirit in my heart right now so strongly I feel like shouting! How come I can sit with tears coming down my face in Burger King, but I hesitate to shout with the joy of the Lord in the same place?!

Somehow the world literally looks brighter today. I know I'll cry a million more tears, but I hope I can be happy for this healing taking place. O, Lord, Holy Spirit, thank You for Your presence in my heart today!

Someone asked me today how I'm doing and I answered, "Real good! For the first time in five months I feel like living again." That sounded so cold — so uncaring to my ears. Why? Let me ponder this for a minute.

Okay. I've come up with another phase to grieving no one's ever defined before. It's Puberty...yep! Cause I feel like crying again

... crying for my feelings of wanting to be "older" yet being afraid to "leave home" (the comfortable.) I'm not referring to the grief as being comfortable, but of my life with Ron as being comfortable. The future is so unsure: will I remain single (it's okay if I do) or remarry? Who knows?! I know one thing for sure. God's my strength and my guide. I want to follow Paul's example of being happy where I am. Sometimes that means reminding myself to be where I am. I can cry and be happy at the same time.

I still miss Ron. That deep chasm is still in my heart, but I think I'll get some wood and begin building a bridge. When I'm more sure of myself, I'll cover it with concrete. I must remember I'm still in recovery — don't want to "finalize" anything right now. I'm still vulnerable.

Tuesday Evening, 8/15/95

I don't want to do this any more! I don't want to be a widow, okay God?! Please, just put my life back the way it was: deeply in debt, two ole clunker cars, an apartment, AND my Ron! Okay? I've given it a try and I'm failing miserably. I'm always running back to You in tears. I must be wearing You out! Maybe I've been in a real bad accident and I'm in a coma imagining all this has happened. Maybe I'll wake up tomorrow. What do You think, God? You'd have to convince a few other people they've been dreaming too, but You ARE God! You could handle that. I don't care how You do it, just please give me my Ron back — *please!* Please, God, don't make me do this anymore. Okay ... I'm bargaining — maybe I'm denying — but I'll do anything in Your will to make it happen. O, God, right now (tonight), I want it all to stop. I want the pain to end. In this stage called Puberty I've decided not to leave home. I want the past back. I don't care if it hurts, I'm going back to last winter, and tonight, in my dreams, I'll be with Ron. (Man, I sound like a brat, but that's okay too. Tonight I don't feel very cooperative with this new life. Notice I didn't say I don't want to cooperate with God cause I know He's got me where He wants and needs me and I'm okay with that ... just having a "moment!")

Whew. I'm glad that's over! Where do these feelings come from?!

Thursday, 8/17/95

You blessed me again this morning, Lord! I was talking to Mom and told her I feel like living again. I went on to say how much I love Ron, but that he's a part of my past and I feel like moving on — that there's a future out here for me. She was so glad to hear me say that. (They don't want me to be unhappy.)

Others may say, "Of course, what else would she say?" but reality knows Ron was her son. It would be easy for her to want me to never move on. (I think I would feel that way a little bit.)

Ron and I didn't always see eye to eye with our parents, but we always had a great relationship with them. (They were usually right when we disagreed!)

Lord, thank You for letting me be me without smacking me around! I was so filled with grief the other night. I meant every word I said, but You let me express my sorrow and get beyond it (and You didn't lay a guilt trip on me).

Friday, 8/18/95

I think it's the computer! I'm working this morning, minding my own business and I start to think about moving out of the garden apartment into the hi-rise — of Ron carrying just about all the groceries up the stairs all at once. (We were on the fourth level in the garden apartments.) I wonder if he was exhausted, or in pain, from over exertion of his heart.

The ole "If I'd Only Known" feelings are running rampant this morning. Try as I may, I couldn't stop them until I gave in and cried my heart out again.

Friends whose husbands have left them tell me of breaking into tears six months later (no one's mentioned seven months). Does that mean all these tears stop after six months? Is that the end of the pain? *Am I crazy?!* Of course you cry for a while! It's good to know that at least I'm having more good days now than bad ones.

As long as there's progress, I can get through this (with God's help). Lord, it's so comforting to know that You'll never leave me — that I can count on You being with me.

I was thinking — wondering if God's got a dump truck like Pastor said one night — one full of blessings ready to back it up and dump it out on us?! Kind of a neat thought. He's sure been busy blessing me! I think about the fact that Ron and I can't communicate (as some have suggested I try doing). Pastor Reynolds did a study on Heaven and gives scripture reference to the saints in Heaven knowing what's going on down here. Since there are no tears in Heaven it seems to be contradictory to think of Ron being happy, knowing how much pain I'm in.

For one thing, he probably notifies God it's time to dump another load of blessings on me when I go through a bad time. (That would bring joy to him.) Then there's the issue of time not being the same any longer. While the last five months have been an eternity to me, Ron's probably still being welcomed into Heaven. Who knows?! All I know (and believe) is that God doesn't make mistakes and He knows what He's doing.

Chapter Six

8/20 ~ 9/19/1995

Grief Becomes So Familiar

Sunday, 8/20/95

I love some reruns — Andy Griffith, Dr. Quinn — shows like that, I could watch about a million times! There's one re-run I'm really starting to tire of. It's the ole "It's been _____ months since I found Ron" re-run. It's so painful. I worked at church on the directory all day today. I was so tired by the time I got to the service. I thought it was from being there all day, but I realized it was because I'd dealt all day with the 5th month anniversary of finding Ron.

I never thought about Grief as being either a friend or an enemy until tonight. In considering that question I don't think of Grief as a friend. (I certainly don't like this pain.) Yet, to call it an enemy is not appropriate for me. I guess I know if I don't deal with it, that it could easily become an enemy, but right now, Grief is helping me to heal. Heal from what?! From Grief. *Man, am I getting dizzy!*

So, if it's not a friend or an enemy, I guess that leaves it being an acquaintance. An acquaintance is someone you meet — work with for a while (or years; *that's scary!!*) and go on without revisiting it again. I think that fits. I certainly will never lose Ron again. So, some day when I've finished this job, "Grief for Ron" will be behind me.

I know I'm healing because I don't suppress the pain (at least, not for long at a time). Even though I've left another song service tonight, I know I'm getting better because I had a great healing this past week. These "moments" are getting further apart so I know I'm on the road.

However, the intensity doesn't lessen. It's still brutal, cold, hard, and so deep that I'm back on top of Cadillac Mountain looking for the end.

I thank the Holy Spirit tonight for sending me to the altar instead of letting me go out the door — for there, at Calvary, was a healing as the Balm of Gilead poured out on me as Joan prayed for me. O yes, God, You are with me the whole way. Thank You so much for a church called Capital Baptist. Thank You!

Monday Morning, 8/21/95

In thinking more about Grief as an acquaintance, I realize it can't be called that. An acquaintance doesn't go everywhere with you. This Grief is everywhere I am — in bed, in the tub, in church, on family outings.

I wonder if I'm the only person who has this need to define things. I'm reminded of being at the doctor when my spinal cord was compressed. I begged him to tell me "what" was hurting. Was it nerve damage, muscle damage, my spine —— What?! He said that he didn't know. I felt that if I could find out what was hurting, I could deal with it. When I finally did find out what it was, we did something about it and it was fixed.

Maybe Grief becomes a new organ in the body, an organ that can destroy this body if I don't deal with it. It's too intangible to say that it's an "emotion." At this point I don't want to deal with defining it any more. End of discussion.

I'm tired today. Dealing with the emotions like yesterday leaves me physically tired. (That's okay because I'm spiritually in shape!)

Wednesday, 8/23/95 lunch

"How Great Thou Art" — what a wonderful song! Yes, some

day God is sending His Son back. What a glorious day that will be! What a blessing it is to be alive and to be glad to be! On this road called Grief I find contentment and peace. Maybe I should label Grief as a road. A road once traveled? Probably not! I think I'll begin to repave it with treasures laid up in Heaven.

I'm really getting excited about teaching. There's a burst of energy welling up in my soul tonight that I can't explain. There's still such sadness in thinking of Ron and our life together being over, but I truly believe that our life's experiences can make us or break us. Please, God, help this pain to make many, many blessings from You come to be for others.

Thursday, 8/24/95

My life feels almost normal today. I feel like I'm standing taller — not bent over so badly by the weight of Grief. I know that down inside I still have tears left. I haven't been through Thanksgiving and Christmas yet, but I'm going to look forward to those days with a positive outlook. I have so much to be thankful for. Without Christ's birth, where would Ron be now?! While there will be a huge hole on those days I'm going to concentrate on the positive.

I wonder today if this is just another phase — if I'll slip backwards a month or so. I really don't think so. My whole outlook has changed to a more positive one. To God be the glory! I'm still hung up on this six month to a year thing, but God reminded me that I've always pushed ahead in life and dealt with things "quicker than normal" (by man's rules).

I realized this morning that at least 50% of my non-committed thinking is spent in conversation with God. When I'm not talking or concentrating on work or something else, at least half of that time I'm talking to Him. *I wonder if this were true before Ron died?* I hope it stays that way for a long time! I believe it probably was true, at least to an extent, because I don't know how I would have made it otherwise.

I don't believe surviving this loss victoriously is an accident. I believe I was where God wanted me to be when Ron died. I know

He set the stage. Without a doubt, He had prepared me before I ever opened that door that night.

Friday Morning, 8/25/95

I cried myself to sleep last night and woke a couple of times crying for Ron. I was so sad and lonely.

It's not that I'm unhappy now, but I am sad. It's those extremes again! I'm trying to accept the pain this time instead of fighting it or bargaining with it.

I'm very happy and at peace with my decision to teach and sing in the choir and do the visitation and the Bible Institute. I was so upset before when every minute was planned, but now that I've made these decisions, I'm ok with it. I want, more than anything, to be working for the Lord. I know I'll never be instrumental in saving hundreds and I know my life will never touch thousands, but if only God and I know how much I love Him and want to serve Him, I'll be okay. I'll never be a "Paul" but I hope I'm a good "Barnabas" (make that a "Brendabus"...*I'm a girl*).

I wish I understood what hit me last night when I went to bed that caused me to cry myself to sleep. What triggers these emotions?! Ron and I never shared the home I'm in now so that can't be it. As I sit here I realize I'm only "half" here. Before Ron died, when you met me or looked at me, you were looking at only half of me. Ron was such a part of my identity, of who I was. Mom said it soon after Ron died — that we could no longer refer to "Mike and Angie" and now the "Ron and Brenda" tie was gone too.

So, "I'm" cut in half and I'm all alone. Man! Ron and I really took our vows seriously in becoming one — but only "til death us did part." We were a pretty good team though, weren't we? We complimented each other; he was 6'4" — I'm 5'1/2;" he was quick to yell — I was slower and so on, but we had a couple of things in common — our love for the Lord and our love and commitment to each other. Yes, I miss him. *I think it's time to visit the cemetery again.*

Sunday Evening, 8/27/95

It's been a wonderful Lord's Day! Experienced a touch of sadness at one song, but, all in all, a peace reigned in my heart.

When I got up I wanted to pretend that Ron would be coming home from his business trip tonight. But, even though I think it would have been comforting for just a little while to slip from reality, it would have hurt a lot more to have to come up with a plane crash or something to explain why he wasn't coming home. Reality seemed a lot less painful!!

God, You're working on me. Seems like I've been wandering in this Grief long enough. It's time to get beyond it and really get to work for You. You've been so very wonderful to me — so very gentle. I love You so much. Choir practice started tonight. I'm so glad I went. It's going to be wonderful. Pastor Eagy has such a wonderful, sweet spirit. He's a very good leader.

Thursday, 8/31/95

I'm finding that I'm missing Ron holding me more and more all the time. I never realized what a privilege of marriage it is to be able to say, "Hold me" and feel his protective arms envelope me. Why do I have to lose something (or someone) to realize how much that entity meant to me? I can be thankful that I know in my heart (and my head) how much we really appreciated each other. He knew it too.

Am I too old to run away? Seriously, why can't I? Or, more to the point, why won't I?! I guess because there's no use.

I believe I finally put a handle on Grief. It's not a friend or foe, an acquaintance or an emotion — it's not a road once traveled or an organ of the body. You know what it is? It's a condition.

I have another condition. I have a 35% permanent partial disability of the cervical spine. Because of that condition, there are some things I do, like sleep with a certain pillow or sit at a certain seat to avoid having to turn my head for very long, etc.

There are other things I avoid doing, like running, jumping on a trampoline, and I try not to run into walls, etc.! Last week at work, I came around a corner looking the other way (at a good clip — I was in a hurry) and ran smack into the very firm chest of a man. He went "Ugh" — I went "ouch" and my neck hurt for twenty-four hours. So, I try to avoid such things — because of my "condition." I will be wearing a neck brace when I'm in anything that moves until God restores my neck to its original condition before the fusion. We have an agreement! If I'm in another car accident without it, the doctor guarantees that I'll be a quadriplegic.

I guess you could say I've learned to live with my "condition." I'm learning to live with this other condition — Grief. I realized today that it hasn't gotten less severe (or less often) or less all consuming. I've simply learned to live with it. That bugs me. I thought there'd be some point where I'd "get through" or "over" this Grief. I don't think I ever will. Oh, I'll learn to live with it (like my neck condition). I see people all the time who have lost a very dear loved one years ago. Say the right thing, or ask the right question, and they're back in tears — back at the graveside again.

Monday, 9/4/95 (Labor Day)

I just don't know how to get beyond this pain. It keeps coming back in waves so high and dense that I'm sure I'm going to get lost again. I didn't read my Bible (or pray much) while I was away for the holidays. That may account for part of my mood. We went to church yesterday. The message was on the faithfulness of God. The Pastor pointed out that if God got Christ past Calvary, He can get us through what we're faced with. How true!

Jane and I walked on the beach before we left for home today. More memories — good ones — good ones that hurt.

Tonight my heart says there's no hope for lasting happiness ever again for me. I'm glad my head was listening to the sermon yesterday. Perhaps while I sleep tonight the message will drop twelve inches to my heart! God, could You carry me on the beach tonight as I go to sleep? Walk close to the surf so I can feel the coolness of the mist as it soothes these hot coals of Grief I'm consumed with tonight. And, God thanks for being faithful! I'm trying so hard to reciprocate!

Tuesday, 9/5/95

The separation becomes more real every day. When Ron was alive, we'd often comment how amazed we were that our love could continue to grow stronger each year. Seems like it would have to come to a point where you just couldn't love the same person any deeper. Guess love is something like faith — the more it's exercised, the larger it grows.

Right now that's how this pain is. It grows deeper each day. What if it's the same as love? Everyone tells me it will heal with time. What I need someone to tell me is how much time? Tell me where the end is and then I can deal with it. I'm so frustrated with myself! It must be me — it must be something in my personality that keeps hanging onto the impossible.

Dear Ron,

Don't worry, I haven't flipped! I know you can't begin to answer the questions I'm about to ask. And, I know you can't give me the strength and comfort I so desperately need today, but since old habits die hard, I thought maybe talking to you would help. After all, you've always been there to listen and advise. We didn't always see eye to eye with each other, but you were such a wonderful sounding board. You kept me grounded.

We always knew we could get through anything as long as we had each other. We certainly saw a lot of diversity in our years together, but we saw a lot of victories too!

Ron, I don't know how to survive this loss. I don't know how to be a widow. I know in my head that God knows what He's doing — that He's going to see me through, but my heart left this earth on March 20 when you left me.

I wouldn't wish you back for anything (not really)! If God gave me the choice today I wouldn't want you back from where you are. Yet, I'd give all I have to be with you again. I wouldn't bring you back, but I want you back! How can I make both statements and

mean them both with all my heart at the same time?! Oh, Ron, I
need for you to hold me so badly. I need for your strength to flow
to me by being held in your arms. Remember right after I was diagnosed with the thyroid condition and something happened at work
that I found out was my misunderstanding? Remember how I ran
to our room and sat against the bed (in the very spot where I would
find you a couple of weeks later) crying? You came and wrapped
me in your arms and held me. You assured me that I wasn't losing
my mind and that I would adjust to the medication and that you'd
be there to help me get through until then. Ron, I need you now
to hold me like that again.

With only a destroyed heart to deal with, I'm left completely
crippled and completely alone. I'm so glad that God is so near
(even though today I can't even feel His presence.) Why can't I?!
Why have I been unable to accept His comfort? I'm so overwhelmed with my need to be with you that I've even shut our Lord
out. I don't understand that, but I'm thankful that He's faithful and
that I can be sure He's with me. I know that He's keeping me in
His hand, safe and protected while I'm in His Intensive Care Unit
with this new heart attack I'm experiencing.

Ron, I love you with all my heart! How can I ever learn to live
and love again? How? We had discussed the "what if" of this situation (as far as wanting the other to live and love again), but we
never discussed the semantics of how to do it. We would have never
thought of that. So, is it any wonder I'm fumbling for so long?! I
love you! I always will.

–Brenda

Wednesday Evening, 9/6/95

I am so thankful for C.B.C.! It's good to be in the Lord's house
this evening. I think I'm becoming a Christian snob cause there's
no church like this one! It's not perfect (sorry Pastor), but it's great!
The church lives up to it's motto, "A Church with A Heart;" our
Pastors preach the Word of God (no more and no less); there's a
gazillion ministries one can get involved in; the Holy Spirit is alive

and well here, and so on.

Yesterday I felt the Holy Spirit telling me two or three times that He could bring me comfort, but I didn't accept it. I'm not sure why. I wouldn't say I was "enjoying" the pain. Maybe I just didn't feel like I had the energy to come alive again. I do know that God didn't leave me alone. His offer of comfort kept coming until I finally accepted it. He's so gentle at times like that. Again, He didn't scold and rebuke me, He waited patiently for me and then wrapped me in His love again.

Thursday, 9/7/95

I think Grief must destroy a certain number of brain cells! It's been over five and one half months since Ron died and I'm still not fully functional at work. Things that never would have gotten past me do. I must wonder at Jeremy's patience. I wish I could find a way to repay him (and AMS) for their care and concern.

Concentration seems to be a problem. I can focus on a particular job, but it's like I have tunnel vision in doing that task and no more. Usually, I'd be analyzing ways to do it better and quicker, as well as ways to double-check my work. This must be what it's like to suffer brain damage that impairs physical activity yet leaves the memory of what you used to be intact (to a much lesser degree, of course)!

Regardless, I don't like it. Part of that may be pressure that's natural with me being the sole breadwinner. That puts a tremendous pressure on someone who has never been in such a position before.

Sunday, 9/10/95

Dear Lord,

Sitting by Ron's grave, I was going to write him a letter, but I believe I'll write to someone who can hear and respond!

It's so beautiful here at the cemetery. The grass is brown from the drought, but there's a cool breeze blowing that gives a peaceful feel to the air (and to my spirit). Forgive me for ever judging others who felt a need to visit a cemetery. It really is nice to come here and remember happier times. It seems to bring that happiness to the present. I can see where only satan could bring fear and spookiness into such a peaceful scene.

I'm not sure where the summer went. It's almost fall. I'm sure glad You've been with me, Lord. It's comforting to know that You'll be with me during the days of fall and winter, Thanksgiving and Christmas too. I truly do not dread the short term (or long term) future.

It's been interesting to realize that it's five to six months after the death that the real Grief sets in. And, I've been blessed with being surrounded by people at work and at church who still support, ask, and care about me.

A part of me wishes I could stay here at the graveside, alive and enjoying the serenity, but I guess I wouldn't be much use to you here, would I?!

Lord, I want to make a difference for You. I want to begin to spend the rest of my life serving You and others the way I've been served these last six months. I won't insult You by saying I want to repay You. (I could never do that, for my debt is too great.) Just as I've asked You to help me do my best at work, I want You to help me to do my best for You. I cry out to You today with joy, love, and total admiration for WHO You are and for what You continue to do for me.

As Les said in Sunday School this morning, we get caught up in tithing the 10% You command, but then we think of the other 90% being ours. That applies to our time and talents too, I'm afraid. Sometimes I tell You that I do this and that for You so "this" night or "that" day is mine. No, God, we're all Yours whether we acknowledge that or not. Think about what this country would be like if all Christians would live that fact! I wish I could always do so, but we're human (at least I know that I am) and no matter how good my intentions are, sometimes (many times) I get in the way.

Lord, why is it so comforting to be here? I don't understand that. Is it the cool breeze rustling through the trees, the sound of traffic passing by, the feel of my full skirt blowing in that breeze wrapping around the tree I'm leaning on? Or, could it just be the peace in knowing that, not only is Ron physically with You now, but that I will be too some day? There are two screws on this grave marker that will some day hold the declaration that my life on this earth has ended. I have some mixed emotions on that, but, You know what? They're about 99% good feelings.

While I don't want anyone to suffer as I have in Grief, it's still kind of good to know that I'll be missed (there's that human self-ishness again). The other point in Grief (at least for a Christian) is that, while the Grief is pretty severe, the blessings have been mighty powerful too!

God, thank You for this visit! It's time to get to choir practice. Thanks for convicting me of that too! I'm excited about the choir!

Love, Brenda

Tuesday, 9/12/95

Allen's asking Lisa to marry him tomorrow (on her birthday). She told me he has some pretty high standards for marriage based on Ron's and mine. That's good. I want him to know our marriage was not perfect, but it was based on commitment and faithfulness, and our Christian upbringing. I want him to understand the responsibility he's taking on — the responsibility for her spiritual well being as head of his household. I want her to know that this "women's lib" stuff doesn't work.

Next Wednesday is when I plan on taking my wedding band off. It's the 20th — six months since Ron died. The 21st was our anniversary. Why is this so hard to do? There's such ceremony around putting a ring on and absolutely none on taking it off. So, I'll meet God at the altar and we'll have our own ceremony. My ring has been off my body once, off my ring finger twice. They made me take it off when Allen was born. When I had carpal tunnel surgery I transferred it to my right hand. I've got a needlepoint picture to mount my ring on.

Wednesday, 9/13/95

Pastor called yesterday to tell me they'd decided to make my class part of the single's ministry for management purposes. I know that I don't want to be referred to as "single" — I'm a widow. I was concerned if I feel that way and don't consider myself to be "Mrs." Fahey any longer, how would an older widow feel?

Older ladies I've met in the past still consider themselves to be married and still wear their ring. We all deal with our identities differently.

Anyway, I got real upset (there was another issue at stake too) and called Pastor back. I have to wonder...if he'd known what an emotional mess he was inheriting when I joined the church, would he have tried to discourage me from joining? We talked for a while. Then, Travis and Renee and I were talking (in general terms) about divorce, widowhood, etc. He pointed out that, according to Biblical terms, I'm more single than a divorced person. And, in our conversation I actually caught myself referring to being "single." So, there I am. I've worked through all that.

Another part of my getting upset was because Pastor told me what they were doing. I didn't have any "control." I finally realized that I was fighting against his authority over me. (Not a good thing to do, Biblically speaking!) Again, not like me.

I believe my strong emotions on the issue of being single stems from my first encounter with a couple of divorced ladies a week after Ron died. They sat and put men (all men) down in such a horrible way. I had just buried a wonderful man. I remember thinking to myself, "If this is what being single means I'll never be single!" *I meant it too!*

Friday Evening, 9/15/95

I worked late. It didn't upset me. I had no real "desire" to get home. Went to the grocery store. As I drove into the development, I was hit head on — no, not by a car, but by something just about as devastating (more so, probably). You know, I believe I could take a major physical pain about a million times easier than this pain, this horrible never-ending, never relenting Grief. I know I could have stood anything on earth with Ron by my side. I wish I'd known how strong he was for me and how weak I would have been without him. Maybe I could have saved some of his strength up in a bottle.

People tell me so often what an inspiration my strength is. To have the strength to be in church Wednesday night, when Ron had died on Monday night, that I "keep smiling," keep working. O, People, why can't you see that I'm quite the opposite!?!! It's because I'm so very weak that, without God, I'd simply melt into the pavement and cease to exist. Yes, my faith is strong. That's the only thing I've exercised, but I know that sometimes God asks for nothing more than that.

I haven't cried all week. Why now? Maybe I'm good at saving things up. (Sure seemed to have enough pain right now to last into the night.) I wish I could go somewhere on a beach tonight and walk in the cool breeze, feel the sand between my toes and the mist of the ocean. I'd even be happy with a visit to the cemetery, but it's just about dark.

I want so badly to back this car up and peel out of here and drive as fast and as hard as I can. Why can't I just pack up and go? *Why did Mom and Dad have to raise me to be so responsible?* Just once, just one time, I feel like rebelling, but I guess I'm safe because I know I won't! Besides, my ice cream would melt. Guess I'd better get inside!

Monday, 9/18/95

I've heard of people with cancer who go in for surgery. When the surgeons get inside they find the cancer "wrapped" around an organ or the spine with "roots" going through so badly that they couldn't be cut out. So, they sew the patient up and tell them it's too late — to pray. I'm beginning to see how the love Ron and I had grew over the years like this. There are so many roots wrapped around my heart (and many going through the very core), that many times all I can do is pray. Sometimes I can pull one out, but it's painful (such as taking my ring off this week).

I've lost my appetite today. I'm trying to eat lunch, but can't. It may be that I'm tired of fast food. I think I'll bring some spaghetti to work tomorrow. That'll be good for the time issue too. I start the Biblical Studies class tonight and plan on using lunch to study. Not leaving the building will add thirty minutes to study time.

I remember, the night Ron died, telling someone who asked how I was that I was numb and, for the time being "numb" was a good place to be. I knew I was in shock (in the Intensive Care Unit). I believe at two months I went "onto the floor" and am only now leaving the hospital, going back as an outpatient occasionally.

There's a new dimension to this though. The pain of our separation is getting much more intense. I guess this makes sense. Seems like I'd feel the pain more as I come out of shock.

There's one more issue I'm new to. It's been on going since Ron died, but I haven't written about it. Since it's not going away, it's beginning to add a real stress to my life, so I believe I need to quit trying to suppress it. As with other things I've felt, I can't seem to deal with it until I acknowledge it enough to write it down.

About two to three weeks after Ron died, I was approached by a man who told me we were going to be together. I only knew him by sight and would never be interested in him (not a put down, there's just some people you "know" wouldn't interest you). For one thing, someone so insensitive to approach me so soon and in the rude manner the approach was made, wouldn't be someone I'd ever see.

I explained very nicely that I was in a lot of pain and it was much too soon to even think about seeing anyone. I thought that would be the end of it, but he kept on "approaching" me. I have someone who's been dealing with him, but he's not getting the message. I'm really scared at this point. I'm going to have to remove myself from the situations where I see him if it goes on any longer.

Plus, Steve and Allen are going to step in if it happens again. I've convinced them to let this other person handle it until now, but they've let me know this is it. Allen pointed out this is how stalkings begin. The guys are so wonderful. They're very protective of me. Yet, they don't live with me and I'm scared enough that I'm calling a security company to look at a system. I don't want to live in fear. I won't live in fear. As a matter of fact, I'm beginning to get miffed!

Tuesday, 9/19/95

The tears come again today. I say that I'm tired of playing this game — this game called "Widowhood." I'm ready for Ron to come home, but I know that won't happen. I know there's no hope for that.

I carry on — making my way alone, yet not. It's as if I'm detached — watching. Surely this can't be me. Surely I don't have the strength to carry on with Ron gone. How in the world have I been functioning? How in the world have I been able to make the decisions and moves I've made?! I stand amazed at God's provisions!! I stand in awe!

I also stand tired and very weary. Why do I have to face tomorrow? Six months — why do I live with a calendar that very nonchalantly calls me back in time? All it does is sit there with the power to break my heart by reminding me of an anniversary I'd just as soon forget. Oh well, forty-eight hours from now I'll be beyond two more dates — six months and what should have been our 27th wedding anniversary.

Chapter Seven

9/20 ~ 10/19/1995

The Six Month Mark –
It's Over Now (Isn't It?)

Wednesday, September 20, 1995, 6 months

Somewhere along the lonely, sad day of yesterday, I remember asking God to give me the "peace that passeth all understanding" today. Couple that with all the people who have been praying for me (they've called yesterday and today) and how could I lose?! God truly blessed me today. There's been a joy in my heart. That curtain still fell when I'd think of Ron (or look at his picture) but that was necessary to keep the peace in place.

I met God at the altar in church tonight. I asked Him to bring Ron over so they could both hear me. There, we had our own ceremony as I removed my wedding band and replaced it with the pearl ring I bought. There was reluctance as I completely removed it from my left finger and hand. A part lingered there for a moment, being held between my thumb and ring finger, but with God's help, I let it go, and there was joy as I recounted to God (with Ron listening), what a wonderful husband Ron had been. I asked God to give him a very special blessing for being so good to me. There were long spans of time when I couldn't be a good wife to Ron because of my pain.

So, another milestone. Maybe this is how things (memories) will all be sometime soon — joyful and glad. I look forward to that day. Oh, God, You are truly awesome! Only You could get me through today singing Your praises! Thank You!

9/21/95, Thursday, 2:30 PM

Twenty-seven years ago, right now, we were getting married. The wedding started twenty minutes late. Brent and Lucille had a flat on the way to the church. He was the best man so we waited!

The sharp pain hits again — the pain of a love gone, of finding Ron, his face so purple and so still. I relive the entire scene again and I cry. I feel so helpless. There's nothing I can do to change this whole thing. And, would I if I could? Sure I would...I wouldn't know the pain and the loneliness.

As I look back on our honeymoon, I should have known I was in for a wild life with Ron. We went to Niagara Falls and the Thousand Islands. It was off-season so the tour boat didn't stop at the island with the castle. Ron thought it would be neat to go to it ourselves. He had this brilliant idea of renting a speedboat (he couldn't swim), following the next tour boat out and sight see on our own. Great plan! Only thing was, we couldn't find our way back. We had no idea for hours which country we were in, but it was fun and we didn't stop having fun. We were married in September, 1968. Allen wasn't born until December, 1970. We wanted to be alone for a while. (We only knew each other three months before we married.)

We had our share of hard times financially and Steve and Allen got broken and torn several times, but we all survived. When we moved out of Mike and Angie's in September or October last year, Steve stayed since he had a job near-by. So, we were alone, and we loved it. We would have taken either son back into our home in a heartbeat, but we'd looked forward to being alone again. It was just another blessing God granted us. It was easier for Steve too. He's said several times that it would have been harder if he'd lived at home and seen Ron every day.

Friday, 9/22/95

Mom goes to the doctor today to find out for sure about what "type" of Lupus she has. She's having a real hard time. I don't believe I could love her and Dad more than if they'd been my natural parents. If the Lord ever does bless me with another husband, I know I want Dad to be the one to give me away.

I remember at Ron's viewing that I realized that the "legal" bond with his parents and me was lying in a casket. I remember telling them of my fear later through tears. Mom let me know I'd always be their daughter. How very blessed I've been with two sets of earthly parents who truly have loved and nurtured me. I get two when so many others have no idea of what a "functional" (I should say "godly") family is. Yes, God is truly the key to ALL good things.

Monday, 9/25/95

I feel I could use a few days off now. However, I believe it might cause more stress if I took time off at the moment. Besides, what I really need (at least I feel I do) is a month off. I want to go to Vincennes, Campbellsville, Ohio, and Indy — places Ron and I have been. I'm not sure why either. I believe I may be trying to recapture or relive my memories. It may be I want to confront them — to show this Grief thing that it needs to let go of the past. Try as I may, I can't seem to get beyond it. There's something holding me back and I'm not sure leaving for a month would give me the answer. Maybe I need some goals. The Bible says that we perish without a vision. Maybe that's what I need to concentrate on and the other issues will resolve themselves.

I think I'll stay home from church tonight and tomorrow night (revival going on) and work on setting some goals. I realized this weekend that I probably wouldn't be able to breeze through the holidays like I originally thought. I need to be more realistic with myself. I don't have any plans for Saturday or Sunday afternoon. I think I'll keep those times free too. Maybe if I get everything straight at home, I'll feel better too.

Something is telling me to keep moving through this valley I'm in right now instead of camping out. I know I need to burn the plans for a "home" (temporary or not) that's been forming in this valley experience. I cannot — I will not let this Grief consume me. There's denial and then there's acceptance. I've accepted this as a condition. I won't accept it as a permanent way of life that hinders my very existence.

Wednesday, 9/27/95

This is it, Lord. I'm going down for the count. Never in my life have I experienced apathy — until today. I can't handle any more major hurts. When I prayed two and a half weeks ago for You to help me at work, You must have literally flipped on a switch in Heaven, because I began doing things that were "normal" for me to do.

This thing with this man (let's call him "Joe") is also getting to me. "Joe" has been told no. The issue's been settled two or three times. Yet, he came back again. No one can assure me it won't happen again. I cringe every time I see him. Except for Larry, I've never felt fear of a man in my life. *Larry tried to drown me when I was nine or ten in the public pool (held me under water) so I think that fear was valid!* I don't like this, but it's an issue who's time to be dealt with has come. I'm thinking a meeting is in order.

I want to go and see Jan for Columbus Day next week. I have to decide if it's worth the additional pressure of more debt to get away. I'm not sure. Please help me to decide, Lord.

God, You have given me so much (so many blessings) that I don't want to fail You. I'm not doing my best in being a Bible Study leader either. The worst pain today is in feeling like I'm failing You when I have such hopeless feelings.

I've decided to confront "Joe" (with Your approval) so that pressure is gone (at least I see it "going").

Thank You, Lord for helping me work through some things. I no longer feel apathy (thank You)! I prayed as I entered the restaurant for Your help and to no surprise, (but with great appreciation) I see You've answered another prayer!

After Church

Well, satan - you took me down for the count this week! But, know what? God was there to soften the fall - He was there to lift me back up - He was there to back me up. you are so incredibly stupid - not to mention sneaky. You hit me between the eyes with something so new I couldn't identify it until today - apathy. If I don't feel I can't be hurt. True - but I also can't be loved. And - you big dummy - don't you realize every time you hit or cut me I will bleed - I will cry - I will feel the pain - but there was some blood shed a long time ago - there were some stripes received many many years ago that will wipe away anything you can hit me with. Sound familiar? Go back with me - let me show you a place called Calvary. Satan - Christ fought my battle this week some 2000 years ago - **don't you remember?** How in this world can you forget that?! Haven't I told you you'll never get me? That's not a challenge, satan - it's a fact. It's a promise AND it's something you can bank on! Why do you keep coming at Christians? Don't you know Romans 8:28 (POW!) What about John 3:16? (WHAM!) What about verses like "Greater is He who is in me...," how about those three "children" in a furnace?! Need I go on? Satan - just save yourself some grief and re-read Revelation - you've lost! But, scripture must be fulfilled. You're destined to go down in the proverbial "burst of flames" (you probably think it really is a proverb)! Oh well - I have come through victorious in Christ. I just checked my wounds - removed the bandages for a check. Guess what I found, satan - my wounds are healed - and, know what, king of stupidity? There's about a foot of scar tissue you'll never penetrate again with apathy. So, put on your seat belt - baton down the hatches and watch what God's gonna do now. We left the stage of Grief this week. You know what I realize? You tried to take Ron's death and make it ugly. You tried to turn it into a tool to be used by your darkness. When that didn't work you thought you'd try something new (it was pretty powerful too), but God took it and I know He's going to make it beautiful. I've gotten a glimpse of Heaven this week. I love God so much. Oh, satan - why didn't you believe God way back at

Creation? Why did you have to fall? Think of how much more wonderful life could have been - (not to mention your own eternity) if you'd only kept looking up. You are a powerful foe, but you're beaten. To God Be The Glory! To Him is the victory.

Friday, 9/29/95

"The End of the World" is playing. I stop ... I pause ... I look at your picture. It's different this time. There's a very deep sadness, but I don't cry. I still don't know why my heart goes on beating, but now I wonder why these eyes of mine don't cry. As I look at your picture, I realize I really am learning to live without you. Guilt ... sadness ... slight panic ... the fear that even the memory of you being a part of my past won't protect me (how could it anyway? - false security) ... all these emotions. I think I'm flipping back to the Puberty Stage of Grief this morning. *Heavy sigh!*

Monday, 10/2/95

Fear ... uneasiness ... sleeplessness, all foreign to me. Yet, today I feel these emotions. We met with "Joe" last night. Lord, I prayed to You and asked You to control my words, emotions, and thoughts during the meeting. I went in with no agenda other than to ask why he continues to pursue me. As with many men who attack women, he made his last advance my fault, all because I was within ten feet of where he was. He perceived that to be me "approaching" him. The anger that boiled within me was calmed, but I left more afraid than ever.

I put my very life in Your hands because today I feel threatened. When I got home last night my garden hose had been moved. I felt uneasy going inside. Stupid? Maybe — maybe not.

I'm so lost in my thoughts I can't even write them down. This is not good!

Ron's death robbed me of my sounding board, my equalizer, my stabilizer, my grounding rod. "Joe" has robbed me of my security, my innocence, joy, and peace.

My joy and peace come from God. Am I letting this human do

this? Is God? Is this Your way, God, to show me what it would have been like way back when — when I was talking about "one Brenda-sized-bomb?" Is this what it's like to be blown to bits — to be blown to smithereens?! I feel there's not one part of my life that's stable right now. I also know (in my head) that You are in control. You haven't moved and I definitely don't have the nerve to turn away from You for a moment! Thank You for that!

Is this all a game? I go to work and I smile. I function. I interact. Yet, I'm in turmoil. I'm really counting on some miracles, some really heavy blessings coming soon. God, would it be too selfish of me to ask You for a blessing or two to help get me through? Oh, God, I don't want to be selfish, hateful, and hurtful, but tonight I don't feel anything good about "Joe." I just want him to go away, to cease to exist. *How awful of me!* I've tried to be Christ-like and "give him a break," "look for the good" but, God, he's so horrible and self centered (as if I'm not right now). Still, I'm not out to hurt anyone.

Tuesday, 10/3/95

Peace reigns! Guess God did some open-heart surgery on me during the night. I sure feel a lot better today. I never realized how calming Ron was on me. I sure do miss him a lot! I'm looking forward to seeing Jan and Jim. I'm glad I'm getting away for a couple of days.

Wednesday, 10/4/95 (evening)

One phrase I would never have applied to myself is "contented to live alone." However, I really am doing fine. Do I want to stay this way? I'm not sure. There's a lot of pain in marriage (I don't mean that in a negative way). *That's a very strange thing for me to say. As a matter of fact, I can't believe I said it.* It's just that lately I've seen some people going through some pretty heavy things. Losing Ron was pretty severe, so why would I want to set myself up again for such a thing?!

There are a lot of great things too. I wonder if my neighbors think I'm weird for sitting in my car so much! It's just hard to concentrate inside with Muff-up, the phone, TV, etc. so I sit here and write. Anyway, yes, marriage (to the right person) is great! I'm glad I'm okay alone and I'm glad I don't have to worry about my future. *That's God's job.*

Thursday, 10/5/95

Somewhere over the last week, my dependency on Ron has been broken. I've spent my adult life wondering when I was going to grow up. (You know, "feel" like a parent, like an "adult.") Suddenly, today I feel "grown up" — "mature."

I'm not sure where this took place (or when). I can now kill multiple spiders and crickets. *(Still don't like it, but I only scream now when they jump right at me!)* Last weekend I washed my car and mowed the grass (cut my hands doing so just like Ron used to do!), wanted to cry a time or two (I'm such a wimp), but I made it through.

I don't have a clue what my future holds for me. I do know that I'm supposed to stay put in my home, in Virginia, in my job, and in my church (thank God)! That's good to know!

I need to plan for my financial future. As for my life, I'm going to do my best to take it one day at a time. Tomorrow is not promised so I really need to live in the "here and now." In case I hang around until retirement I need to plan for my future as if I'll remain single. (Did you hear that, Pastor?! I called myself "single.") At least I'm building equity in my home — that's good. Beyond that, it's probably going to be a year or so before I can start saving anything substantial. I just think it's great how God's providing for me now. Maybe now that I feel grounded He'll see fit to let me build up a bank account. He's been so wise. If I'd had much more than I do, I would have been out of here. What a waste that would have been. I know I can serve God anywhere, but I really want to be in His perfect will for my life. He's got the Master Plan...why should I get in the way?!

Friday, 10/6/95

I'm in the plane approaching St. Louis. As I look below, I see a neat pattern of houses and streets, streams, railroad tracks, etc. From up here it's all neat and laid out and orderly. *Is this how God sees our lives?* Is this what it's like to see the Master Plan? Look! Over there is March 20. And here — right here is now, October 6, but, look closely and you can see ten years from now.

God can see our entire lives at a glance. To get from here to there is so easy. Yet, for us, we have some turns to make — some rivers to cross (some rivers to cry), but the streets are so straight, even with the turns we have to make.

The announcement said not to leave your luggage and walk away and to report any bag you're asked to watch. Yet, the lady next to me doesn't hesitate to say, "Sure" when asked to watch another's bag. We really don't believe it can happen to us…she's a professional looking person, neat, and clean. How could she be a terrorist?! And, he's healthy and young (and handsome). How can he die tonight?! Surely it can't happen to me. *Yet, it does.*

We're getting ready to land. For some reason, I don't want to. The last time I was at Jim and Jan's was two summers ago. Ron had returned to work in Vincennes at Midwest. Steve and I came south to do the last fair with the Spaceball. We stayed at Jim and Jan's between the two fairs in Tennessee and Louisiana.

Maybe I should go everywhere Ron and I have been in one swoop through the U.S. That way, I could get all these "1st times back" done and be finished with all this Grief work. I came to get away from pressure and find myself "working!" I really don't want to do this. I don't want sadness attached to everything I do. It's a real bummer! Just had a thought ... do tears shrink you? Maybe that's where all my weight went. Maybe I cried so much that I shrunk myself! (I agree - I've flipped! Must be the altitude! O well, here we go!)

Saturday Morning, 10/7/95

I believe my subconscious knew what waited for me on the ground last night. I had completely forgotten how very much alike Jim and Ron were. I'd forgotten the call from Jan when she and Jim had fallen in love when she talked about how their sense of humor, choice of clothes, etc. was so much alike. They were the same height (6'4") and weighed about the same and even had the same build. They definitely had the same sense of humor! It was such a shock to walk beside Jim in the airport and to hear the jokes, etc. And, there was something about his hand on the steering wheel ... I could see it clearly in the light of the full moon from where I sat in the back seat. It was a hand that was alive, capable of holding Jan's (as his right hand was doing). It was capable of building things and fixing things and of bleeding when he cut it doing these things. It was a hand with life flowing through it. *There was just something about his hand.* It's also taken for granted that it, along with the rest of him, would still be living the next day. And, so it is!

I wanted so badly, as I sat in the back seat crying so hard, to ask Jim to stop the car. I wanted to jump out and run — to physically run away from the pain. I knew they'd catch me. Maybe that's what I was after. Maybe, if I'm to be honest, I wanted Jim to catch me and hold me as I cried. Maybe it was comfort from one so much like Ron that would have brought peace. After all, I could very easily have slipped from reality (there in the moonlight) and believed that it was RON holding me. I do know I'm not being covetous of Jan or Jim. It's not Jim (my friend's husband) that I wanted last night. It was Ron I wanted and Jim's the closest thing to Ron on this earth. So, do I stay away from him and Jan? No, because within a couple of hours down the road, these feelings had passed and I was able to look at his hand on the wheel and feel nothing, and look to his right hand holding Jan's and smile with a peaceful remembrance of Ron's hand holding mine as we drove down the road of life together, hand-in-hand.

I slip into bed after a wonderful day of friendship and fellowship and a few good interactive talks with Jan, I'm thankful that I came.

Jim had asked Jan before I came how wise it was for me to see him since we all knew how much alike he and Ron were. He thought it might be too painful for me. Such insight on a truth that was buried deep inside of my subconscious mind that also knew the shock of what was waiting for me on the ground.

How many times have I asked God to let me remember physically being with Ron even though I knew it would be painful? Once again God grants my wish and in a much more demonstrative way than I could imagine. Another tidal wave endured — another first now past.

There are so many people hurting, bearing pain so much worse than mine. Their burdens are so much more severe. Even though my pain and grief are deep, I've been so blessed. Oh, God please help me to see what I'm to do with this pain. I don't want to make it any bigger than it is (to do so would bring You dishonor), but to make it seem smaller than it really is would be harmful to me and also dishonor You.

Monday, 10/9/95

So, here we are Lord, on the plane ready to take off to return home. Thanks for this time of running away. Of course You made it a time of running "to" instead. I found an answer or two, received many blessings and I find pain is universal. It comes in all sizes, shapes, and disguises. I find that I really do need to stop looking for someone whose pain is so much more than mine that it negates my very own. I am in pain, I will be for a while. I need to accept that it's not like something that can be operated on and done away with.

I also know I've been suppressing memories of "the physical Ron" but I also don't have a great "need" to deal with that fact. As I can handle the pain, please let it flow through. And, when I do need to deal with it, I'll trust Your Spirit to nudge me in that direction. Thank You for the time with Bro. Stevens this morning. I walked away with the feeling that I need to quit looking for Your "plan" for my life, be faithful in the "little" things and You'll take care of the rest.

Disappointments can be so many in life that we can get bogged down. I believe I've set myself up for some by expecting too much too soon from myself. While I claim to be living in the "here and now," I've actually been looking to the future much too often. How many times has Your Spirit confirmed to me that we're doing okay alone, You and me? I don't need to look beyond this point. I borrow too much trouble from tomorrow. I guess You're changing my personality somewhat, maybe making the Desidrea Prayer more of a reality to me. I give lip service to "accepting what I can't change" but fight against needing time to recover from an extremely severe loss. So, I pray today that You keep my course steady and straight, taking detours when needed, but understanding the extreme need to stay focused on being where and when I am.

Tuesday, 10/10/95

I'm finding myself to be insecure right now. Guess I have been since Ron died. I recognize my total loss of Ron's protection, whether real (his physically being there when the smoke alarm goes off) or imagined (safety felt in wearing my wedding band) is beginning to be complete. That's somewhat unnerving. Something else that he provided me with that I hadn't realized was a great deal of self-esteem. I don't remember him ever being "flowery" with praise and words, but somehow he made me feel worthy of his love — special in a way no one else could be to him. Guess that's the way it should be, but I still didn't take him, or our love, for granted (except in the fact he'd be with me a lot longer). So, I'm left feeling incapable of going it alone.

Wednesday, 10/11/95 (lunch)

I realized this morning that I've taken a pretty hard blow. Last Friday night I lost Ron all over, just as sure as if I had walked into the bedroom again and found him. It hurt a lot more this time. I always thought experiencing something the second time is easier (maybe it is if you know it's coming), but I had no idea of what it would be like to experience the pain of remembering Ron completely and totally again. I didn't "see" him, or even "feel Ron's presence," but I did remember what it was like to be walking and talking with him.

Therefore I knew what pain there is in not being able to share a life with him any longer.

Lord, I'm sure thankful that You relieved me of the burden of being concerned over tomorrow. I'm having trouble taking care of today!

Friday, 10/13/95

The Lord really lifted another burden from me on my trip to Louisiana. I hadn't even realized I was carrying it to such a personal level. I'm talking about the burden of trying to justify my pain being bad enough to continue feeling it.

I look at Dave and his wife. Surely losing your son, who was trying so desperately to help the teens in trouble that spring night in California, only to be killed, with a bat, by one of them who slipped away, is pain much worse than mine.

What about the single parent who's lost more than one child or the couple who lost five of their six children? How bout the O.J. thing? or the Oklahoma bombing?

What I knew in my head, God's now planted in my heart. None of those tragedies change the facts. Jan said the words last weekend that no one other than I have said, "Ron - is - NOT - coming - back." A simple, basic, undeniable fact. No matter how bad someone elses pain is, my pain is still wrapped up in that one sentence, "Ron - is - NOT - coming - back." I'm still amazed at the impact that fact has on my life to this day. It's astounding how much we became one. If his leaving me has done so much to my life, I can't begin to imagine what would be left if God ever pulled up roots and left me. Ron was as much a part of me as is possible for two separate beings to be. Yet, God's Spirit really does live in me. Maybe I don't have to be worried about His leaving (and I'm not), but I must think about the application here to truly appreciate the fact of His faithfulness. Just as awesome as God is, so is His presence in my life. I continue to stand amazed at His love and power — even more so at the blinded eyes of those (such as the teen with the bat) who refuse to see.

Monday Evening, 10/16/95

I was thinking about something I'd written earlier in my journal. As I was going to bed one night I wondered if God had taken Ron so I'd serve Him more. I quickly added I didn't think God worked that way.

I guess I've heard some (a lot of) sermons lately on facts like we're created to worship God and that we should always be seeking to be more and more Christ-like.

If I believe, truly believe, that I really am created to worship Him, then my first thoughts, desires, goals, and so on should be towards that end. Christ certainly hurt. He suffered a lot of injustices from others and from life itself. Certainly He suffered a lot for obeying His Heavenly Father!

So, bring it home. I ask, "What if Ron was created (one reason, anyway) to more closely perfect God's love in me by his being taken from me so early in life?" What if I was going to be too weak to be used by God to minister to others? Let's say for a minute that that is one of the reasons God created Ron. What are the implications? The unsaved might say, "if God's a God who causes such pain as you've suffered in the loss of Ron, then I wouldn't want to serve Him." The Christian might say, "He's too loving (as I originally thought) to be so cruel." (He could never be cruel!)

To the former, I would say to look at all the good in Ron's life. He lived a long life with his birth defect. He gave a lot of joy to others and he gave the world two wonderful young men. I could write a book on what he's done for me in my life. No, former person, the good that God gave far outweighs the seeming cruelty.

And, to the latter I'd have to say to come to where I did today — back to the Bible where God tells me that I'm created to worship and glorify Him. That's my purpose and reason for being on this earth. Not to be happy with (or devastated by) the loss of Ron. Those are just "side" emotions, gifts (and costs) of being a person who not only has the duty, but the privilege, of being able to praise such a wonderful God. After all, I could have been created as one of those rocks God said he could make to cry out if I wouldn't!

Yes, I must keep focused on my very purpose for being here. All the rest pales in importance. I'll still hurt (Christ did), I'll still bleed when cut (Christ did) but I will rise again (as Christ did) and then I'll be truly fulfilled as a person created by an all-knowing, sovereign God.

Thursday, 10/19/95

Sometimes I sit and stare at my left hand. It, like my heart, is empty. I see the crease, which must now be permanent where my wedding band used to live. Except for the time in Louisiana when I was feeling Ron's loss again, I don't reach to twirl it. When Ron was alive, how often did I feel for my band, somehow sub-consciously feeling Ron's love? Now that he's gone, I know that's gone too. So, how come my sub-conscious is so far ahead of my conscious mind?! Somehow I'm out of sync with myself! I've got to get these two minds of mine together. Doesn't the Bible talk about not being a "double minded" person? (I know - I'm out of context - it was just a thought!)

But, I look at myself in the mirror sometimes and wonder who I am. What makes me tick, live, and breathe? What makes me — me? Hum......

Chapter Eight

10/20 ~ 11/19/1995

Life Is Precious–
Even Muff-up's

Sunday Evening, 10/22/95

Lord, the last few days have been hard. I pretended on Friday that I was ok, that seven months was "no big deal." Reality knows it hurt. Muff is in bad shape again. She couldn't even stand up when she got out of bed yesterday. There has been no improvement today. I had a church visitation I'd put off already and Steve wanted Allen and I to go car shopping with him. So, I left Muffin, knowing she wouldn't be alive when I returned. After all, she's "just a dog." Yet, reality also knows that I've had her half as long as I had Ron. So, to say good-bye to her isn't going to be easy. Yet, I still chose responsibility to humans over her needs. I came home and she was still alive. (I was very glad.) Allen could tell that I was down.

Tonight, on the way to church, I went by the apartment we lived in. There was a car there when we moved in that had a scripture verse on the car tag. It was from Deuteronomy. Ron and I would often comment that we needed to look it up, but we never took the time to stop and do it. A couple of mornings after he died I'd gone out early to Roy Rogers restaurant for some time alone and when I came home, I parked across from the car. I opened my Bible and read the verse. It ministered to me so much that day, but I had forgotten the passage. I went tonight to see if I could find the car. I couldn't. I'll try again sometime. *(I found it months later. They'd gotten a new car! The verse is Deuteronomy 31:8 "And the LORD, he it is that doth go before thee; he will be with thee, he will not fail thee, neither forsake thee: fear not, neither be dismayed.")*

Driving into the development stirred up such memories. Memories that were so bittersweet. It hurts so much. I'd watched a romantic movie today. I guess I should stay with the Waltons and Dick Van Dyke! I really am feeling lonely. The choir practiced our Christmas musical tonight. It's called "Come Home For Christmas." How I wish Ron could come home for the holidays. Facing Muffin's seemingly impending death — it's all too much. Yet, I need to focus on all the good (past and present). God's got my future in His hand, but I'm in the run away mode again and I'm afraid some day God's going to let me do just that, only to find out I really don't want to. So, tonight I ask You, Lord, to keep my path lit with Your lamp. Keep me safe and in Your will! Father, I've got so much I need for You to take from me, from my mind and my heart. I want to focus on You and not so much on my needs. Where is the balance of taking care of myself and becoming self-consuming? Help me, God!

I prayed in church tonight for all the couples sitting in front of me. It's my prayer they'll never know separation on this earth — that the Rapture will take place first. I could see Pastor Reynolds on the right side of the church and Debbie sitting at the piano. Just seeing them separated physically caused some strange anxiety in me. I want all those in my life happy and appreciative of what they have in life.

Wednesday, 10/25/95

I dealt with the issue of life and my right to take it away from Muffin this week. I always felt it was the "humane" thing to do, to put an animal out of its misery. Somehow though, life has become very precious to me — even Muff's. I called to ask Pastor Reynolds if I have the right to have her put down - scripturally speaking. In talking (he said no one's ever asked him this before), he asked me to call a vet he knew was a Christian, and ask his opinion.

I called, and he said that they take the same oath a human doctor takes, but they feel that we can, even should, relieve suffering in an animal if it can be done painlessly.

I asked the question at the Bible Institute Monday night. I've come to the conclusion this is something I can do based on:

Pastor pointed out that it's not addressed in the Bible, which leaves it up to us to decide. Human life, and the preservation of it, is dealt with extensively.

We're given dominion over the animals.

An animal does not have a spirit (even though an animal lover has suggested they do). I sure can't find in the Bible where I'm to evangelize Muff-up!

Muffin is getting worse. She kept me awake last night, literally thrashing around in the bed. I've got pillows all around the edges so she can't fall out. It's not fair to keep her alive like this. So, Saturday I take her in. I really had prayed God wouldn't ask me to do this and He still has until Saturday not to. But, since He's in control, is sovereign and doesn't make mistakes, I trust that he will cause more good to come from this than the pain that will be in holding Muff as the needle is inserted into her vein to end her precious life. I hope to be focusing on how she'd lay her head down on your chest on command; on the way she could jump up to four times her height; how she could outplay any human in the game of fetch; how she'd play reverse ball on the stairs and finally, on the blessing she's been with her pro-longed life to help me get through Ron's death. God's been so good to me. *I must be getting stronger to be able to handle this.*

Saturday, 10/28/95
Emotions are funny things. They can feel, they laugh, cry, act

silly, they worship and celebrate — sometimes they get angry — spiteful and sometimes downright hateful (but I don't like to think about the last two). And, sometimes the emotions shut down. I see the curtain coming slowly down this morning, shutting out the light. I just wish it could shut out the Grief. But, I'll go behind this curtain for a while to get through what I have to do today.

Muff is "just a dog," isn't she, God?! After all, it's not like losing Ron (and, it's not - no comparison! I haven't completely lost my mind yet — thought I had a time or two lately, but it's still intact). But, God, she really is a dog, an animal you've given us to love and enjoy for many years. So, if she is "just" a dog, how come it hurts so much? How come Kristie called from Williamsburg this week to tell me I'd been on her heart so much all week? If Muff's "just" a dog how come everyone I've told about what I'm doing today has given me condolences and told me I'd be in their prayers? Why have several people offered to go with me? And, how come I feel I need to go alone to the vet with Muff?

God You're already there. You've gone before me and I'm so glad You have. You've made this possible for me to handle. You've been so good to me!

It's time to get inside and get ready for what lies ahead. O, Father, how I wish You were here, physically right now. *The tears are blurring the page as I write now.* O, God, please be with me and with Muff. Don't let her suffer or be afraid. Whatever You do with the Muff-ups, as they breathe their last breath, be good to her. She sure has been good to me all these years. Thank You so much for her life and companionship (especially the last seven months). Thank You, God.

Sunday Morning, 10/29/95

Muff had several symptoms of a pretty severe brain tumor. Most of them didn't manifest themselves until the last two or three weeks. It was hard to do, but she died peacefully in my arms. Dr. Tyrrell was so kind and gentle. I had a coffin I'd used in a talk for a ladies meeting a few years ago. Muffin fit in it, so Allen came over and dug a grave for her. For some reason I don't really feel good about having her buried in the yard. That's been strange to experience. I'm not sure why it bothers me to have her out there. Something to ponder.

I gave Muff a bath yesterday. I got the hair dryer out I always used. It's a neat hair dryer. It has a stand and it's at least forty-years old and, it still has the original cord on it. It had frayed a long time ago. I'm not sure I ever mentioned it to Ron. He wouldn't have let me use it if I had. Anyway, as I went to plug it in yesterday the thought crossed my mind that I really shouldn't use it like that, but, I said to myself, "You've used it before and after all, this is the last time you'll be using it." I answered, "Sure, and it really could be the last time you use any hair dryer if you burn the house and yourself up!" Did I listen to me? No! Like a dummy, I plugged it in and, as I feared, there was a great pop, bang, and fizzle as the sparks flew. I found out how great circuit breakers are. *I must listen to the Holy Spirit when He speaks to me!* The feeling was so strong not to plug it in. Do I give myself the benefit and blame it on my emotions of preparing to do what I did? NO!!! I can't blame this major mistake on anything except not listening to God. I'm thankful He protected me. The sparks could have started a fire.

Monday Evening, 10/30/95

This is no big deal! Grief is finished hurting me! As I stand on top of my table at Fuddruckers with my hands on my hips and my cape flying in the breeze (stay with me here) I cry out, "I am woman — hear me roar! I - am - invincible!" Thought you could take me down again, Mr. Grief?! Well, I'm here to tell you that I laugh in your face — I scoff at your ability to EVER hurt me again. I don't feel ANY grief for Muff-up! So there — what do you have to say to that?! - - - - What's that? There's tears in all of your eyes — why are you crying? - - - - You're crying for me?! You say I'm cold hearted? Well, isn't that better than being so vulnerable that Grief can take me down with his hands tied behind his back? All he has to do is utter words like, "I'm sorry" or "She has several

symptoms of a brain tumor" or — don't say a word — just give me
the ole "TV" shake of the head. That's all it takes to break my heart
— again. Oh, you knew it was an act, huh?! Okay — I'll get off my
table. You're right, you know. It's not an act though — it's the old
suppression technique kicking in again. If I grieve for Muff-up, the
loneliness will drag me in and I'll be like the little boy in the commercial who sucks so hard on his straw that he's pulled into the
bottle. I don't pretend to explain these crazy emotions. I feel a little guilty for being relieved that I didn't have to go home to feed
Muff and let her out before coming to class. I've actually got time
to relax for an hour — here at Fuddruckers. I really have shut down
though. I'm afraid if I feel "Muff-up Grief" it'll reopen the "Ron-
Grief" — just can't handle that anymore.

After class

So, I go to class. The professor was talking about God's attrib-
utes, and he pointed out that to love means you will be hurt. So,
God, why do I cry out to You in my loneliness for someone in the
future to love again? Why can't I just be content with the love Ron
and I shared? Why do I search for an emotion that, while it gave
me so much joy, has also given me pain immeasurable? Why would
I want to have such pain again? Is it my need to be loved that draws
me in? Talk about unconditional love, Muffin sure gave us that. Yet,
I've lost her too. Oh, God, I had the physical ability to at least try to
save her if I'd found her dead. Where were all of the heroic measures,
the adrenaline pushing strength that lifts cars and refrigerators and
2,000-pound boxes off a loved one? Why couldn't I get Ron in a
position to try CPR on him? Am I forgetting that You orchestrated
it? *I think I am.* It just hurts so much to see my loved ones leaving
me. I love Ron so much. I realize I don't have a vision so I keep looking back. Lord, tonight I pray for a vision for tomorrow, for the
proper balance in being "where I am," yet having a vision for tomorrow. I can't begin to live in the past now. You've brought me too far
to go back. Help me, Lord! Note: In the statement above about balance it doesn't speak of the past, but of being "where" I am and the

future. Hummm.... I'm tired. I'm going to bed!

Wednesday, 11/1/95

I'm re-reading my journal from beginning to end. I've just read my entry of August 15th about the coma theory. I really do think that would be a great way for God to undo all this. If I am in a coma I sure do have a vivid imagination of sitting in Burger King: it's November — there's a mist in the coolness of the day. I see the elderly lady in her white sweater walking in and the Mom and young son talking beside me (wish he'd quit kicking the seat) and the cute guy in front of me (sorry). Oh well, I guess if I cried out, "Where am I, in a coma or a Burger King?" They might not understand! Someone might be tempted to take me away. (I still think God could make the coma thing work!) Guess I'll get back to reading!

Friday, 11/3/95

Steve and Allen bought me a kitten so I wouldn't be lonely. This little 3 1/2-lb. ball of fur has won my heart! She's also put numerous scratches all over my body! She flexes her claws as she walks, never stops! And, she wants to be held and loved all the time. She's so full of life! It's good to have her. However, my new furniture (not to mention my numerous body parts) couldn't take the claws so I took her in this morning to get her de-weaponized! I didn't know how much I'd grown to love her in these five short days. I worried about her surviving the surgery. She'll be at the vets until Sunday. I took a short lunch today so I could go and see her after she wakes up this afternoon. *Now if I could just come up with a name!*

Monday Evening, 11/6/95

I went to Angie's Friday night. It was already dark when I left work. It had been raining and was still spitting ever once in a while. The Beltway was traveling at a "rolling stop." There was something about the traffic and the taillights shining on the wet pavement that caused me to relive the night Ron died in vivid detail. I'd gone to bed, slept a couple of hours, and finally started this journal some time after 1:00 a.m. I think I slept a couple of more hours before finally getting up around 3:30. I decided to go into the office and get my desk and work organized so Jeremy would know where I was on everything. I remember (realizing that I was in shock) taking Rte. 50 instead of getting on the Beltway. I drove the speed limit and remained very aware of my surroundings. I knew I'd be a lot more stressed if I didn't go in and also knew the necessity of reducing stress as much as possible. The roads must have been wet because I remember seeing the taillights and traffic lights on the pavement. I remember how "foreign" everything looked. Things so familiar. Even my desk looked so - - - "detached" from me. I could feel myself going through the motions of what I'd been doing only a few short hours before with a strange new outlook. I remember praising God for all the blessings He'd bestowed upon Ron and me. I remember feeling so alone — crying every time I'd think about the fact of not having Ron to hold me and get me through this pain, yet feeling so pro-tected by Steve and Allen. They had asked me to move in with them and let them take care of me. What a blessing children are!

So, is it any wonder that I really haven't "grieved" over Muffin? The grief in that situation was before she died — not after. I real-ize she was "just" a dog, but I sit here wondering if anyone's death will ever affect me again. After experiencing what I have to believe is the ultimate pain, how can anything ever come close again?

I finished at work. I remember walking past the security guard entering and leaving the building. I wanted so badly to tell this stranger about my life and the drastic change that had taken place. I didn't. I said, "Good morning" and walked on by. Months later he told me he knew something had happened that had come as a real shock to me that night.

I drove home, stopping by the McDonald's where I'd go most mornings to get a coke. The sweet, precious lady who was always there saw the pain in my face. When I answered her question, she came around the counter, gave me a hug, and offered a shoulder if I ever needed it. She remained very supportive to me until I moved from the area a couple of months later.

I see now where the time alone that morning, away from the home Ron and I shared, helped me to face what lay ahead that day.

I called Ron's office and said, "Hi, this is Brenda, Ron's wife." The dispatcher said, "Oh, hi. Ron's not coming in this morning is he?" I thought to myself how astute he must be to get that fact just because I called. I didn't know at the time that Ron hadn't felt well the day before. When I said no, that Ron wouldn't be in — that I'd found him dead the night before, I'll never forget the disbelief, the shock and the tenderness of his words, "Ron?...OUR Ron? No, not Ron!"

I called Jeremy. He'd never met Ron, but we had talked a week or two before about our "true loves." He told me then (and called back later that day to reiterate), that I had nothing to worry about — that they would work with me — to take all the time off I needed. He let me go into negative leave so my check would continue.

How in the world did he know that I was feeling a heavy responsibility of being self-sufficient now — of being solely responsible for paying the bills?! He (and AMS) has done so much for me. I'll never forget the support. Just as C.B.C. helped me as if I'd been there for years, so did AMS!

Mom, Dad, Karla, and Mike came around ten. They went to the funeral home with Allen and me. Money and King has to be the best funeral home in this area. They were so tender and caring and there was absolutely no sales pressure on anything. They showed us the casket room and left us there. I really appreciated them so much.

Thursday, 11/9/95

This is going to be a very cold winter! I realized last week when the time changed and it got dark so early that this is the time of year Ron and I would double up on our cuddling! I remember statements like, "It's getting cold — time to cuddle more!" I also realized this morning why I'm wearing socks to bed when I never had before. No matter how cold it was, Ron would let me warm my cold feet on his legs when I got into bed. Talk about true love!

Friday Morning, 11/10/95

I cried at work again today, not sobbing — just tears coming up in the eyes. I remember a time or two thinking that if I would start to cry I'd never be able to stop. Now I wish I could cry like I did in the beginning. I remember sitting in a chair crying until I had doubled over, got on the floor and somehow was sure if I could get down low enough, I could melt into the floor and stop the pain. I just wish I could cry until I washed all of the sadness away. But, I guess just as I've grown and matured in my life, so has my crying matured from those infant stages of Grief. *I just hope I never get so "grown up" that I quit crying altogether.*

Finally gave Brat Cat a name — Zipper. She flies through the house! I didn't put her in the bathroom last night. Big mistake — at 2:00 a.m., she jumped into bed and into my face. Guess she'll stay in the bathroom a while longer at night! She's such a joy for me. It really does help to have her there when I get home.

Monday, 11/13/95

Yesterday I got up to a slight snow and ice storm. I got out of the car at church and was reminded of another memory of Ron. Because of my neck, he would always come around and support me when it was icy. Falling can cause great pain for me. Just another case of missing him. He did so much for me. I always thought that I appreciated him completely. I see now where that was probably impossible to do until he was no longer with me.

The messages on marriage yesterday were great. So much can apply to many relationships outside of marriage. Last night was extremely painful though. As Dr. Wemp spoke about things like love pats, etc. it brought up a lot of memories of things like Ron helping with the dishes, etc. He'd swat me with the dish towel — I'd fling water on him — he'd tickle me — Muff would bark, run and get a ball and continue to bark with it in her mouth. We'd laugh, kiss, and hug —- stuff like that. Sometimes Ron would swat me just to aggravate Muffin. Tonight those memories bring a smile to my face. Last night, it brought extreme Grief. As Dr. Wemp shared from his knowledge and experience, I cried for those who can't begin to fully realize just how blessed they are (including Dr. and Mrs. Wemp).

He spoke of the husband telling his wife how nice she looks in the clothes she has. He says it keeps the clothes budget in check! Ron went one better. I'll never forget the one time a beautiful fur coat caught my eye. (I've never been into furs and wasn't "buying" then either.) Ron, very quickly said, "Dear, haven't you ever noticed how fur coats add a lot of pounds to a woman's looks? You don't want to look fat, do you?" I turned quick enough to catch the smile on his face. That became a standing joke with us, and advice he frequently passed on to other men!

Wednesday, lunch - 11/15/95

Life with Ron is coming back in detail. Last night when I left work it was sleeting a little so I went to Penny's to look at something and to see how it was when I finished. Coming down the escalator I wanted to reach behind me and scratch Ron's leg. *I didn't realize I used to do that.* He'd usually be behind me to make sure I was holding onto the rail (in case it jerked) so I wouldn't fall. He'd stay behind me so no one else would fall on me if the escalator happened to jerk or stop suddenly. He was so concerned over me not hurting my neck. The doctor had told him to take care of me — to never let me ride a horse, etc. because of the possibility of being a quadriplegic if I was thrown. Ron took him seriously! So, I guess I must have reached back as if he was behind me. I got outside and the ice was piling up on my windshield so I went home instead of going to church. I whimped out! Would I normally have gone? Yes! Because - - - I would have Ron to drive home, or come and get me — whatever. I can't live my life in fear. I've got to keep going, with or without an instruction book!

I no longer have the luxury of being in shock. What a shock absorber shock is! I find myself less willing to express my feelings verbally to others now. I guess I feel like everyone is thinking it's time to be beyond this. (It's been almost eight months!)

Saturday, 11/18/95

I am so blessed! I'm overwhelmed today by God's greatness, compassion, provision and, most of all, His peace. It's the "peace that passeth all understanding." I've been in a valley since I had Muff put down, but today I think it's time to check out. It's time to pack the ole tent up and hike on out of this place. (I actually did stop and stay a while in the valley this time.) It's time for Thanksgiving. It's a time for reflection, not only on the year past, but also on the one ahead. I feel such an assurance of some excitement to come in the next twelve months. It'll be fun to look back from there to here. Something tells me I'll utter a comment something like, "You had no idea how wonderful it would be, did you?" (A touch of de-ja-vu as I say that, wishing Ron were here to enjoy it with me...*heavy sigh!*)

We shouldn't live in fear of losing someone, but I believe it should be in a spirit of "I really believe it can happen to me, but I don't "expect" it to." I need to look at all those I hold dear to me like that. It makes you careful to remember to say, "I love you" and not to leave any angry words between you. (Seems like I've read that before — in the Bible — not letting the sun go down on your wrath.)

Chapter Nine

11/20 ~ 12/19/1995

It's Time To Give Thanks

Monday, 11/20/95

Way, way, way deep inside I'm sad, but something within me keeps those feelings where they are — way, way, down inside. And, I ask myself, "why?" I remember when I was a teen and a romance would end, we were famous for putting on the saddest song we could find and sitting and crying our eyes out — on purpose. Maybe that's the difference in "puppy love" and the real thing. You sure couldn't have convinced me then that anything could hurt worse. So, does that make the pain I'm in now a "mature" pain?

5:05 P.M.

Something drew my eyes to the clock. According to the paramedics, it was eight months ago right now that Ron died.

I go into the vacant office across from my desk and look out the window. On the 9th floor, looking down on a busy intersection, I see so many cars going in so many directions. I pause and look out. It's not quite dark, yet the sun has set. The headlights and taillights look so interesting as they race by. The lights on the stores are Christmas red — pointing forth to a month from now.

Every car I see represents at least one person who probably has, or eventually will know Grief. If I could only turn back the hands of time —- what would I do if I could? If God were consulting me (you know how they "freeze frame" in the movies) would I prevent Ron from leaving? Or, would I stand in agreement with what God has done? If I was there with Him as Ron begins to experience his confusion, or as he's falling forward onto the bed, what would I do if God gave me a choice? Didn't Ron tell me just two weeks before he died that he hoped to be dead when he hit the floor? We had talked about how George was suffering with cancer. Ron said, "I hope when it comes my time to go that I'm dead when I hit the floor. I know where I'm going and there's nothing to hold me here. I don't want to stay in a body decaying and suffering with cancer." (I said, "Thanks!!" when he talked about not having anything to stay here for! We both laughed as I said I knew what he was talking about.)

I'd like to think I'd stand in complete agreement with God, but I'm not sure I'd be strong enough to do that. *I wish my "wisher" wasn't working!* What good does it do to wonder or wish things to be different? I'm so thankful God didn't give me a choice because I'd never want to "play" God. The burden is just too heavy. I'm so thankful I can just be me and let God be God. Guess I still have to master the art of "Letting Go and Letting God" though.

Wednesday, 11/22/95 (Thanksgiving Eve)

God lifted my heart. I didn't tarry long at the cemetery. Winter is setting in. The "scene" there is turning cold. Loved ones have put fall flowers on the graves. I pull the lilies from the vase on Ron's grave and turn the vase upside down. It's too cold to visit here often now.

Church was good. Fifty people gave praises in the service so it lasted over two and a half hours. The power of God, His grace, mercy, and love; His faithfulness, goodness, and kindness all rang true with each testimony. I was truly blessed. So tonight I go to bed with the peace that passeth all understanding in my heart. I called Mom and Dad to see if I could stop by and see them tomorrow. Since the dinner at Lisa's parents isn't until supper, Mom asked me to come for lunch with them and Karla. *I really need to spend some time with them tomorrow.*

Thursday, 11/23/95 (Thanksgiving Day)

It was a good day. I enjoyed lunch and playing Rummikub with Mom, Dad, and Karla. As I left, I thanked them for letting me come. The ole eyelids begin to moisten as Mom tells me she's glad I came. I confess I didn't know whether to call yesterday or not. I didn't know if it would hurt too much to have me there without Ron. She gets a little choked up as she tells me how much it helped to have me there. As I pull away from the house, the tears are not to be held back any longer and begin to flow. By the time I get to the Beltway I have to pull off and cry. I watch for a policeman so I can pull away if one were to stop. (Just don't feel like explaining that I'm just "having a moment.") The pain is so severe.

I'm in my usual writing place — the car. It's raining. Between songs, I get a touch of a memory of being on the road as the rain hits the roof. While I'm not exactly ready to go Spaceballing again, I sure wish I had Ron to hold me tonight and listen to the rain on the roof with Muff cuddled beside us — Steve in the "loft apartment" — Allen working hard and safe. Yes, all was well then. (Or, so we thought.) How were we to know the strain Ron's heart was under?!

As I drove down Rte. 66 on the way home, the sky was gray from the combination of spray from the cars and the headlights reflecting from it. As cars were rushing by, I wonder if I'd be satisfied if I could physically get hold of this "condition" called Grief.

In the movies, the Lady Lovely receives some devastating news. As she tries to run into the burning building to get her child out as it explodes, the he-man grabs her to stop her. She begins to beat his chest — screaming until she finally realizes that she can do no more and melts into his arms crying.

Maybe if I could hold this Grief it would finally quit beating against me and just "get it all out." Maybe then I could go on without the continual pain. (Maybe I've been watching too many movies!) *Still, it's a thought.*

Wednesday, 11/29/95

I am such a scream. I really make me laugh sometimes!

Another new emotion hit this week — one I didn't have a clue on how to handle so I let it just about drive me crazy! I must admit that for about twenty-four hours, I was very deeply in-like with someone. It was a riot! It made me feel childish, it scared me, it made me giggle (almost), it made me nervous, made me feel good, warm (and fuzzy), it confused me — made me feel just a little guilty. I literally didn't know how to handle it ... so I talked to Pastor Reynolds. That made me feel completely stupid! He just stood there grinning at me. I still wonder what he was thinking. Was he thinking he knew who it was, or was he laughing at me or, maybe he was actually happy for me ... who knows?

There was one emotion I realize I didn't experience in this event. I wasn't in-lust while being in-like. Maybe that wouldn't surprise anyone else, but for some reason it does me — a little anyway. Just as I haven't had any training for being a widow, I haven't had any for being in-like with anyone but Ron for many, many years.

I can definitely say one thing. Not even the good feeling of maybe coming alive again takes the pain away. If I were Lot's wife I'd be fulfilling scripture of "being the salt of the earth" cause I keep looking back so much, Virginia would be covered with salt!

It's funny, but tonight I must be either getting use to these crazy emotions or I'm numb. Guess I could sit here and conjure up some tears if I had a mind to but I don't — so, I won't. Wouldn't it be great if I was beyond tears — beyond all the pain? I know it's silly, but I don't feel like I'll be completely healed until I do find someone else to love (and be loved by) and he holds me as I cry one last time (or two) for Ron. That seems silly to say, but it brings back the memory of wanting to have Jim and Jan stop the car that night and running until Jim caught me and I'd fall into his arms crying, pretending he was Ron. If only there were some way for Ron to hold me in his arms and let me cry for him maybe then I'd be healed.

(I've struck a nerve somewhere cause the ole eyelids are getting wet again!) Lord, thank You so much for the balanced diet of joy, tears, laughter, sadness. What would I ever do without You?!

Sunday Evening, 12/3/95

We sang Christmas carols at church tonight after having the most wonderful potluck ever! I got a touch of the Christmas feeling tonight and it hurt. It really brought out the fact that I came home tonight, alone. I'll get up Christmas morning, surrounded by family. Yet, I'll be alone. O God, why can't I just be happy that Ron's with You? Why do these selfish, 0, poor me feelings creep in? I know I'm human — that this is "normal" but I still don't like to hurt. If man's imagination can create a six-million dollar man, can't You create a soft heart that doesn't break apart on the impact of every sad song?

Monday, 12/4/95

God, if I could give up my future eternity in Heaven today in exchange for ending this pain and sadness I feel, would I do it? If I could simply cease to exist on any level, would I? I hope not. I hope that if that were an option, I'd choose to "tuff it out" today, but I'm not sure I would. If only I knew that today is the one when the pain would end, I could handle it, but I know this isn't the end. I know there's a lot more to come. And, even though I can't feel it emotionally right now, I know there have been (and will continue to be) so many blessings.

Wednesday, 12/6/95

You know, God — I was suggesting some improvements on the construction of the heart the other night, but tonight I was thinking about how incredible the heart really is. Our skin is so easily cut (and it's a "living" thing - so to speak) — our bones can be so easily broken — our very skull can be shattered with a swift hit — we can even "concuss-our-brains." All of these things are direct hits and can easily hurt us, and even kill us. You made the heart to love and to feel and to bless — and to be blessed (as a side benefit it pumps blood through our body to keep our bones, etc. going). Yet, it can take a pretty severe blow (like losing Ron) and it keeps going. I realize that I'm giving the functions of the heart a bit more credit than it probably deserves, but allow me to be a bit romantic here for a moment. *Beats wearing a cape — standing on tables!* Tonight I really pray that Your plans include someone else for me in the future — the near future (like — before ten tonight) would be nice! But, seriously, I know that's probably a while away. I'm glad You're faithful and strong and true and loving and kind and patient. I sure do love You! (Wish I were more like You!)

Thursday, 12/7/95

Life is so interesting! *Boy, could I use some dull!* Went to church last night — met Dawn at Taco Bell — came home and was minding my own business. At 10:30 there was a hard knock at the door. It took me by surprise. My door has a window in half of it and is locked with a key. I raised the shade to see a young man waving his arms trying to get me to open the door. I instinctively turned to reach for my key. I stopped, turned and shook my head. He was talking to me. All I could make out was "fire wood." I told him no twice and he walked off around the side of the house. I immediately called and got Steve on the phone while I looked outside again. I couldn't see anything, including a truck. I called the police. They came out pretty quick (another woman had called too). My screen was open — it was still locked, but it was open. The police said it was bazaar for someone to be trying to sell wood at 10:30 at night.

Allen called to see if he could come and spend the night. I told him no, that they can't be running to Virginia all the time. He called ten minutes later to tell me he and Lisa were on their way. I really was glad. I've got appointments with two security companies — I guess I'll get an alarm put in.

The funny thing was Zipper's reaction. When the police left something knocked on the ceiling (from the neighbors above me, I guess). Zipper went crazy. She ran from bedroom to bedroom and through the living room, crying in a tone I hadn't heard before. She was wild and very aware of any noise, until Allen and Lisa arrived. I didn't realize that cats were sensitive to things like that. Of course, she's a useless weapon. Without her front claws, she wouldn't be

very effective if I threw her in someone's face! The police department suggests getting a dog, but I'm not up to that again. Oh well,
something else to deal with.

Speaking of useless, I heard a useless Factoid on the radio this
morning. Heinz Ketchup leaves the bottle at a rate of twenty-five
miles — per year. That's about how fast this grief is leaving my
heart! Ketchup can be made to flow faster by adding water. *Wonder
what can be added to water down this grief?!*

Friday Evening, 12/8/95

It's supposed to snow from three to five inches tonight. Why
does that concern me? I'm working tomorrow, but I live four miles
from work. I guess knowing Ron could drive me there and back
made snow a "no big deal." Oh well, I have my trusty front wheel
drive Saturn to depend on. Somehow that's not as comforting as
having Ron!

Death doesn't make a lot of sense — at least it hasn't lately.
Children aren't supposed to die at twenty-four (like Dave's son);
women aren't supposed to die first (like Mary Lou), and, when men
do die first, they're not supposed to do so at forty-eight, like Ron.

Monday, 12/11/95

The weekend was rough. Yesterday, especially. The more I try
to "get into" Christmas, the lonelier I am. Ron was such a part of
everything I did for the holiday. I never realized it. He thought the
commercialization was horrible and fussed about it often (I'd call
him a Scrooge, even though I agreed with him). Yet, he was the
biggest kid on Christmas morning opening his gifts and watching
others open theirs. Of course he was there to help the kids "check
their toys out." It's so hard, Lord to concentrate on the joy of Your
birth when I'm used to Ron celebrating with me. I'm so sorry!

I just can't get my tree decorated so I'll take it down tonight.
It's good not to feel like I "have" to have one.

I don't know who I am anymore. I'm living…I'm breathing…I'm "going through the motions" but I'm so detached. I don't

recognize myself today. I want to call someone and ask them if I'm awake or if I'm in a very long dream (or, even if I'm real). There's got to be some way to connect Reality with myself. But, to "feel" Reality hurts — to really know that I know — that I know I'm a widow — that Ron is dead (not "gone," he's dead) isn't something my heart can grasp today. Just wish my head could go into denial with my heart. *R.F. would just be on a business trip or something.*

Tuesday Evening, 12/12/95

There's one class I missed in school — "Hookin 101." I tried to cut class last night, but I couldn't do it. I'm glad. God had started dealing with my very sad heart. He reminded me of why I was born — to praise Him. Dr. Sly confirmed when he feels like God's not enough that he concentrates on Him and His power. So, I feel better today. At one point though I felt my heart was so heavy it reminded me of carrying the extra weight of a child in pregnancy.

Wednesday Morning, 12/13/95

If I could just get my brain and my heart to connect on one simple point, I believe I could conquer this condition called Grief.

I know (in my head) Ron is dead. I know by my actions that "life does go on." (We're all expendable, right?! - - - Well, aren't we?!) My head knows my heart will be happy again, but my heart looks at Ron's picture and just can't connect the two words "Brenda" and "widow" together (words like "alone" and "lonely" come up).

My head tells my heart, "Brenda, you know Ron's dead. You need to feel it and know it and believe it just as surely as I do. I was there with you for those twenty-six and a half years. I never left you, so why can't we get together on this thing and get beyond it?"

My heart answers, "Because I'm the one who feels, loves, cherishes, cries, grieves. **I hurt!** You're just 'head knowledge.'"

"Sure I am. I'm the one that's learned all the facts in Hospice training and by reading and learning how to grieve. I'm the one who God's allowed to absorb the knowledge so when we got here you'd be helped to get through it."

"True, and I appreciate that, but I'm the one who lives the reality. It's my emotions that want to be held and loved and just to have Ron to share my day with. Someday we'll get together. Believe me, I want it more than you do. I'm the one in pain!"

"I know and we'd better cut this conversation out before they come and take us both away!"

Interesting, but not very helpful. Reality "feels" Ron should be alive — yet, Reality knows he's not. As hard as I may try, I can't deny the facts!

Sunday Morning, 12/16/95
Our Christmas program is this morning.

It's 6:45 — I'm waiting for Roy Rogers to open. We have to be at choir practice at 7:15. I realized this morning that I really have shut down emotionally in a way that's new and strange to me. I'm not sure how to describe it. I'm still "feeling," laughing, loving, and caring. But it's superficial (yet real). It's coming from my heart, but there's a place in my heart that has shut and double bolted the door. It's the room where tears flow — it's that place that really deals with Grief. I can't say I'm "cold" but the feelings aren't going very deep. Christmas has always been my favorite time of year. Of course, this year there's such sadness in not having Ron to share it with. Is there any wonder?!

Monday Evening, 12/18/95

I have a peaceful feeling tonight. Or, maybe it's an acceptance in my heart. I'm sad. I'm very sad, but that's okay. My God knows that I love Him and that I'm also thankful for the birth of my Lord and Savior. He also knows that the pain He felt as He watched His Son die on the cross was a very temporary separation. For me though, it's probably going to be a while before I'm reunited with Ron. God knows and understands where I am tonight. Yes, I'm overwhelmed with the love and devotion of the Trinity. I stand amazed at the grace they continue to impart to me.

Chapter Ten

12/20/1995 ~ 1/19/1996

1995 Comes To An End

Wednesday Evening, 12/20/95

It takes nine months to "make" a baby. I remember being pregnant and feeling it must have become a permanent condition! Seemed like the baby would never be born! Allen was three weeks late — Steve was induced on the due date.

I find my Grief at the nine-month stage tonight. I'm sure it will never end. *At least my heart does!*

Just as the pain of childbirth brings such inexplicable joy, I'm sure I'll learn to be happy again. And, after being so sad for so long, I believe that happiness will be felt with a new appreciation too.

Thursday, 12/21/95

Wish I could remember what it's like to feel the "Christmas Spirit" — to remember what it feels like to be waiting in excited anticipation for Christmas morning. Just as looking at Ron's picture had seemed so distant, so does the memory of Christmases past.

Why can't I be happy? Romans 8:28 is a promise I've held onto through so many problems. I believe it with all my heart, except this time. My heart is so heavy with sadness. I want to cry, but the tears stop just short of a full blown crying frenzy.

Friday Evening, 12/22/95

Holy Spirit, thank You for the internal hug You've given me all day! I woke with Your light and love shining within. I'd asked for a Christmas miracle and You've given me one today. (Although I had a very different one in mind, I thank You for this one!)

My heart is still hurting for the loss of my Ron to share Christmas with, but, instead of my heart getting hit with a Louisville Slugger, it's being hit with one of those big yellow Nurf bats. I still "feel" it, but it certainly won't split my heart wide open every time it deals a blow. Thank You!

Wednesday, 12/27/95

I'm not sure where my emotions are today. I almost feel like I don't need to keep this journal any longer. It seems like an extreme range of emotions are necessary to be able to write and I just don't feel strongly either way — which makes me think maybe I'm not dealing with things. I don't mean that I have to feel either "great" or "horrible." I do, however know that I'm emotionally drained right now.

When I left Angie's on Monday I realized just how emotional the holiday had been. I remember wanting to pull off the side of the road to cry and then to go to sleep for a very long time. But, both Mom and Dad and the guys were about five minutes behind me. While a part of me wants the world to know how badly I still hurt, I don't want the ones I love to be burdened by my continuing tears.

So, I shut the tears off and kept driving. And I've kept the tears back ever since. Jeremy's grandmother passed away yesterday. I feel so badly for him and for his family. There is such pain in the loss of those we love. This is true at any time, but during this time of the year, everything is magnified. The cold — the long nights — the "joy" that should be present only serves to make the Grief sadder.

But I know that things in the future will be better and that lifts my spirit today. Who would want to remain sad forever?! I sure don't!

I stand here from my ninth floor vantage point, looking at the near-empty parking lot and wonder why I'm here. Not just at work, but on the earth. Surely the emotional jolt I received when I found Ron was enough to stop my heart from beating.

I know I'm being incredibly selfish, but I'm so tired — not necessarily physically. It's more of an emotional tired. If I were to die right now I wouldn't have the energy to fly to Heaven. The angels would have to transport me. Then, all they'd find outside the Pearly Gates would be one blob-of-a-Brenda on the ground.

O well, guess that as long as this ole heart is beating I'll carry on with the motions. At least I'm starting to feel again (an improvement over the last few days).

Ron, if you were here with me tonight, what would you say or do? I'm not sure how, but I know you'd help me. How did you do it — comfort and strengthen me so much? Just as I stand in amazement at my parent's parenting skills, I stand amazed at your impact on my life. I've decided to take March 20 off. I hope to be able to bury this Grief then just as I buried the shell of your life on this earth a year before. I love you so much, R.F.! I really wish that we had talked about how to go on living without each other, but I guess we wouldn't have known how to then either. I really love you!

Friday, 12/29/95

Allen and Lisa were born tonight — spiritually speaking! They asked the Lord into their hearts! Praise God! Then, her soft, tender new heart in the Lord was immediately broken for her parents — so sure that they could never be reached and broken hearted at the meaning if they can't be. Oh, God, please touch them — please save them before it's too late.

Sunday, 12/31/95

New Year's Eve (heavy sigh). I don't want to leave 1995. It's when I lost Ron — it's when I buried the love of my life — my joy, my comfort and strength, my best friend — my lover. I guess it's not too strange to feel that way. Will a part of me always want to stay in 1995?

I know a very big part of me wants to go forward. I know (in my heart) that '96 is going to be an exciting year, full of wonder and surprises beyond my imagination. There may (probably will) be some pain, but it's time to come alive again. It's warm today. I feel such a spring in my heart. So, as I say good-bye to '95 it will probably be said with some tears, but I am so excited for the joys ahead. And, if it should be the year that I'm called home to be with the Lord, it's my prayer that my loved ones will smile through their tears — that, not only am I reunited with my "brother" Ron, but I'll at last be with my Lord! Would it be too cold hearted for me to say how thankful I am for the joys I've felt since Ron's death? God has blessed me so much. I can't begin to express my love for Him for all He's done.

Wednesday, 1/3/96

Until March 20, 1995, I would have said (probably had said) that it's impossible to feel total joy and total devastation at the same time. I've come to realize that's just not true.

I am overjoyed knowing that Ron is in Heaven. I'm so proud of him. It brings great joy knowing where he is. Yet, there is such pain in his absence from here and from me. That pain really is lessening all the time and I'm grateful for that.

Church was real good Sunday evening (New Years Eve). I went from there to Lisa's parents and spent the night with the guys. The whole crew went to Mom and Dad's for lunch Monday. I'm so thankful for such a wonderful family.

Thursday, 1/4/96

There's a restlessness in my spirit today. I can't figure out where it's coming from. I awoke several times during the night thinking of Ron. I know I dream of him almost every night. My bed also needs to be burped!

I realized last night that I really am healing from this condition of Grief. I'm not sure how this process works. It's been a while now since I've cried. I know I still miss Ron from the depths of my heart. Yet, I can't seem to remember the extreme pain that causes — something like childbirth pain. Once you hold that baby, it does something to your memory of that pain. Yet, in the case of Ron, my arms are empty. I sure hope I never get to where I like being alone. Even though God and I are doing okay, I hope I don't have a future without someone to share it with here on earth.

Maybe that's where this restlessness is coming from — wanting to begin to really live again. I'm anxious to see what '96 holds for me. I think a part of it is that I'm beginning to get my self-esteem back. I didn't realize it had been so badly damaged in losing Ron, but he seemed to complete anything missing in me. I wonder if everyone in our lives fills such a place in our being — in our personality. I certainly never believed I could survive on my own, either emotionally or financially. I've had a lot to learn about budgeting, etc. but I am learning. It's forcing some self-discipline in my life too!

I wonder if God will let us play "house" in Heaven. Maybe Ron could play the part of my husband and I could do it all right this time. Since everything's perfect in Heaven, we could be like that family in the commercial on TV now. It's in black and white and takes place in the 50's or 60's and in a "perfect world" — until the oven blows up. They head out to Best Buy to get a new one, but in Heaven the oven wouldn't break — nothing would, especially my heart. Oh well, time to get to work.

Tuesday Evening, 1/9/96

"The Blizzard of '96." Finally, I'll get out tomorrow. Steve came over Saturday. We thought he'd be able to get home Sunday even if we did get the two feet of snow they were predicting. We were wrong! He left two and one half-hours ago and hasn't called yet — I'm such a mother! I'm concerned.

Looks like Steve may be moving in with me in a couple of months. I'm glad — he'll be a big help to me in many ways. When he told me Friday their lease would be up in two months I said,

"That's impossible — you just moved in!" They moved three weeks after Ron died. It's so hard to believe that's been ten months ago! *When will my perception of time come back into sync?!*

Wednesday, 1/10/96

I made it to work today. We're "officially" closed, but reports are still due Friday so I came in and got the faxes out to the guys. Getting out of the neighborhood was a challenge. Hope I can get back in tonight.

I want to go to church tonight, but I have an unnatural fear of going. Unnatural because if Ron were alive, I wouldn't hesitate to go. So, which is worse — false security in Ron's existence or an unnatural fear? The former sure offers a lot more freedom. I'll probably drive home just to be sure I can get into the complex and then go to church. *I really refuse to live in fear.*

Thursday, 1/11/96 - 6:30 A.M.

Live in fear? No, but being practical is another matter. There was no gas at the service stations and I had less than a quarter tank so I didn't go to church. Tried to go to the grocery on the way home — didn't do that either. So, I'm at the grocery now. Due to lack of help, the twenty-four hour Safeway is closed until 7:00. At least I can get in then. (I called — they have milk!)

Dreams are good. They can take you to worlds where things are different — great — wonderful — even a little silly sometimes. They can even bring Ron back to me — at least for a little while each night. I'm very thankful for that. For however long I dream, Ron is alive and well and, very much himself! We laugh, shop, goof off — make love! And, even when morning comes (or the alarm calls me back to reality), I'm left with that warm fuzzy feeling. *I like that.*

Monday, 1/15/96

January is so cold. The snow is such a mess. It's beautiful to look at in the beginning when it's fresh on the ground — before the plows and cars and sleds and kids (and dogs) get to it. Those things mess it up. It's necessary to get out, but it still messes it up. I guess that's the way death is. It's beautiful (for a Christian) to die and meet the Lord. But then, for us who are left behind it gets messed up with the Grief, tears, new responsibilities, and all that goes into it! But, just as the snow melts, life goes on. Somehow we muddle through.

Wednesday Evening, 1/17/96

Where did it go — this condition called Grief?! Somehow I feel like I'm finally through the cloud! I don't know whether to shout for joy or give a really heavy sigh. This is strange and new and all of a sudden and I don't know how to deal with it. For at least ten years now - - - what? No, you're wrong — it has been ten years, not ten months. It must have been. I've gotten so used to this grieving thing. Hum - - - for some reason I feel like going back to the lower case when addressing grief - - - yeah, I like that. It feels good (strange - but "good").

I know that if I got out a stack of old 45's and an old one-at-a-time record player and put on some really really sad songs I could muster up some tears to cry — and I think that would feel good. It would be an "I really did have it all and I'm thankful I did" sort of a cry. Not an "I'm so devastated" type of cry, but a good, soul cleansing type. (It's time to have a slumber party!)

I even think I could pass the "Jim" test tonight. I believe I could see Ron's "twin" and not fall apart. (Where's my private jet? I need to go to Louisiana!) Boy, am I feeling brave! It's probably a good thing I don't have a way there cause I might get body slammed! But, it's very good to be coming out of the total sadness that's been behind the smile I've been wearing. Loneliness is still running rampant, but that's part of it.

Friday Morning, 1/19/96

What is it about a thunderstorm that causes my thoughts to wonder back through time? Maybe it's the songs. "The End of the

World" played earlier — "Never My Love" plays now. No, I think it's the weather. It's almost dark outside. The temperature was in the 60's this morning — it's dropping into the low 30's by this afternoon. Thunderstorms are passing through now. It's supposed to snow later. So, my mind drifts back to a time when Ron and I would cuddle up during a thunderstorm and reminisce about a time when my Mom (and his dog) would run with fear during a storm, so afraid of what "could" happen. There was no fear for us of the raging storm outside, or of the possible storms life would hand us some day. We sat, safe and secure in our home, in our love for each other and in the Lord. It's so comforting to know that nothing will happen to me that is not in His will. Only God can allow (or cause) things to happen to me. And He's there to see me through. As I look at Ron's picture, that familiar curtain blocks my heart from the memory of having his arms surround me during the storm.

I've taken a step back this morning. I need to cry, but I'm just too sad to. *Bummer.*

Chapter Eleven

1/20 ~ 2/19/1996

I'm Such A Yo-Yo!
Up...Down...Up...

1/20/96, Saturday - Ten Months

I was making the bed this morning at 8:00. I began to realize that ten months ago at that time I'd seen Ron alive for the last time. We'd said our final good-byes. Even though he was still alive and others would interact with him, our relationship was gone — over. A sadness set in, but I still couldn't deal with it. Later, Cecille called to let me know she was praying for me today. What a blessing she continues to be.

Steve had a trial workday and got a job so he's moved in with me. What a blessing! He noticed something sad in me last night. I guess that behind these walls maybe I'm more honest with my feelings. I wouldn't say I'm "dishonest" outside — maybe a more proper adjective would be 'distracted'. As children, Steve and Allen would be fine during the day, but let the distractions of TV, playing, etc. be gone and they'd "feel" the illness again. Guess that's what I feel at home.

Monday, 1/22/96

This new life I'm living is funny sometimes. As I go further along this path of recovery, I find I don't know how to deal with some things, such as dating and romance. (Not that I've been asked to yet!)

I'm beginning to really hope that God will bless me with someone else in my future. I realize that most of these emotions are coming from the depths of loneliness, but I'm still starting the thought processes. And it's funny how "out of touch" I am.

Point: Someone suggested I ask a guy to the Sweetheart Banquet at church. Answer: I'm too old fashioned...I could never ask a guy out. Besides, who would I ask?

Point: When I re-enter the "dating game" do rules that applied in my teen years still apply? Such as — do I meet the guy at the door if "Mom and Dad" aren't home? Since I am the Mom, there's no one to fit the role there! Seriously, though — is it okay to have someone in when we're alone? I know I've regressed here, but aren't emotions, feelings, "the neighbors talking" the same? I still believe in the "refraining from the appearance of evil" thing. It's sad to say, but I doubt in today's world that anyone would even notice or care or talk.

Guess this point was driven home the one time I did let a guy in when Mom and Dad were gone. He wasn't there for five minutes before I was ready and we left, but Mom and Dad had a trusty reporter around who failed to mention the five minute part, but they said it didn't matter anyway — what did matter was my reputation. So, I didn't do that again.

Point: Guess I would still handle an "out of control" situation the way I did that one time it came up. Mom had taught me all I needed to know. "He" and I were on a double date with my roommate. I had reached up and changed the other guy's radio station (rude maybe — but...). He responded by pulling a knife on me — really, he did! I grabbed his wrist and began to dig my nails into it as he gets close to my face explaining how "No one touches my radio!" My wonderful date responds to my question later of why he didn't come to my defense by explaining the other guy is his friend and I really shouldn't have touched his radio. I was new to Washington, DC — had heard all the horror stories of being eighteen and female and defenseless, so I felt I was safer staying with them than getting out of the car. (They wouldn't take me home.) I was wrong!

We got to the drive-in (I miss drive-ins) and my date decided to "get pushy." So, I had to inject Mom's proven method of taking him down and, I'm glad to say it worked beautifully! He had to explain to the couple in the front why he was screaming, but we got to watch the movie. Can you imagine his nerve?! We'd both lived in Campbellsville and dated there. For some reason he thought I'd "grown up" since leaving "Mommy and Daddy." I explained how it was he who had regressed. Oh well —

Point: Then, there's the kissing issue. (No — not, "Do I?" I have matured enough to know some answers!) When Ron and I kissed the first time or two our noses got in the way! I'm sure we're the only ones in the world that ever had this problem! But it's something to think about. Wonder if that problem still exists today?

Tuesday, 1/23/96

I believe I understand why God didn't make emotions tangible entities. It's because we'd do away with them. We'd beat-em up — kill them — run from them or otherwise delete them from our existence. Then we wouldn't learn to deal with them so we could learn from them or be able to help others. Even if I can help someone else with their Grief it still doesn't negate their need — their responsibility — to work through their own pain. So, even though I know how others have helped me, I'm still not sure how much I can help any one else. And — nothing — no-one can make it possible for me to have Ron hold me right now. (There's something strangely familiar about this feeling of Grief. It's been a while since I've experienced it. Guess that's the way it goes from being Grief to grief.)

I believe I'm at a crossroads today. As I write that last part, I realize that a big part of me doesn't want to leave the "Big G" Grief stage. It's not because I like to hurt (remember I'm the original chicken — yellow through and through), but it's because I'm so afraid of forgetting Ron. I still love him with all my heart. I don't want to forget him.

So, at this crossroads — do I stay stuck here in the past or do I trust God? Do I trust His desire for me to live again enough to turn around and walk, facing forward? God, I know it's possible to go forward with my memories. I've trusted You to keep me going in the right direction while I faced backwards to March 20. Help me now to face forward into the future. I'm just so afraid that the "Lot's wife" in me will turn and look backwards again and You'll zap me like You did her. (I'd like to discuss that with You face to face— I don't mean any disrespect, but that had to be almost impossible to do — even though she had her "Ron" alive and well beside her!) Oh well, please help me pass this crossroads victoriously. I really am frightened! hum...what is that verse about "love casting out fear?"

Thursday, 1/25/96

There's only eleven months until Christmas! (Sorry — I'm eating lunch at Wal-Mart. I love Wal-Mart!) I met with Pastor Reynolds last night about the directory, teaching, and other things. I don't know why, but I brought up the feelings of wanting to have someone to share my life with. He pointed out that with Steve moving in I wouldn't be so lonely. How do I explain to him — or to anyone that the loneliness isn't from "living alone" but from not having Ron in my life? How can anyone who hasn't "been there" understand that I can be surrounded by people — even people who love me and still be the loneliest person in the world? This is one emotion I pray Pastor and Debbie will never understand. After I left him I had the horrible thought that maybe he was thinking I was talking about "that other thing!" I hope not! I hope not cause I wasn't. Remember that I've reverted back to my teen years in this dating thing. No, I miss Ron more than anything because of the totality of our union — not just the physical. I'm glad to see that the love we had wasn't based on the sexual part of our marriage. It's the opposite that's true.

Later that evening...

Faith — think about it for a minute ... It's been a literal life pre-
server for me. Tonight, I remember walking up to the casket for the
last time to tell Ron "Good-bye." I stood, thinking about our lives
together. I remember rubbing his hand — it was foreign to me —
cold, leathery feeling, hard. Just five days before it had held me so
gently, as we awoke together one last time. Now, life was gone from
it. As I stood there, Mom walked up and put her arm around me.
I started crying softly. I remember telling her I didn't know how I
was going to make it without him. I remember she said to me,
"Brenda, you have a very strong faith in God. That's what's going
to get you through." Then, it felt as if I was back in the room as I
found Ron — I remember asking him to wake up — asking God
to let him — but, I wasn't "remembering" it, I was calling out to
him to just wake up! Mom gently turned me away from Ron and
we took a couple of steps and I passed out. Why remember that
now, Lord? Except to tie that truth she spoke into my feelings
tonight. Seems like people everywhere are in pain. I want so badly
to see the joy. Tonight I want to remember the faith — the goodness of situations. Without Allen's total rebellion and rejection of
us, and our "rules," I wouldn't know the total joy of that relationship being restored a few months later. I couldn't fully appreciate
our relationship today. Without being a month from being a quadriplegic from spinal cord compression I couldn't know and appreciate the joy of standing and walking or going over a speed bump
without yelling in pain. Without knowing a great marriage, I
couldn't appreciate the pain of losing it (which is better than losing
a horrible marriage)! Without the tunnel accident, when I faced
death — only to walk away from it, I couldn't know there's nothing to fear about being dead. (Dying still holds some qualms for
me!) Yes, it really is time to face forward — to face the future. Time
marches on and it's time to greet it once again with love, app007cia-
tion, and anticipation — and with lots of faith! Faith is all it takes

to start building. I'm not sure where my faith comes from. The Bible tells me to exercise my faith. Yes, I'm strong, but it's in You, Lord — not in myself. Guess you could say I'm physically strong though. Well, I am! I know I'm 5' — not much else and I weigh in at a whopping 107 lbs., but I've been known to put a drunk twice my size down with one hand (my left hand at that)! Sobered him right up to see me looking down on him. He didn't know what had removed him from the Spaceball! Just ask me about a town called Skowhegen! That's not a challenge. I don't enjoy having my entire body sprained! Think I'd rather be spiritually strong anyway! Thank You Lord for refocusing my concentration tonight! I love You — all three of You!

Saturday, 1/27/96

It's raining today. The sun is shining inside though. I really love Ron. I love remembering him. Guess my emotions are still working themselves out. I had some pretty heavy dreams about death last night. Remembered the early emotions and pain of losing Ron. I'm in the car waiting for Steve at the body shop. I just looked in my rear view mirror and caught a glimpse of someone who looked like Ron. It was the color of shirt he had on — one like Ron's. While I instantly knew it wasn't Ron, it still felt comforting — natural. How many times did I sit in such a place waiting for him (I hate auto parts places), look in the mirror and see him coming? Yes, life (walking — breathing) is natural. It's death that isn't. There is a real sadness in knowing Ron's not going to ever walk back to the car, but even that sadness isn't quite as bad. The Son-shine reigns today — even though there's a cloud or two in the sky.

Sunday Evening, 2/4/96 (In Church)

We're having a missionary emphasis day today. Claudia sings a song — sings so beautifully of a Lord and Savior who walked the road to Calvary — to die on a cross — for me, and for you. He laid down His life, and He had the power to pick it up again. Ron, because you chose to listen to God's calling on your heart as a child, tonight you're with our risen Savior. Oh, Ron, how I long to be with you tonight, but I feel a calling on my heart to be happy being here a while longer. God's got something for me to do. I have an idea what it is, but time will tell. I'm just so thankful that you're okay.

Tuesday Evening - 2/6/96

There are things I can do now that I couldn't — back when Ron was alive. I can put my feet on the furniture with my shoes on — or lean back in a chair — give anyone I want to $1,000 (Don't line up ~ I don't have it to give away. But, I could if I did!) — eat out at McD's any time I want (He hated fast food!) — a bunch of stuff like that. I can do it all now without Ron fussin or teasing or whatever — but even that freedom doesn't bring joy. So, how come I'd do those things when he was alive, except the $1000 thing?

If I wanted to, I could even walk all over the hood of my new Saturn! But — I don't want to. I bought a condo with people over me and beside me. Ron would never have done that — even though this is a very quiet place. (Steve's like his dad. We'll be watching TV and he'll jump and go, "What was that?!" I'll look up and ask, "What's what?" It's just a dog barking or something being dropped. *Steve's a lot like his dad!*)

I'm not complaining about the sensitive hearing thing. Ron's hearing was very sensitive. A long time ago he, Michael, and his co-owner was at their waterbed store. (Ron was their accountant.) They were in an inner office with the door open. Ron finally told them that the buzzing was driving him crazy! Mike and Dave listened for a moment, looked at each other and said that it sounded like a smoke alarm (they were both paramedics). Sure enough, a customer had let his cigarette ashes fall on a bed upstairs. The entire upper floor was fully engulfed. The fireman said it was ready to flash over and that the fireball would have gone down the stairs, around and out the opened back door right by the office they were in. They would have been incinerated! None of us ever fussed about Ron's sensitive hearing again! It had saved their lives.

Freedom is a funny thing! We think as kids that we can't wait to be grown up so we can stay up late (or out all night) with whomever we choose — don't have to go to school (work's okay — we'll get paid for that!) — junk like that. Then, we grow up and grumble that we have to go to work. (We don't stay out so late any more — and we try to choose our friends better too.)

There's something to be said for freedom, but there's a lot more to be said for hearing just one more time, "Brenda, get your shoes off the sofa." (It was a sofa — not a couch!)

Friday, 2/9/96

A trip to the grocery with Steve last night — seems like a harmless activity. Yet, as I stand in the chip aisle waiting on him to get some munches, I turn and my eyes are drawn to something on the top shelf behind me — I say out loud, "Severe flashback — memories flooding in — major Grief returns!" He asks, "What." There's such a look of concern on his face as his eyes follow mine to the cheese and peanut butter crackers that his dad liked. I see the three packs that were in the box of his personal things I picked up from his office. And, I remember the bottle of antacid they say he was taking at work. I didn't understand — he never took it at home and I didn't know he was taking it at work. Dr. Byers said it wouldn't have any connection to his birth defect or his death.

I can't shake it — this inner turmoil. This is what I mean when I say I still don't know how to be a widow. How can a pack of crackers cause such turmoil?! By now I should know how to handle these emotions, but I don't. Maybe it was the other things at the grocery last night — the chicken croquettes we used to eat — the cheese fondue — and more. The things we used to like and used to eat — things I hadn't noticed until last night. Didn't realize just how much spaghetti and cinnamon rolls had become my diet over the last ten months — those things and McD's and Boston Chicken and Taco Bell! Maybe it was the young family in front of us at Taco Bell where we ate on the way to the grocery. The two boys were the same age difference as Steve and Allen. I asked Steve if he remembered being that age. He said no and he was sure he never swung on the poles and chains like they were doing either! (Right, Steve!) They swung, okay — but only one time each trip! I just didn't enjoy those trips to the emergency rooms we took so often to get them put back together and sewn up! I wanted so badly to tell the couple to enjoy those boys and, more importantly, to enjoy each other. But, they wouldn't understand if I tried to explain. (How could they?)

There's got to be more to my feelings than I'm seeing here. It's just too severe to be caused by a pack of crackers! I remember as a child we'd go to the movies on Saturday afternoon to see an Elvis movie. The movie was so exciting — we'd get caught up in the idea of being swept off our feet by ELVIS! We'd cheer as the curtain came down — so excited — but then, step outside into the bright sunlight. Reality seemed so "unreal." Our emotions were still inside, melting as Elvis sang that love song to us. The inevitable heavy sigh would break forth as we headed home — alone, without Elvis. As the years passed by, the matinees would be replaced by the dates to the drive-in or ball games.

The grocery trip was something like that last night. It was good remembering buying the things Ron liked — cooking for him (for us) and us eating together. But, Ron won't be sharing these things with me again — I stepped out into the bright light of Grief again.

Think I'll write myself a rulebook: Rule #1 = Once through a feeling — thou shalt not revisit it. (Right, Brenda!) We had a Rulebook when Steve and Allen were kids. It worked then. It could work again.

They'd ask why they couldn't go out to play at night — we'd answer, "It's in the Rule Book." That would end the discussion. Of course, as they grew older they'd question the validity of this "Book." So, Ron began quoting page and paragraph number. It was the day Allen asked to see the Rulebook that we knew they had (and probably had had) our number! They'd play along. Ron was great at inventing things — like juicy water. When the boys would want sodas Ron would suggest water. Yuck! - - until he suggested juicy water! They'd always take juicy water over regular water! They loved the banana pancakes and the green eggs for breakfast and the colored milk. They could choose blue milk or green milk or chocolate milk (each of which came from a different color of cow, of course). Come on now, why are these things any worse than Santa or the Tooth Fairy or Easter Bunny? Ron had an imagination and the kids loved it.

Saturday Morning, 2/10/96

Wonder what's bringing up memories like yesterday again, or why I haven't remembered things like that earlier. It's nice to have twenty-six and a half years (and the three months we knew each other before we married) of memories to recall now.

It's a comfort to have Steve with me. Even though he was fast asleep last night, it was still good to know there was someone there. I must stay aware of the fact that I was okay before he came though. I would never want him to feel "obligated" to stay with me. I don't want to become dependent on him either — not in the "need" for him being there to make me happy way.

Zipper was spayed yesterday. We both missed her last night. She's such a funny little nuisance to have around! As I write this, I realize that if Ron were still alive I would have never "met" Zipper.

Tuesday, 2/13/96

God continues to bless (and protect) me! I could really kick myself for not keeping track of something, but I never would have thought of it. I wasn't sure when Ron died about whether God would expect me to tithe on the insurance policies from his death. I asked Pastor Reynolds. He very quickly gave me a scripture reference. *"Thou shalt truly tithe all the increase of thy seed, that the field bringeth forth year by year"* (Deuteronomy 14:22). (That's BEFORE taxes too!) He also was just as quick when he found out that I was selling the RV and Spaceball to call me and tell me that unless I made a profit from the sale on those things, I wouldn't tithe on that. And if I did, I'd only tithe on the profit — not the total sale. God has blessed me so much. He's proven that I can't out give Him. I love it!

I'm not normally a careless or stupid person — especially in the area of fires. But this case was in not knowing how to do something.

Ron and I never had a fireplace and I had no intentions of using the one in the condo I bought — until it got SO cold with my "wonderful" heat pump system. Allen had offered to get me some wood last summer, but I declined. So, I decided to quit buying those three-hour fake logs and get the real thing. I called the number on the mailbox and, to make a long story short knew I was paying a high price, but I wanted some wood.

The following Saturday night, Lucille called and invited me over for a movie. I'd put the last three-hour log on to get rid of it about an hour and a half before. I threw a wet (rung out) towel over it. Ended up burning the towel up!

I was telling Glen about it at church the next morning. He laughed (having been a fireman) and said, "it's really scary what people do with the ashes." I told him I'm very careful with them — I faithfully empty the fireplace every night before I start another fire. He about died when I mentioned that I put them in a plastic bag and put the bag in the trash when it's full! I had NO idea embers can stay hot for a couple of days! Not only could I have caught my house on fire, but could have started a fire at the dump! Glen also told me not to buy any more wood — that he has plenty. So, he brought me a supply last night. It was SO cold — he'd loaded the truck himself and had delivered some to Lucille and Keith too.

Friday, 2/16/96

Suddenly, as if in a time machine, it's 1992 and I'm standing in the front yard of 14 Meier Circle in Vincennes, Indiana. It's a brisk evening — the sky is clear — about a million starts are out. Inside Mom lies — dying — slowly, but surely. I look at the partial moon and wonder when her spirit will rise so high she'll look down on it and our front yard. She has so much trouble breathing and endures horrible tests so often. She experiences the humiliation that only an invalid (or caregiver) can understand. Yet, she doesn't complain. I love her so much. I'm so glad I can share my pain (and fatigue) with Ron. He's such a comfort (so loving and caring) with Mom and me.

Wait — the time machine is revving up — lights are blinking. Now I'm in 1995 — in our apartment — in our bedroom. Ron lies so still — his face is so blue. (Why isn't the rest of his body blue?) There's peace in the room as I cry so gently for the love of my life — wanting him to get up — wondering what could have taken his precious, vibrant life from him. Things that I can't begin to imagine now will transpire over the next year. I know God will get me through, but it hurts to know Ron can't be there to comfort me.

But, it's not 1992 or 1995 — it's February 16, 1996, and I'm so alone. God IS here — He IS getting me through, but for the first time I can say — without guilt or disrespect to Him, that I really feel like I need more. I believe it's okay too. God made Adam and Eve. He made man and woman and joined them together. I believe it's okay to acknowledge that I need and want someone in my life. I believe that's His plan for most people. I don't believe He's called me to become a Paul — for I'm told He's the same yesterday, today and forever. Therefore I don't believe (not here — not right now) that He would change my make-up at this stage. Maybe it's time to begin thanking Him for the person who is walking ever so slowly towards my life.

Chapter Twelve

2/20 ~ 3/19/1996

Every Emotion I've Felt So Far Is Revisited

Wednesday, 2/21/96 - Lunch
Dear God,

Please don't make me do this again — feel the deep unrelenting pain of Grief. I know it's been months since I've felt this deep pain and, I'm thankful for that. But I can't bear the pain anymore — even spread months apart. Concentration is unattainable today. I'm back to robotic actions and feelings. If only my heart would become numb!

I know all things work together for good and I know there's something to come out of this pain I'm feeling today, but God, DADDY, please help me! I need You so much! I truly can't bear it. A part of me today wishes I was a bum cause I could just pack up and go. There are things I need to do for others today, but I literally can't. I don't understand.

Friday, 2/23/96
It doesn't make sense that everything is still the same since everything has changed...let me explain. It's getting warmer outside

135

— the days are getting longer. One of these mornings I'm going to walk out the front door and hear birds singing. One of these days I'm going to "feel" spring in the air and, it's going to hurt. It already does!

Last Spring, I had Ron. A year ago we had less than a month left to walk this earth together. How quickly I remember how very special our lives were then. So, even though it hurts to the core, I want to concentrate on the joy of then — not the pain of now.

Saturday, 2/24/96

The sun is out and a coat (while may have felt good) wasn't necessary this morning. I'm very happy to announce that on this "springish" morning my joy is alive and well. I've had a pretty rough week, but God's kept me facing forward, as my heart looked back. I'm so thankful for a Lord who loves me and keeps me and protects me.

Monday, 2/26/96

When I got back to work after lunch I sat in the car and cried as I did in the first couple of months. The Grief consumed me once again with a fire so hot it reminds me of my fireplace. Steve and I are learning how to build some pretty neat fires as we experiment on how to lay the logs, and all.

This fire in my heart today was soothed as the tears flowed over the flames, cooling the burned logs down until there were only embers left. And — tonight I feel the heat of a couple of those embers. But, the flames have once again gone out. So, I choose not to put any more logs on tonight. I could very easily build the flames again. I'm not suppressing — just staying away from that "teen-age" need to cry. I think I'll shut the glass doors on the fireplace of my heart tonight and go to bed in peace knowing the Gatekeeper will keep me safe and secure. To God be the glory!

Wednesday Evening, 2/28/96

Now, I need help on a different decision. I'm going Saturday to look at a knitting machine. I want to get one and do some knitting for some additional income. I'm praying hard for God's guidance on this. God, You are so awesome! I can't begin to comprehend Your presence, power, compassion, faithfulness, love, peace, - - - I could go on and on. Tonight I'm so touched by just what a PERSONAL God You are to me. You have kept me exactly where You needed me to be this year. I've said it before — if I had any more money I would have packed up and been gone several times. If I had any less I wouldn't have the peace You've given by supplying my needs.

God, You've even begun to give me a peace over the anniversary date of Ron's death. I want to spend some time at his grave. I want to read my journal from beginning to end and write some letters to some pretty special people. Then, I believe Jamie and I will go to the Italian Inn for a pizza for lunch. The perfect ending to a great day will be to go to church. I love You so much!

It's hard sometimes to take things one day at a time. It's so hard to believe that I'm still alive and well and even "coming" alive again with new desires, feelings, and plans. God, You know the future. You hold mine in Your hands. Oh, God — You are so worthy of praise and honor and glory. Why have You chosen to bless me so much?! How in the world will I ever be able to pass on all You've given me?! I want to sit in the car all night and sing along with the CD player. BUT, it's getting cold and my eye lids are getting heavy so I guess I'd better get some sleep. Thank You, Lord!

Thursday, 3/7/96

I guess we all have a passion for something. Allen loves four-wheeling. He can pull an engine at the drop of a hat. He has about a million "Bronco parts" — rebuilding one.

Steve's passion is stereo equipment. When we were in Indiana he had a '79 T-bird. It was a nice car — a "classic." He had a burglar alarm put in, but it wasn't for the car — it was to protect the sound system (which was worth more than the car). Ron and I bought his "old" system. When anyone of the "younger" sect gets in my car they always go, "Wow, what a system!" They really are wowed when I tell them it's Steve's "sluff-off" system. I have a Pioneer tape — 6-CD changer — radio, etc. The CD changer lives in my trunk. Installing it was part of my purchase deal with Saturn.

I like to put the CD player on random play. I have some oldies, along with Christian music in it.

Life is like a CD changer on random search. The song playing now speaks of heaven. There's no more looking here on earth — no more worries in heaven. It speaks of life being over and seeing Jesus.

God, what is it that You put in us that fights so to stay here? We lie in bodies that are in pain and dying — yet we don't give up. We keep on fighting even though we know what's ahead for us.

Now another song speaks of being shackled by a heavy burden and being touched by Jesus. I could use a touch tonight. I'm so thankful Ron didn't suffer with me by his bed watching — hoping against hope for a miracle. My burden lies in not wanting to face (yet wanting to get beyond March 20). I know God will make me whole again some day. *I just don't know when.*

Yes, I have a fantastic stereo system and, at the touch of a button I could choose a happy song or a love song — or a really really sad song, but life (real life) is more like the random play (at least it is to my finite mind). God's got the plan — nothing in my life is played at random even though it seems like it is on this side of the curtain.

I'm remembering Ron more all the time. And, I want to more and more. It hurts so badly, but it's like I've GOT to feel the pain. I can't keep dealing with it in this abstract way. I really want to get to the other side of March 20 in every way — not just on a calendar.

Sunday Morning, 3/10/96

It's a beautiful morning. A crisp 20 degrees. I sit in the sanctuary listening to some very heavenly music. The Griffith Family sings of heaven, God, Jesus and it's so peaceful. Sadness fills my heart as I think of Darla and Terry. They stand by the deathbed of their only daughter. The doctors tell them the time has come. By "man's" guess she'll be with her Lord by the time this service ends.

(By the time the morning service had ended, Michelle had gone to be with her Lord. There's so much sadness. No matter how glad we are to know she's with the Lord, the pain for her family will be so intense words can't begin to describe it. God, please back Your dump truck up to the Blessing Loading Dock — they're going to need it!)

Monday, 3/11/96

Our Spring Jubilee started yesterday at church. Michelle's whole family was in church last night. There were tears of joy — tears of grief and just plain ole tears. Dawn's grandma died five years ago today. The songs made her cry. Jamie cries beside me — Cathy cries on the other side of Steve — Jimmy cries in front of me. Are those sniffles I hear behind me? And, of course, I cry.

Hum, seems like you can tell what some things are by the way they smell or look or feel or act. This sure feels like a valley I'm in. Just as sure as I can tell a rose by the smell, I have been in enough valleys this past year to know one when I see one. This one's different though. It's the Valley of the Shadow of Death. I don't like it here — think I'll check out. *Wonder what the quickest way out is.* I guess a sense of humor could do the trick. I used to be a clown — yep, a real Clown for Christ. I made people laugh (scared some). *No, that's not the ticket.* I definitely need to laugh though. Rest assured I'm not doing denial or suppression here. Again, I was body slammed by Grief tonight at church. But I also heard the message about sometimes "choosing" to be happy. It would be real easy to stay here in this valley and cry and become help-less, but I believe I'd rather be happy. I'll still feel the pain — that's for sure. But, I can take it and go on. I choose tonight to look for the blessings and the joy. Think about it. Ron's been in Heaven for almost a year. I love him — I'm happy about that. I've been kind of Home sick lately, but I think I'll keep working here for a while. In the mean time, I'm sure if you asked Hillary Clinton that she'd tell you she's proud of her husband for being in the White House. Well, I'm proud of my husband. Ron's in heaven! He's with our Lord. He doesn't have to make an appoint-ment to see God — he's there. That's pretty neat.

Monday, 3/18/96

I'm an optimist. I don't believe there are too many problems in life that can't be solved. I also live in a real world and I know that this doesn't always work out to be true. However, that's how I attack problems or issues in my life. Ron was the same way.

Within a week of his funeral, I had bought a new bed, re-arranged the apartment, started looking at new cars, and had given his clothes and tools away.

I decided last week to handle Wednesday as a celebration of Ron being in Heaven for a year. There's going to be some pain — I know that. No one has to tell me what happened a year ago. My memory was forever complete in finding him. I'm going to take some friends to the Italian Inn to have pizza for lunch. He loved their pizza more than any other on this earth. We haven't been there since he died. It's time to go again. I guess this is a strange way of dealing with his death, but that's okay. We all should grieve in our own way. For me, this is working.

I have a problem though. My sub-conscious mind is out of sync with my conscious one again. I keep having flashbacks to the summer of '93 when we were on the road with the Spaceball. It's bringing reality to the forefront and I get horrible, stabbing pains in my chest as I once again realize that Ron's really dead — that he's not ever coming home again.

I also realized that I've been thinking all wrong about having feelings for anyone else. It was fun being a teenager again, but I'm so thankful God hasn't allowed any kind of emotional interaction with anyone. I'm not ready to deal with that yet. Maybe I will be soon, but I'm so thankful that God has protected me.

I walked out of the house this morning and it happened — I heard the birds singing — even heard an owl "owling." And, I smiled. It's so good to be alive — even with all the pain. As I sit here in Fuddruckers tonight, I'm getting into the cape mode again. I remember being on Cadillac Mountain wondering how deep the ocean (and my pain) was. My focus was on going down looking for the end. Tonight I'm coming up out of the water as Superman used to in the movies – with my hand extended up over my head with a fist made and looking up. Superman's neat, but God's neater!

Chapter Thirteen

3/20/1996

A Day of Celebration and A Few Letters

Wednesday, March 20, 1996
One Year Today

Yesterday was the first day since Ron died that I could remember what we were doing one year before. It was a Sunday so we were in church in the morning and evening. Pastor Reynolds preached on "How To Put Life Into Your Prayer Life" on Sunday morning.

I was at peace yesterday. I worked until after 7:00 to get things cleared up. I was up until 1:00 a.m. getting my journal entered and edited. I wanted to read it today. I'm in the same McDonalds that I came to so early the morning after Ron died. Nalanee is still here. She remembered me and asked how I've been. Her dad died a month or so ago so she said her Mom is going through what I am. *I'll never forget Nalanee's kindness that morning and the mornings after.*

I believe my plans to celebrate today have been honored. When I woke up at 6:30, I had a joy in my heart as I looked forward to a wonderful day of celebration. I know a lot of people are praying for me (What would I do without them?), and I know we serve a God who answers prayer!

Today is the first day of Spring and it's snowing. *Guess I won't spend a lot of time at the cemetery.* Right now I don't even feel a need to go there so maybe I won't. I was getting ready to leave home and walked through the bathroom to the laundry room. Coming back out I found a card on the mirror. Steve and Allen had given me a beautiful sympathy card, their love, and enough money to pay for the pizza today.

These two young men are the best blessings of the union between Ron and me. Maybe all parents feel that way, from a natural relationship, but when the rubber met the road a year ago today they hit the pavement running. They've protected me and supported me in so many ways, I can't begin to comprehend what this year would have been like without them.

One year - - - suddenly time has come into focus fully and completely for me. HOW can it have been a year?! NEVER has God's power of protection seemed as real to me as it does today. He has brought me through a year that I can't comprehend living through. I have a mountain of blessings to be thankful for.

Love immeasurable — pain incomprehensible — blessings abundant — I've experienced them all this year. I'm so thankful for this day of celebration.

Choices. We all make them. I believe now that many times all I have to do is make a conscious decision (in faith) and God takes the driver's seat from there to fulfill that plan. He's sure been doing that. And, lest I forget, part of my prayer was for Him to let me feel the pain that I need to feel today. I don't know how He'll do it, but if I need to cry, I will and He'll be there somehow to wrap me in His protective love. You know — sometimes His love means putting the blanket of care around me — and around the pain — locking it in instead of out. Sometimes I MUST feel the pain and, without His protective blanket of love, I'd push the pain away and cease to move forward. WOW!

Today was good. Lisa G., Jamie, Lisa P., and I went to the Italian Inn for lunch. It was good. We had an enjoyable time. I called the cook out to thank her for the wonderful pizza and to tell her why we were there. I told her that Ron had told everyone who ever bragged about their pizza that no-one could top the Italian Inn's! She really appreciated that. Our waitress (who's name was Lisa too) said they could hardly get her to keep cooking!

Yes, today worked. It's interesting, but I really do feel like the largest hurdle has been conquered. So many have told me that once today is passed it will get better. Tonight I believe that. Can't explain it, but I believe it.

I remember "counting Mondays" for the first few months. Then I counted the weeks. All of the weeks and months have led to this first year mark. It must be the first anniversaries that hurt the most. The first holiday — first Thanksgiving — first Christmas — first birthday (yours and his), on and on. They are all special days that, once survived, just can't hurt as badly anymore. As I draw this first year to a close I want to write some open letters.

To Grief,

You've been a hard taskmaster this year. I end this year with great respect for you. Your name shall always be capitalized in my eyes for you have become something to be respected.

You've been an enemy ~ an unwelcome guest ~ a comfort ~ sometimes actually a friend. Most of all, you've been a teacher. You've taught me that I can lean on my Lord. I don't believe it was ever your intention to separate us from each other and I'm thankful for that. You taught me what would happen if I tried to ignore you or to put you in one of the dark, hidden sections of my heart.

You've taught me survival at it's best ~ through Christ. Grief, thank you for all the lessons you've given me!

To satan,

My heart breaks for you tonight. Not like a few years ago when Jan got so scared when I told her that I felt sorry for you. No, my sorrow for your destiny doesn't make me vulnerable — it just makes me sad. You really thought a couple of times this past year that you could destroy me, but my focus was upward from the moment I found Ron. You never stood a chance.

You, and the millions who have been snookered by you will spend an eternity paying for what you've done. I really hate you for your power of deception, and you certainly deserve what awaits you.

To Capital Baptist Church,

"A Church With A Heart" ~ how awesome you are! I'm sure there are other churches just as compassionate and caring as you, but I sure have come to love you.

Pastor Eagy, I'm glad Pastor Reynolds was out of town when Ron died. He would have been fine too, but I wouldn't have been able to experience your care and compassion. I believe your Spirit that night set my feelings and reactions for this entire year into motion.

Tonight, as I looked up from the songbook and saw you there, I stopped and was transported back a year. I couldn't help but wonder if you were aware of what this date was.

Pastor Reynolds and Debbie, you all have been so wonderful to me. You really helped me through this year.

There are SO many others at CBC who have helped me ~ I won't even begin to name names. I'd end up hurting feelings and I wouldn't do that for anything. Thanks to everyone!

To Ron's Parents,

Thank you for giving life to such a wonderful man! Your marriage was an inspiration and guide for Ron and I, always holding hands ~ helping each other ~ loving each other verbally and in public ~ your dedication to God ~ the rubbing of the head (Ron really loved that part)! I could go on and on.

Just as my parents did, you all seemed to have the gift of parenting. I know by experience that doesn't come naturally. It takes an Agape kind of love to be so wonderful. No one is perfect, but with four wonderful parents as role models how could we ever loose?

You welcomed me into your family when Ron and I met and you've let me know that I remain so even tho Ron's gone.

It is my honest and earnest prayer that you will never have to experience the pain I've come to know. May you have a long ~ long life until we're raptured out of here! God bless you all!

To My Parents,

When you all went to be with the Lord (ahead of Ron), I thought my heart would break. When Ron joined you all, it DID break.

But, with the childhood and upbringing I had with you, how could I loose?! You taught me all about God and how He could be trusted and leaned on. You taught me to serve Him.

Thank you for somehow knowing when to hold on ~ and, when to let go. I still don't know how you did it!

Bet you were surprised to turn around and see the RF with you! God bless both of you! Take good care of him until I join you!

To God,

You are SO awesome! I sit here and I'm speechless. I can only say ~ "You know ~ You know."

To Our Sons,

Dear Allen and Steve,

Tears come to my eyes as I even begin to think of you guys and what a blessing you've been to me. You've known when to call ~ to come ~ to care ~ to help ~ to hug me.

As your mother, I stand much taller than my physical person! Your Dad and I could only guide you in life. You have both made the choices to become the men that you have.

Allen, your Dad would have loved Lisa as much as I do. If I

may speak for him ~ "we" approve! Steve, hold on. God's got someone truly awesome for your future. Be patient.

Our Lord will greatly reward you both for your dedication, especially after the way you've come through for me this year.

Remember to always look up to your Heavenly Father before you look out. Love Him first before anyone else.

To Ron (a final good-bye):

Dear, dear Ron,

You're such an angel! My spirit has soared several times this past year as I would think of us being reunited as we rise to meet our Lord.

Thank you so much for your gentle spirit the morning you died. You took time that morning to hold me in your arms before we were to start that last day ~ a day when I'd need the memory of those first few moments together.

Ron, what's it like to die? Were you scared? Did it hurt? Did you call out for me? Did you think I'd failed you when I didn't respond? Somehow I believe that, by the time it came for you to leave, your focus was on Someone much closer to you than I.

How did you go to Heaven? What was it like? I'm sure your fear of heights was gone, but did an angel (or ten ~ or twenty) come for you? What's it like to actually meet our Lord? Remember when we were in New England, in that gorge, (can't remember the name now) and we commented on the beauty in comparison to Heaven? Is Heaven a million times more beautiful? Is it?!

Neither one of us was perfect, but we were faithful to our love. I'll never forget your sense of humor! I said something last week to Steve and he commented that was something you would have said. *Thanks for leaving a part of yourself in me.*

I can see you and Dad at their kitchen table in Kentucky. I'd walk in. You'd been up for hours, talking and drinking coffee and Dad would say, "Well, Ron, if we don't get up from here, this day can't get started..." He'd have an errand to run in town. You'd give me a hug and tell me good morning.

All in all, I think I've done okay with my decisions since your death. I know I've done a few things I shouldn't have (or, should I say that you wouldn't have done). But, I believe on the major ones that you'd approve.

Ron, I love you and I miss you so much. As I look back at our lives, I realize we accomplished everything (except being financially set) that we ever thought or dreamt of doing (which is why we were never financially set). Yet, I wouldn't change one thing we did. I'm not left with memories of what "we wish we'd done." I'm left with memories of all that we did together.

The strength you imparted to me has helped me deal with your death so much. You taught me to be independent while I remained completely dependent on you. If I had written an order for the perfect husband I could never have described you. Even with your faults (I know, "What faults?"), you were too good to be true.

I know I don't need to do this, but since you're still such a vital part of me, I want to ask you something (even tho I realize you can't answer). Ron, may I have your permission to move on ~ to get beyond the Grief and the pain - - - and, the loneliness? If our Lord chooses to bless me with someone else, is that okay with you? I know we had discussed this ~ given each other permission, but we thought it wouldn't be an issue in our "older" age! I guess I need to know in my heart that you'd really be okay with me finding happiness with someone else. It'll be a while yet before this becomes an issue, but somehow, today seemed like the time to ask you.

There's been such a peace and joy in my heart today. The pizza is still as wonderful and unique as it always was. *Did you see the cook's face? She was beaming!*

There was a time in our marriage when I would have described your personality as basically negative. Since we'd gotten back into church I saw you change before my very eyes into a gentle, calm spirit. I'm so thankful for that. Again, I believe knowing you really helped me survive this year.

Ron, I love you. I want to go on and on writing to you, but it's time to let you go. I don't want to end this year on a sad note, but there IS sadness in saying goodbye. People say, "I'm not saying good-bye ~ but goodbye for now." Reality knows that when we leave someone's home we say "Good-bye - - - period." And, so it must be with us. However, I just remembered something that brings a smile to my face.

I love you ~ I always will!
Good-bye!
Brenda

Chapter Fourteen

3/21 ~ 5/19/1996

The Black Hole

Wednesday, 3/27/96

I am suddenly overwhelmed as I realize I don't know who I am! For twenty-six and a half years I was "Mrs. Ronald Fahey." For the last year I have been in the very dense fog of Grief. I've come out of the fog, but I don't know where I am (in this journey of life) – who I am – or where I'm going. And, I'm scared! I'm really scared.

I don't remember ever going through an identity crises before – why now? I'm still Brenda Fahey. I'm still a Christian. Beyond that (and the usual Mom, secretary, etc.), I don't know what's left.

More and more, my memories float back across time to Ron and our lives together. I'm starting to have nightmares – of Muffin being killed by a German Shepherd – of someone grabbing me and Steve not hearing my screams – stupid stuff.

Am I so terrified of being alone that my mind conjures up some horrible existence?! None of this makes sense. I no longer want to live my life in moments or days. I want to fast forward into living weeks (or months) at a time. I know it's wrong to wish my life away, but I'm frightened of the present. If "being out of your comfort zone" is a sign of growing and stretching then I'm going to be a very tall person very soon! Basically speaking, Grief has exited and Loneliness has entered.

Saturday, 4/6/96

Dear Lord,

Surely I've caught a glimpse of Heaven this week! The Passion Play is wonderful! I'm glad I get to play one of the "good guys." Even in a play, I'd hate to have to cry out for Your crucifixion! I really get into the part. I get such a joy as Matthew walks on stage. I know this isn't even beginning to touch what the reality of seeing you will be like, but it sure feels good to know that day's coming!

Wednesday, 4/24/96

We find ourselves outside again at work. There's a fire somewhere in the building. I got to the garage in time to get my car out before they locked the doors. I'm behind the fence of the church parking lot across the street. (It beats standing outside in the wind with heels on!)

It's a strange vantage point I find myself in – looking at many of my co-workers through a fence. Reminds me of the new Federal Maximum Security Penitentiary in Indiana that Steve and I toured before it opened. It was very sobering to sit in a cell with only a small window – doors bolted behind you and a fence (or two) on the other side of the window.

Prison – I've been in one. Its name is Grief. As I sit on the inside of this "fence" I don't like it – can't wait til I'm free. Yet, I've been given a life sentence. *Ron's never coming back.* I'll never get free.

Prisoners sometimes get out on a life sentence for good behavior. But they still wear the title of former inmate. It'll go with them to the grave. Many choose to turn their lives around as I'm choosing to do. I must quickly add that I feel more positive than negative on my journey and imprisonment. God has been so good to me. Still, the application is applicable. I feel bad for prisoners. I'm a widow and society looks a lot kinder on me than on a former inmate. Hum . . .

Wednesday, 5/1/96

I figured out a pretty important role that husbands play today –

decision making! It was so easy to put my two cents worth in and let Ron carry the burden (and responsibility) for making major decisions. Sometimes I didn't "think" it was easy to follow his choices, but now I see just how tough carrying that load is for a man.

I've got a semi-major decision to make and I've really lost on how to make it. I've done the basics – researched, budgeted, prayed, etc. but I'm not finding peace on what to do. Maybe the purpose is for me to get to where I am today – to seeing what a responsibility it is to be a man. Maybe I needed a real good lesson on wifely submission. There's got to be a lesson in this because I've really prayed a lot – I've even tried crying and whining. *That didn't work either!*

Monday, 5/6/96

I know what it's like to be lost in a black hole. The oxygen keeps pumping into your lungs – so, life continues. You wish it would stop so you could. There's no way out of it. Somehow you ended up in this hole. It wasn't anything you did – or didn't do – it's not your fault. There's no one else with you – it's so lonely!

There's hope that someday someone will join you. That's selfish because for them to join you they'll probably have to go through the same trauma you've been through. Still, you don't want to be alone forever. You realize suddenly that this must be how someone waiting for an organ transplant feels. Hope – guilt – lonely. So many emotions.

Some day it will be better. Could someone please send a balloon with a message telling me when?! If only I knew I could look forward to it – I could plan for my future. In the interim I'll hang here in oblivion – in this black hole. (There must be something useful I can do while I wait.)

I also realized what holds this black hole together – an entity called "Empty."

Sunday, 5/12/96   (Mother's Day)

The Lord is so good. Even on special days like today when I

miss Mom, God gives comfort. So many of my loved ones have left this earth. It leaves one feeling pretty lonely and empty sometimes. Thankfully I don't dwell here long.

It's been a good day. The guys and Lisa took me out to lunch. I'm so blessed to have them. But sometimes I long to have Ron to share my pride with. The many times we'd sit and reminisce over their childhood are very special. Allen had such a temper and was so independent. Steve was so laid back. They've both become very fine young men. I'm so blessed on this Mother's Day. *And, I'm lonely.*

Chapter Fifteen

5/20 ~ 7/19/1996

It's That Yo-Yo Thing Again

Monday, 5/20/96

What is it about today being the 20th AND a Monday that has me concentrating so much on Ron's death? I keep remembering last Monday night and a meeting with Pastor Reynolds. I had quit the Bible Institute two weeks before (after Dad had the T.I.A.). Just couldn't handle the pressure anymore. Truth is that I'd taken control of my life from God. *Why I'd do such a thing is beyond my comprehension..*

Since the one-year anniversary date I've been lost – not knowing who (or why) I am. I've really been floundering. Finally, I decided to go in and see Pastor Reynolds. I'm back in the Institute and out of the hospice group. I'd already quit that. Pastor Reynolds said something that's had me a bit shaken. I don't remember his words, but he told me it was time to get on with my life. *I sure wish that someone would share the secret to doing that with me!* I'm ready – more than willing – even anxious to do that, but, for the LIFE of me, I don't know how! Ron was my life! My "life" is gone. I'm left just as helpless to this new life a newborn is to his. No one expects a toddler to be self sufficient so how come I'm expected to be?!

I guess I need to quit talking to people – maybe rely more on God and less on "man." I'm not sure that I know how to close a part of myself off. I've always been so open with others, but maybe that's a new lesson I need to learn. I sure don't like the feeling I'm left with.

Wednesday evening, 6/5/96

You know, I was happy when Ron was alive. Life had its problems that would come and go (as everyone knows), but "life" was good. I have come to the realization that life — once again — is good. The memory of Ron – the loneliness – the "burdens" of being alone are just today's versions of yesterday's arguments – or being sick or having a bad day at work. *Is this Spring I feel in my soul?* Somewhere in the crevices of yesterdays-gone-by I can remember the pain of the last year, but I can truly say my focus is forward and not backwards.

Sunday, 6/9/96 (after church)

It's raining "cats and dogs" – "like bullets" – "it's coming down in sheets" – all those clichés that we humans conjure up are all happening right now so I'll take time to work on some feelings in my heart tonight. I've really been avoiding dealing with some things lately. Today Bro. Brock gave the "singles" a plan and some goals to look forward to. And – my heart broke once again. Just last week I was reminded that I don't have a clue on what it's like to be "single." *Have I not been saying that myself for over a year now?!*

Sunday p.m., 6/16/96

Father's Day – how I missed Ron today! Again at church I was told that I was being prayed for yesterday. People are so sensitive to my feelings. Tonight I was talking to Glen and Ginny came up to me to ask me to be her Mom at the Mother/Daughter Banquet next Saturday. What a wonderful blessing! I was so honored.

Steve and Allen worked on things around the house yesterday while Lisa studied. They're such a blessing to me!

Tuesday, 7/2/96

Things are progressing so well in my life! Jeremy gave me a

"quick" review and a good raise last week. I got an overall Excellent on performance and showed great improvement in all areas.

Steve and I went out two Fridays ago to get him a dog. Turned out not to be the breed he wanted. Since we were out, he wanted to swing by the Ford dealer. He's been in so much pain with his Honda. He's just too tall to fit in it. We drove out at 2:30 Saturday morning in his new T-bird! It's beautiful. I ended up trading my Saturn for a '96 wagon. It has several options I wanted and I'm doing this knowing it's not the wisest thing I could do. But, I prayed and asked God if it was going to do anything too harmful to my budget to stop me in some way. I realized this weekend that I have become contented with my life!

Sunday, 7/7/96

- - and then, I came to Louisiana! Maybe content isn't the word. I took time to stop and found out that I still miss Ron more every day. I want him and our lives back so badly that surely I must be the most selfish person in the world! Everywhere we went this weekend was with other couples. (What do I mean by "other" couples? – a slip of the tongue!) I'd been in these situations before — without Ron, but with other couples. Yet, I knew he was alive, so, I too was a "couple." It was different this time. Lord, will I ever fit in again? At least, seeing Jim wasn't traumatic like last year.

I'm in a tiny toy airplane. It has a total of two seats in each aisle! You know, life can change in an instant. As we finished lunch today the call came from a friend of Jan and Jim's. His wife had left church ahead of him to get dinner going. An older woman in a Cadillac thought she had time to make the turn in front of her, but she was wrong. She hit their friend's Ford Tempo and she's in surgery now. The doctors don't know if they can save her leg or not.

Lord, what was happening in Heaven when the two cars collided? Did Your eyes close on impact? I know You bent down and picked her, her family, and friends up as they came upon the accident one at a time. Her father – holding her still as she thrashed about from the pain as they worked for over thirty minutes to free her – what was that like for him? Lord, we never know from one minute to another what awaits beyond the next tick of the clock. Please help me to live each moment for You, Lord.

As we taxi down the runway in this tiny toy airplane, the road is bumpy — the engines are loud and drowning out all other noises that surround me — and, as we go faster and faster, there's a rush of excitement. There could be fear at going so fast and knowing we'll be leaving the ground soon, but there's no fear ~ just a calm assurance that all will be well as we glide off the runway. And, so it is with my life right now. I leave Louisiana with a new found prayer that God has someone for my future, but also with a new found and deepened prayer that I'll find many opportunities to serve God.

Wednesday, 7/10/96

I wonder if Ron ever thinks of me. He probably does. (At least my finite mind wants to believe he does.) I wonder what kind of eyes he sees me through now. Are his eyes the same as Christ's? Does he see only the good in me – in my heart? I'd sure like to think of Ron thinking of me with a total – complete – and perfect love in his eyes. To think of Christ loving me enough to die for me. Now, on this side of Calvary, He can look at me without the pain of the cross facing Him. It's all behind Him now. I'm sure He's not in therapy for all the injustices He's suffered at Calvary! So, He's left to the time when we see each other face to face. Is Ron like that? I remember us looking at each other at different times of our marriage with the look of total love and devotion. Think of that kind of look – now perfected! I'm so overwhelmed with God's love today. *Makes me a little home sick!*

Lord, there is such a restlessness in my spirit! What is it, Lord? I have things I'd like to see happen in my life, but I truly want to be in Your will.

Your Spirit asked me tonight if I really meant it when I prayed a year ago for You to spare my future love the pain I was in even if it meant spending the rest of my life alone. With everything inside of me – from the very depths of my loneliness I answer, "Yes." Of course I can rationalize it to say that I've survived and that I'll have a much greater appreciation for him.

I sure am glad I don't have to worry about these things since You're in control. I love You and I trust You with my life, my love and my future. (You've done a pretty fabulous job with my past, You know!) So, I'll go inside now and wait for Your peace to permeate my very being.

Friday, 7/12/96

If I believed in reincarnation (which I don't), I'd be sure I'd been a race horse in my "prior" life – a stubborn – full speed ahead – no holds barred race horse. It's funny how I want to fast forward to the future. Yet, I'm the first to say I'm glad I didn't know what 6:05 p.m. on March 20, 1995, held for me until that exact time. If I'd known Ron was going to die, I would have been so filled with Grief we could never have enjoyed our last days and months together. It's the good parts of the future that I want to know now. However, being the stubborn horse I'd have been – I'd jump ahead and mess it up by trying to make it better – or quicker – or sooner.

I'm glad I'm me. I'm glad it's now and, I'm really glad God's in control!

Wednesday, 7/17/96

I'm reading the book *Living Through the Loss of Someone You Love* by Sandra Aldrich. I am so overwhelmed with thankfulness that I wasn't asked to watch Ron suffer here on this earth!

I've been sick since Sunday, but I'm feeling better today. I realized this morning that I'm making progress. I often wanted to be left alone when sick…not ignored, just left alone. I realized this morning that I've thought several times the last couple of days that I wish I had someone to leave me alone! Not Ron, but "someone." *Does that mean I'm looking to the future more?*

Since coming home from Jan's I realized how "normal" it is to want to be with Ron. We'd never gone more than three days without talking to each other. We'd been separated for a week or two at a time, but at least we spoke by phone. It's been over a year since I saw or spoke to him. Why do we think that just because we know we'll never see our loved one again here on earth that we automatically get over wanting to?

God is so good. My book is beginning to sell. I still hope to be able to help others through it – and, it looks like there may be a sequel. I'd sure like to read the last chapter to see how (or who) I end up with!

Chapter Sixteen

7/20 ~ 10/19/1996

God's Waiting Room

Saturday Morning, 7/20/96

Lord, why does having someone to share things with enrich those things so much? I'm sitting in the car waiting on Steve, and a rainbow from the sun in the window fell on the book I was reading and it made me feel good inside. The bright colors – beautiful shades (You did a great job with the colors of the rainbow) reminds me of happier days. It really has been a sad year. I've laughed and had fun, but all that's been covered by a sadness. The coating is getting thinner and, sometimes (like last night) it actually breaks that thinning cover of sadness. Kristie and I were talking and I was telling her of Muffin's first seizure and how Ron thought He'd killed the dog. We laughed so hard in the restaurant, people thought we'd lost our minds. But, it was good to laugh again – to really laugh again. And, it's good to see the rainbow. I'd like to believe that's Your sign of my future and having someone to share it with, but I remember Pastor's message Wednesday night so I won't read anything more into it. I think maybe things like the sadness, the laughing again, the rainbows are lessons You're giving me – special moments so I'll remember to hang on to the important stuff when You do bless me with someone again and he does something stupid (like putting the TP on the roll backwards)!

Oh, Lord, I have so much love for my future husband in my heart! I don't even know who he is, but my love for him – my appreciation for

161

him is growing in my heart daily. You know my heart and my heart trusts You to lead me to the one YOU have chosen for me.

Wednesday a.m., 9/4/96

It only takes one phone call to change everything. It was 4:00 yesterday when I called home to check for messages. There was only one. It takes only a few seconds to relay a message, but time slows to an incredible crawl as I hear Aunt Gerda's voice. I can only imagine her call is about Grandma. (There's hesitation – concern in her voice so I know it's not good news that she's called to share.) The words I'm waiting for finally come – it's not Grandma, but my cousin, Allen, whose life has ended – tragically ended in suicide.

Allen took such good care of Grandma. He'd do her spring-cleaning. He was there for her when others couldn't be.

Once again AMS comes through as I ask permission to go to my Grandma. I'm so concerned for her. She raised Allen from an infant so this is very hard for her. She said Uncle Bill (Allen's dad) sits and cries – wishing he'd been a better father. It's so easy to blame ourselves at times like this, wishing we'd done more when, in reality we've done what we could. It was Allen's decision to take his life. It's that choice thing again. We all make choices in our lives. This one – this suicidal choice impacts so many others. In the final moments when he felt no one cared why couldn't he see how everyone DID care? Maybe we all need to be more demonstrative in our feelings with others.

Friday, 9/6/96

Funeral homes...it doesn't seem to matter where they are – from New York to Ohio to Kentucky – they all seem to be the same. So, at my funeral (I need to put this in writing), I want that CD changer – on random mode playing. Put some Beach Boys and Elvis in with the Christian tapes. And – I don't want it to be real low playing either. It would be really great if they could have a Spaceball there – giving free rides to all who dare! (OK, I'm getting carried away, but I really want my passing into Heaven to be a celebration.) Still, I should remember that it's those who are left behind that the funeral is to minister to.

O, Lord, I really do love You and I believe I may be doing that suppression thing again because a time or two I've gone back to Ron's funeral and, as the tears begin to flow, the flood gates drop and the curtain falls. Why do I do that? Why do I fear the emotions that have not failed me yet?

We have returned for the evening viewing. I've retreated to the basement to be alone. I find (if I'm to be honest) that I want Ron to be looking for me and to find me and to hold me as I cry over losing him. *Emotions really can be crazy at times!* Still, I want so much to feel the pain that is so deep within my soul tonight. Only then can I deal with it and get back to the peace and contentment I'd been feeling lately. Ok – so I change my mode of thinking to wanting Mr. Wonderful-of-my-future to find me and we begin to talk of life, pain, death, God's blessings and, before I know it, he whisks me off on his white horse and we live happy ever after! How come that desire is about as useless as the former?

I've been asked a couple of times this week if there's any one in my life. It's almost embarrassing to say no and, why should it be?! I know in my heart that I haven't been in any condition to have anyone in my life. I'm very thankful that God's in control.

Saturday, 9/7/96 p.m.

I'm finding myself in airplanes too often, I think. Yet, here I am again, getting ready for take off to head home.

Allen's funeral today was very nice. So many tears – many holding back the feelings of anger at him for doing this to himself – to us. Now is not the time to be expressing those feelings I guess.

Mr. Wonderful never showed last night. I went upstairs to find that I'd been missed. I made an appearance and went for a walk to get a coke. It was dusk and it didn't take, but one catcall to make me realize that this walk was probably not the smartest thing I'd done all day. Still, I walked on – asking God to protect me in my stupidity. I ask myself what was going on. Was it blind faith – the feeling of, "it can't happen to me" – or just a plain ole, "I dare you to even think about it!" Who knows?! I'm thankful for a Lord who protected me. I asked Uncle Bill about the area later and he said it was definitely not a good idea to go for a walk in that neighborhood.

Friday, 9/20/96 (1 1/2 years today)

I was thinking yesterday morning that I must be all out of "sad." I guess I'd tried earlier in the week to muster up some tears and had failed so, I figured the sadness was gone. But, yesterday morning Gloria asked me why I was so down! Go figure! I wasn't even thinking about today – just doing my job. Guess I really do wear my heart on my sleeve.

Yes, I am still sad, but it's not to the horrible depth as it was last year when I described sadness. You hear how people who have suffered a crippling accident. They fight it with all their energy until finally, they give in and begin to adjust to what they have left. Many will even maximize on what they have. THAT's the person I want to be. I want to maximize what God has blessed me with. Even though it's 'normal', 'okay', (maybe) 'expected' for me to be sad today as I remember that eighteen months ago, time stood still for me, I want to rejoice that, for Ron time ceased to exist! Glory be to God!

Wednesday, 9/25/96

I'm experiencing some new feelings. I can't even identify how I feel, so as in the past, I thought maybe if I put it in writing it wouldn't be such a mystery.

I remember last week trying to cry and not being able to. It feels like I want to cry – could cry – maybe even should cry. I can't remember the last time I cried for Ron. Maybe it was the anniversary thing last weekend. Maybe it's the epitome of loneliness hitting. (It is, but I'm not devastated by that.) Maybe I'm beginning to depend more on me and less on Ron (good thing since he's not very dependable these days)!

Monday, 9/30/96

I went to Lisa's bridal shower yesterday. It was a lot of fun. She's so shy when it comes to being in the spotlight! I am so happy for Allen. He really deserves someone special like Lisa

I decided that God must have me in a holding pattern in just about every area of my life. I'm not sure why, but I hope I learn the lesson completely.

There's sadness in not having Ron to share this time in our son's life. There is so much joy in seeing him so happy. We have prayed for years for someone special to come into Steve and Allen's lives.

Tuesday, 10/1/96

There's no doubt. I'm definitely in a holding pattern! He taught me that He's all I need and now He's asking me to wait. I ask, "For what?" He says, "Hold on. I'm working on something." I ask, "Can I see?" He says, "You 'can' but, you 'may' not – not yet anyway." So, I go back to the waiting room and sit down, hands crossed – thumbs twiddling. But, there's an excitement in my spirit. After all, it IS God who's in the next room working on something for me. I could never be disappointed! He's the greatest "Gift Giver" ever! So, I wait. (Hope He doesn't forget that I'm here – He knows how impatient I am!)

Saturday, 10/5/96

I really wish someone would publish a rulebook on widowhood! I found myself in another situation tonight without knowing what's "proper." I know that it's "my" house (Ron never lived here with me) and, it's "my" car – but what about Steve and Allen? I caught myself calling them my kids tonight. It didn't sound right. They're "our" sons. But calling them "ours" insinuates there's more to me than me. So, does calling them my children tell the world I'm a widow?! Who knows? No one will write the rules – it's all conjecture!

Sunday, October 6, 1996

It was only last Tuesday that God sat me in His waiting room. Tonight He called me in for an examination. He found my commitment lacking in a couple of areas (like praying and reading His word). Can't argue with Him on this one!

While He may still have me on hold, I have a feeling I've got a test or two before being released to work on the project He's working on for me. *Man, I wonder what it is!!*

Chapter Seventeen

10/20/1996 ~ 1/19/1997

Eagles Soar and So Can A Widow

Sunday Night, 10/27/96

Dear Ron,

I'm so thankful to my heavenly Father tonight. I'm so very blessed! I know you were with us in spirit tonight as our son was joined in Holy Matrimony with Lisa. Wasn't it a beautiful service? The way Lisa cried as she came down the aisle. Not everyone knew why she cried. It wasn't because she was having second thoughts as some were thinking. Natalie was a half hour late and then the bride comes down the aisle in tears! Her young, tender heart was truly broken by the meaning of gaining Allen as her husband.

It was a beautiful service. I really appreciated them honoring your memory! Allen wanted to do that. The Pastor said that Allen and Lisa wanted to pause for a moment to remember you. Then, Allen took a white rose and put it on the altar beside the picture of you they had placed there. I missed you, but it was nice to have your picture to look at.

I was so proud of Steve too. He took his position as best man seriously. He and Allen were so handsome! Jerry was a blessing too. People were surprised to find out that he was the father of Allen's former fiancée! What a great relationship they have.

Ron, it's now natural for me to refer to Steve and Allen as "my" sons instead of "ours." Guess I'm really beginning to move on and to realize that being without you is now "normal" for me. It's good to be feeling secure again. With God's power (and by His grace), I've come to realize I really can make it "on my own." I still love you with all my heart though! Take care!   Brenda

Monday, 11/18/96

Last week was incredible! We had a revival with Bro. Dan Ondra. He's a fantastic chalk artist. He preaches a sermon and then draws a picture about it. For one thing, I learned that the author of Footprints is now known. Her story is so moving (as I always knew it would be).

Bro. Ondra has a screen mounted to the top of the easel he's drawing on. The lights are turned out in the sanctuary. As he begins drawing, a slide projector begins and projects onto the screen. There may be a narrative or a song or information going on. Then, when he's finished, there's another projector he starts. All lights are out and the narrative and slides project onto the finished picture. It's really incredible.

I asked if I could take him and his wife out for dessert Sunday night and, to make a long story short, he ended up asking if he could draw my story.

Wednesday, 11/20/96

I was thinking about my cats tonight – asked someone at church if they get their cats all these shots that's suggested. It's time for Zipper Cat to get one or two. I may have the money, but I'd rather spend it on something fun! She and Charmin are never out so I think I'll pass. *Wonder if they know they've been saved from getting a shot?* Sure wish Mom and Dad had spared me! Some of my most horrible memories of childhood are of Dad driving up to the Health Department for those shots! Took some kind of persuasive action to pry my wee little fingers off the car seat! What a wimp I was. (Okay – I'm STILL a wimp!)

Anyway, got me to thinkin about when I'd wake up to find that my cats hadn't come home or that they'd died. Somehow Dad would remind me that they'd been sick. How I grieved for those cats. AND – Mom and Dad didn't go right out and replace them either! They'd let a lot of time pass before finally giving in to getting another. (A lot of time had already passed before I even wanted to get another one.) Hum – seems like tonight that Mom and Dad taught me how to Grieve for Ron in those lessons. Once again I'm amazed at their parenting skills and at God's lessons in life that have brought me to today.

It wasn't until I was in my 30's and said something to Mom about how neat it was that the cats always seemed to know when to go off somewhere to die. Mom said, "Those cats didn't go off and die – your father gassed them!" When they got so sick he couldn't stand to see them suffer anymore, he'd put them in a shoe box, unhook the gas line from the stove he'd put in the bathroom for the winter, and he'd put them to sleep. (Sounds better than "he gassed them" – don't you think?!)

Hum – somehow tonight I remember the pain I felt then – as a child. Felt a lot like how my heart has broken in losing Ron. Hum - -

Tuesday, 11/26/96

It's time for Thanksgiving. As I reflect on this past year I see where I really have a lot to be thankful for.

I'm really excited about my journal going to print. It's taken a lot of work getting it ready. I've already sold eight copies!

Over sixteen hundred families participated in the organ donor program in Virginia last year. Out of those sixteen hundred, sixty have been invited to Richmond next week for a ceremony with Governor and Mrs. Allen. He will present us with a medal of life. Mom and Dad are going with me.

Wednesday, 11/27/96 (Thanksgiving Eve)

Once again I look out from my ninth floor vantage point – same as this time a year ago. And, you know what? So much is the same. The lights on the building across the way are still Christmas red. The traffic still rushes by with their headlights and taillights flashing. And, I'm sure each car I see has, does, or will know the pain of Grief.

Somewhere, deep inside I remember the severe pain at this time last year, but I can't quite feel it. I see that a year can make a big difference. Somehow I believe my sub-conscious still remembers because concentration just hasn't been available to me for a couple of days.

I'm looking forward to the next two days. Lunch tomorrow will be at Mom and Dad's; dinner at Lisa's parents; dinner Friday at Mike and Bev's. AND, I don't have to cook a thing for any of them!

I wanted to go to the cemetery tonight on the way to church, but it's already dark. I'll go tomorrow.

Angie has a date Saturday and Steve has met someone. Maybe their Christmas miracles are on their way! *How bout me?!!!* (Heavy sigh.) Guess if I can't have "What's his name" I'll just have to wait! (That's okay.)

I got the proof of my book today. It went to print this afternoon. Kind of exciting to see it come together. I showed it to Kathleen. She stood and read parts of it for several minutes. She was impressed with it. *It's so personal!* I guess that's what journals are supposed to be! It's truly faith in putting it out for the public to read – that it's God's will – that let me give the go ahead!

Sunday, 12/1/96

Thanksgiving was so good! A few healing miracles took place. Maybe it was the wedding, but both Steve and Allen seem now ready to get on with living is a world where Mike and Bev are a couple. Also, Karla went to dinner at their house Friday and really seemed to enjoy herself.

Steve's date didn't go well, but Angie's did. She's found a home too. She'll be moving in soon. It's so good to face Christmas with our family safe and happy. I'm so thankful for Allen and Lisa's marriage. She's such a blessing.

There's an extremely deep emptiness in my heart this holiday season, but it's not so deep that it pulls me into pain as I feel the emptiness. I remember saying something about not wanting to live at one point. I can now understand the helplessness and hopelessness that one feels at the point of death by one's own hand. I still don't understand even forming a plan, but I can understand feeling so alone. Had someone remind me that I still have my two sons, but think about that for a minute. "Society" says the ultimate pain is losing a child. Until Ron died, I may have agreed, but, from the moment a child is born and they cut the umbilical cord, our children begin to leave us. We spend the next eighteen to twenty years training them to leave us. Even God tells us in Genesis 2:24 and in Matthew 19:5-6 that a man shall leave his father and mother and cleave to his wife. And, in those same verses, He tells us that we become one flesh when we marry. So, it makes sense that we would have more trouble losing a spouse since we've grown together.

Tuesday, 12/3/96

Again this morning I'm reminded of all the blessings of how I lost Ron. The man in charge of Security here lost his forty-three year old sister-in-law on Thanksgiving morning. She'd had pain for a couple of months. The doctor told her it was in her head. And – she died. By the time they got inside and found the blockage, the gangrene had spread through her entire body. What a senseless waste! Not all doctors listen to their patients. Think of all the anger and frustrations this family faces – the teenage son who can't begin to understand why his Mom is gone. How can he understand?

Lord, please let me reach out to others. Please find me worthy of being used to help a million others. God, You've been so good to me. My heart breaks for this family and for so many others who are hurting. I'm really going to be listening to Your still – small voice so I don't miss any questions on what I need to be doing to be found worthy to be used by You! Help me to help others, Lord.

Friday, 12/6/96

Meeting Governor and Mrs. Allen was a fantastic honor! There are five organ transplant consortiums in Virginia. Each one was asked to invite twelve families who had donated organs and/or tissues in 1995 to a ceremony and reception with the Governor in Richmond. The new State Library will open in January. This was the first event held there. Mom and Dad went with me. The families were presented with a beautiful Medal of Life to honor the donation. Governor and Mrs. Allen are a very warm and caring couple. Their compassion really came out. There was some sadness. As Mom said, there were so many people, each with their own pain, in one place. Makes you stop and think.

Sunday, 12/8/96

Pastor Eagy preached on "The Grinch Who Stole Christmas" this morning. He told the Dr. Seuss story and related it to Christ's birthday – and our Christmas. I realized I was letting Grief become a Grinch for me. I know that I can't be consumed with so much sadness that I forget the Reason for the season. Yet, how do I stay balanced between that and suppression? I reached out to someone this afternoon and got shot down – that didn't help!

They say you can count on one hand the people who are really "close" friends. I've found that to be true. But, I also see where you can probably count even fewer on the other had who really despises you. So, why did today hurt so bad?

That ole Grinch has surfaced big-time tonight. As I was driving here to church, I seriously considered running away (at least partially so). I could do that. Since I can't justify walking out on my debts, I have to be at work five days a week. But, I could run away from home and church. So, I ask what those places have done to me! I know I can't run – but – if I could, I would.

Well, there's no time to run away tonight – gotta get to choir practice.

Tuesday, 12/10/96 (lunch)

Between Friday evening, when I returned from Richmond, to Sunday night, several people with major hurts crossed my path. One message I got from our Sunday School class brunch was that, to plant seeds, I need to count the costs. I believe God's been helping me. So, I've been counting the cost of speaking and sharing the pain of losing Ron with others. There's going to be rejection (as I saw with the Christian sister I tried to talk to Sunday); there may be some anger (like witnessing the accident Friday night and the bozo who caused it blaming the young lady who was SURE her life had ended – or would once Dad got there); there will be others' pain taken on by myself (as there was with the brother in Christ as we held each other and cried for his lost supervisor killed in a car accident); and then there's the pain of reliving the emotions of losing Ron as I share and talk with others. I had completely forgotten that I had trouble sleeping after Ron died until Mom reminded me. After the first night, and until I came out of the deep shock, I DID sleep well. It was once Reality began to creep in that I began losing sleep. (Guess I've been focusing on the positive nights!) I do remember in those early days thanking God for letting me sleep so well. It was one of the blessings He gave me.

By yesterday I was asking my heavenly Father for a hug. And, know what? He's given me two! One lady has suggested a sequel. Does that mean I'm "sequeling" right now? When I gave Kay her book this morning, we talked for a couple of minutes. We talked about the Internet. She told me to get prepared to hire help to mail orders! Then a few minutes later she told me she can't see me at AMS a year from now. She believes I'll be able, financially to quit and travel as I'd like to. WOW! Something for my "Hum-Box!" WOW, could it happen? Could I ever step out faith that far? I mean, I'm it. It's not the same as when Ron and I did it. I'm alone now. Could I ever leave the security of a steady income? H-m-m I sure could! Cause I've learned (without a doubt) that security in anyone, but God is not real. If He ever gets me to that point, I'll follow Him. It is so neat not to have to worry about such things! I truly trust God with my future. Awesome!

Friday, 12/13/96

So many emotions rush through my mind as I hang the phone

up. It's been one year and nine months (a week from now) that I asked again if Ron's heart valves were used and I got my answer.

Lisa (from the Washington Regional Transplant Consortium), was so careful as she explained that they weren't used. (*She must deal with all kinds of reactions from people at times like this.*) She gently (almost too much so) dealt with the fact it was the medical examiner's decision not to use Ron's valves. She went on to explain that 80% of valves from a forty-five to fifty-year-old are not used anyway due to plaque buildup. She mentioned that with Ron it was because his was a sudden death with no known illness. I tried (also gently) to ask if it was because they wanted to be sure he wasn't murdered (and I recall my own questions that night and "waiting" for the detective to come out and ask me that very question). She confirmed that that was the reason.

So, I feel confused. To realize that I wasn't the only one asking that question that night upsets me – why? I believe it's because it takes my emotions back to feeling so helpless and not understanding. Yes, that's it. I'm back to not understanding. The wounds of "I don't understand – I don't know how to be a widow" resurface so strongly I almost break out in tears. How can this be?! How on this earth can Ron be dead?! *I still don't understand!*

Suddenly I can see what they mean when they talk about taking three to five years to get through such a loss.

Yet, I feel protected. It helps having my emotions of that evening affirmed. To realize the police found it as incredible as I did seems to help me deal with it. I'm so glad they were there to do the investigative part of finding the inexplicable explained.

Monday, 12/16/96

It's been a rough weekend. I began baking at 9 a.m. on Saturday and sat down at 4:00 p.m. I was going to the cookie exchange at church, but didn't make it. My neck was in pain from over working it. I should know better by now. When I crushed a cookie with the oven mitt I found myself wanting to call for Muffin to come and eat it. *Bummer.* Then, there was the lack of the Cookie Monster (i.e.

Ron Fahey) after every tray coming out of the oven. *I really missed that part too.*

Steve and I went to see Allen and Lisa yesterday. We had our Christmas dinner and carol sing at church last night. My heart is as gray and sad looking as the sky outside – better get my tent and some wood and set up camp. Looks like I'm going to be in this valley a while. I've certainly tried to find my way out for the last two days, but I just keep gong in circles. *If only I could find the Christmas Spirit of years past!*

Wednesday, 12/18/96

I decided to take a field trip today – here in the valley. If I'm going to be here a while, I may as well check it out. That was always one of the first things Ron and I would do when we moved – go in and explore the neighborhood and how all the roads came together.

I wonder why I'm always so anxious to get out of the valley so quickly. Maybe there's a blessing or two here that I've been missing out on. I've heard some pretty neat comments on my book. People are really being blessed. That's so amazing to me! I want so badly to be used by God. I'm waiting on Him to open the doors. Yes – call this the Valley of Excitement.

Friday, 12/20/96

It got real cold in the valley last night so I hiked on out. Besides, those valley experiences could turn out to be pretty deceiving. Sometimes it's easy to get conned into staying in the valley instead of exerting the needed energy to climb out. But, I found that as I climbed out this morning I was too warm to worry about being cold. Hum. Again, the tried-and-true method of concentrating on something other than the pain helps get me through. Amazing!

Monday, 12/23/96

You can't see my heart. (You see evidence of it, but you cannot actually see it.) There's things covering it up – muscles, blood vessels, tissues, bones, more stuff and, finally – fourteen layers of skin.

(At least they tell me there are that many – never had the opportunity to actually prove that fact!) Add the layers of clothes and you've got a pretty good camouflage of there actually being a heart somewhere in there. If someone wanted to touch it – or fix it – or see it, they would have to work for a while at getting to it.

I think loneliness-at-Christmas is like the heart. Maybe it lives beside my heart. After all, it's an "emotion," not a "thing."

Let's see. There would be a layer (a thin layer) of denial to break through. (*I've been working on this for a long, long time.*) There's the mind to remove (it keeps "reminding" me how lonely I am); and, don't forget that other part of the brain that registers the images of pictures onto the plat of loneliness; oh yeah – what about the dreams? *They're SO real.* When I wake up alone, that hurts. But, maybe I'll keep this part for now. At least, for some *(unreal)* part of the night I'm not lonely. Why rob myself of those moments, smiles, and the "I'm okay's?" Guess they cover this loneliness up too. It's not that I *mean* to lie – it's just too much trouble to explain the continuing pain.

Tuesday, 12/24/96 Christmas Eve

It's been a good day. They let us out of work early. Steve and I went to church at Capital. It was a candle light service with a lot of music and a great message on having peace in our lives.

I had dinner at Peg's last night. She reminded me of something her mom had said earlier – that God is enough – that He wants to be the husband to the widow. I really know that God is enough and that if He chooses for me to spend the rest of my time on earth without someone to share it with, He will be enough. He's just not all I want. I am so lonely. But, I'm still willing to spend my life as God leads. That's where peace enters in. Peace of God and the peace from God.

Sunday, 1/5/97

I was thinking this morning that maybe I should be more "mature" in my thoughts of someone being in my future. After all,

I am almost forty-seven years old now! So, what do I replace these teen-age-ooy-gooey-feelings of wonder with?! What do I substitute the "I-want-to-be-swept-off-my-feet-by-an-incurable-romantic-type-person-who-carries-me-off-into-the-sunset" feelings with? Seems to me that to substitute any of these feelings and wonderments with anything else would be the same as a person who feels Christians should walk around with a somber face all the time – never laughing or enjoying life. I think I'd rather be a person – both spiritually and personally who finds wonder and excitement and fun in life. Why else would God have given us the feelings of joy and happiness? Yes, I'll remain just a bit childish in my expectations.

Sunday 1/5/97 (11:59 p.m.)

Dear Lord,

Tonight I kneel beside my bed and I pray one of the most important prayers I've ever prayed before. Tonight I lay myself – my future – and the one I will love some day on the altar to You. Lord, my flesh cries for someone to hold me and love me and cherish me. My flesh cries out to be able to spend the rest of my life caring for him – making him happy – being a godly wife for him. That, God, is my earnest – wholehearted desire in my flesh. But, God, You know what's best for me (and, for him). Lord, You know where You need me the most. I prayed at the altar this morning for You to prepare me for what lies ahead. I truly believe I could be used by You with someone else at my side, but Lord, You know how You want to use me. That is how I want to live. I've given lip service to wanting to be in Your perfect will – tonight I submit my will to You. Mold me – make me, Lord what You need me to be.

How on this earth can I say to You – God – the personification of Perfection that You're not all I want? How on this earth can I feel that someone else can serve some purpose that You can't? While You don't have the physical arms that can hold me, or the human body that can talk to me, You have the Spirit that can live in me and fulfill any need I have.

Tonight, Lord I want You to be all I want...I want You to be all I need. Period. Again, I pray for Your perfect will – even if it means saying goodbye to the lifestyle of marriage that I've known, and so deeply wanted again. Thank You Father, for Your patience and guidance. Whatever my future holds – no, let me rephrase that. Whatever You hold for my future is what I want – it's all I want. If I can't trust You, Lord then who can I trust?!

Thank You God – thank You!

Love, Brenda

Monday AM - 1/6/97

"Victory in Jesus" – what a triumph! What a glorious feeling! What excitement! "Praying through" – what a concept! How rewarding! "Shouting" – how unwise a thing to do sitting at my desk. Yet, it wouldn't surprise me a bit if, from somewhere deep inside of me, a victory yell came forth! Last year I wrote of a pressure building inside of me til I felt I might explode. That was of Grief. This is from victory. (Maybe I could just do a victory dance or something.) Oh, Lord – how wonderful You are! I am so excited for what lies ahead! You and I are it. I'm going to depend completely on You! You are SO awesome! You know those ooy-gooey feelings I spoke of yesterday? That too is a neat concept. You know I respect You and who You are (I don't mean to be disrespectful). I just feel so good to the commitment I made to You last night. As I think of You choosing not to bless me with an earthly mate again I pause to examine my true feelings and – I say - - - "Yes, victory!" Whatever You say is fine. After all, You really are all I want or need. It's up to You to change my feelings on that if You bring someone else into my future. *It's so neat to have You back in control.* I'm not sure I've been trying to "control" my emotions. I believe it's more of a matter of adjusting to this new life I'm in since Ron's death. And, it's been a major adjustment to make, but victory came as I fell to my knees at 11:59 last night. Finally, I've been able to let go of the Grief and pain and loneliness. Wait . . . yes . . . loneliness. . . it's gone! Wow! Even that hole has been filled by Your Spirit,

Lord. That's a victory I feel I may need to remind myself of as this future unfolds. Please help me to remember that, Lord.

I know what a racehorse feels like! Cool! Suddenly, I'm at the Kentucky Derby. (I love Kentucky!) – we're in the starting gate. While I don't understand all the semantics of what's about to happen (After all – I'm just a horse!), I feel such an eagerness to break out of this gate. I'm waiting for that Man to open the gate in front of me – to let me out to do what He's trained me to do – to run the race - - - to win! My heart is racing – it's pounding – there's the proof of the air as it explodes from my face – I can't wait to get out! It's good there's Someone else in control of that gate. If the gate wasn't stopping me, I'd rush out and be disqualified for starting too soon. That would be tragic!

And, I know when I go over that finish line that it's the One I serve – the Man with the reins who will get the glory – for HE knows when to hold me back and when to give me a nudge to break forth. Oh, I'll get treated well for my part. My name will be in the papers and on the news, but isn't it great that it's the One on my back who will get the ultimate glory for winning the race! That is down right awesome!

Wednesday Night, 1/8/97

I am so glad this is Wednesday! I feel like I'm going to explode with excitement. Someone asked me right before I left work how I was. I told him that if life gets any better I literally won't know how to handle it! He said, "Wow! What a statement!" I said, "Yeah, I know!"

You know what I feel like tonight? One of those punchin bags you buy your kids – you know, with the weighted bottoms. No matter how hard you hit em, they bounce back up. You can sit on him and keep him down a while, but that stops you too, and you can't sit there forever, so you get up and – wha-la! He bounces right back up – and, he still has that silly little grin on his face. He never did lose that – even while he was being held down.

Yep, that's me – a re-bounding – pop right back up sort of a guy - - - uh, make that "gal!"

I got this victory in Jesus Sunday night and have been on such a high that I've been untouchable. But, satan's been there to "knock me down" a time or two yesterday and today, but I just took it to my Lord – to my first Love – and He fixed it for me. And, I bounced right back. (Yes, with the silly little grin plastered on my face!)

I've been on the mountaintop many times the last year or so since Ron went to be with our Lord. But early Monday morning I left the mountaintop. This time it wasn't to descend into the valley. I got caught up on a high soaring eagle's wing and we're flying above the clouds.

The really neat thing is that this trip I'm on won't have any devastating side effects like drugs or alcohol. And, it doesn't cost an arm and a leg – or a job – or a marriage, my children . . . as a matter of fact it pays great dividends! Wow!

Friday, 1/10/97

I wonder if we are to God as ants in an ant farm are to us? Walking down the hall today at work I saw several people coming out of an office – others going into one, speaking and smiling as we passed one another. Everyone doing their job. Everyone (like the ants) knows what their job is. And, we both have an ultimate Authority – at least we do – God. Bees have a queen bee (can't remember right now if ants have queens or kings or what – *doesn't really matter*). They know where they're going and what their job is. *Wonder if they ever rebel or feel lonely.* Seems like there ought to be a government study done on that. Makes as much sense as trying to prove what an infant is thinking. I don't really think infants think. God's given each species a thing called "instinct." We muck it all up by trying to figure everything out. Like me – if I'd learn to live one day (no, for me one minute) at a time, I'd be a lot happier. I worry too much about being happy in the future instead of remembering to be happy now – where I am. Hmm – ants and ant farms – humans and office buildings . . . wonder if God laughs when two of us collide coming and going?! *Ants never seem to do that. I wonder why...?*

Chapter Eighteen

1/26 ~ 5/25/1997

Year Two Come to an End...Life Continues

Sunday, 1/26/97

Super Bowl Sunday. Yippee! Actually, I wouldn't even have known who was playing if Pastor Reynolds hadn't mentioned the Packers. I mentioned to Debbie after church that I think I know their uniforms are green, but I have no idea how I'd know that. She pointed out it could be because they're called the "Green" Bay Packers! Hum . . . guess I pay more attention to those things that I thought.

Hurt my neck this week. I just turned my neck while in the phone at work Thursday morning and it popped real bad. I'm really hurt, but I won't go to the doctor. I'm afraid to. That would mean therapy and wearing that dumb ole brace for a while and maybe other stuff if don't want to remember from before - - back in that former life I had.

I've been reading my book, which has produced some pretty wonderful dreams of being with Ron again – on the road with the Spaceball – stuff like that. What a privilege it was to look into his eyes and convey true totally sold out love to him and, for his eyes to melt the very heart in my chest that held all that love for him. O Lord, tonight I pray for that privilege again and I promise – I promise to be a godly wife to him (even when he's not so "Mr. Wonderfully" acting)!

God called me a dummy in church today – affectionately so. He

181

did! Pastor's been trying to get me to teach Sunday School, but there's the visitation issue. His message was on commitment to ministry this morning. Since I know I have the gift of teaching and, since I've been praying for God to open doors for me to speak to ladies groups and, since there's a need at church, it was like God was saying, "You big dummy! I've called you and you say you want me to call you and we keep going in circles here." (Isn't it great how diplomatic He is? "We" haven't been going in circles. He's been standing still with me running around Him saying, "Please, please, please let me teach!")

So, I see where I haven't been taking the local call – the "ho-hum" sort of call seriously. Still don't know where He's leading exactly, but I'm going to start pretending to be a teacher – go to Wednesday night meetings and on visitation and maybe, when I grow up, He'll find me worthy to teach!

Gee, I wonder if that philosophy will work with finding someone to love. And when I do, why won't I be able to tell him? I love being a woman, but sometimes I don't like being on hold – waiting on him to make the first move. Men can be so slow! Honestly! *Where's my cape?* On behalf of women everywhere – I stand on my table and ask you guys what you're waiting on?! You're the ones we want to live for and spoil rotten and dote on! Don't you realize how many cookies you're missing out on – how much total devotion you're missing out on?! Why are you so practical?! Oh, you want to be sure?! - - - Well, we're sure! You guys are a riot!! Just say the word and you'll have one cape wearing, fully devoted lady flying off this table into your very strong, manly arms! *I think it's time to go inside now!* (It's kind of neat to be out here writing again tho.)

Wednesday, 1/29/97

I go to the doctor this afternoon. Just can't ignore it any longer. I was in bad shape Monday and found out I was being put to sleep by the Aleve I was taking! Guess that's why I slept so well Saturday and Sunday nights!

It felt so good to be awake yesterday! But, the pain is alive and well – woke me up several times during the night. I'd just like to find out what happened to cause this injury. Why now, after so many years do I hurt myself just turning my head?

Monday, 2/3/97

Forty-seven today. Don't feel a year older than I was yesterday! Also don't feel any more "grown up!" I've been in a major slump since I hurt my neck. The doctor said it will hurt for a couple more weeks and that arthritis may be setting in which would account for getting hurt so easily. The pain is better, but it's affected every phase of my being. The "sole-support" fact hit again. The ole "what-do-I-do-if-I-become-disabled" issue hit. I was talking to Steve over the weekend and shared my concern. He told me he didn't want to call me stupid – but, what do I think; that he and Allen would let me sit on the street?! Of course I don't, but I just don't "naturally" think of my kids supporting me!

Thursday, 2/6/97

Lord,

Today, sitting on this small hillside eating lunch, I've gotten a glimpse of what my life is like when I try to help You out. It's not that I've been trying to control life. I've just kept enough of "me" in things that I can now see You turning to help someone else – saying, as You do, "Brenda, when you want to let go, call me and I'll work things out." God, You are so awesome! So now, I stand amidst the mulch and between the split trees and, with my head bowed, ask You for total forgiveness. Looking down on the road below I see a few cars heading toward me. Those, I'll call opportunities and blessings coming my way. Those heading away from me I'll call satan and all his angels packing up their bags and heading on down the road. Sure, he's the master of disguise, but I'm going to be checking things that come my way very carefully. Lord, more and more I'm seeing the reality that You really are the One I want to please here on earth. Thank You Lord, for the sunshine and these times alone with you. Most of all, thank you for the view from this hillside.

Monday, 2/10/97

Our sibling dies – we say we don't expect them to die before Mom and Dad. Our child dies – we certainly don't expect that! Ron dies at forty-eight. Maybe not as much of a shock as a child, but - - - still, not an expected thing for a perfectly healthy person to do.

All that to say this: When is it "okay" or "a natural thing" for someone to die? When are we okay with losing someone? Is it okay for Mom or Dad or Grandma or Grandpa to die? That's certainly more "understandable" - - at least if they're older (like in their eighties or nineties or one hundreds). I don't think it's ever okay to lose someone. I don't think God's okay with death, so it makes sense that we shouldn't be either. He didn't design us to die. He made us to live and commune with Him – to walk in the Garden at night with Him.

So, why do we always seek to "qualify" a death as "okay" or "expected" or "worse than?" It seems that everyone does this. I wonder why. It's certainly not a competition anyone wants to win!

Thursday, 2/27/97

Cheerleaders! They come in all sizes, ages and degrees of expertise. Some are famous, some are never known. I was never "known" but I was a cheerleader – for a short time – for a junior high football team in grade school. I wasn't very good, but it was fun (the team wasn't very good either).

Ron was a cheerleader – my very own personal, private cheerleader. I miss him sometimes. Sometimes I want to go home and pout about how I was mistreated that day and hear him tell me how I'm the greatest!

It's different with your children. They put you on a pedestal and get upset if someone upsets you. But, a spouse seems to know when you just need a hug – when you're just being a crybaby. Yeah, I miss my very own personal, private cheerleader!

Sunday Night, 3/2/97

It is well with my soul. And, so it is, Lord! I thank You for the new found peace in my spirit. Sure, there is pain from time to time – for I'm still bound by this earthly body. But God, You know and You care! And, I realize that when I'm hurt – You're hurt. True peace has come this year. God, there's so much I still want to do for You, but I'm no longer putting You on my time frame. Lord, You've given me a burden so I now wait on You to bring it to be. Thank You for Your peace and Your patience.

Our Spring Jubilee began today. The Griffiths and Dr. Lovett are here. I have been waiting for this for months and it's been everything

I knew it would be. Dr. Lovett has grown a beard and mustache. I begin to laugh as I realize that nothing really does stay the same – not even Dr. Lovett's face!! Oh well!

Wednesday Night, 3/12/97

I sit tonight and ponder the words "healed" and "forgotten." I would have to do a word search on the computer to lay my hands on the entry last year where I discussed "healing from my loss" and "forgetting" being the same in the end. It's amazing what Time (is that a capital "T" I just used?) – anyway, it's amazing what Time does with our memories. I really am healed from the Grief, but I realize tonight that I haven't "forgotten" Ron or his memory.

Sunday afternoon, 3/16/97

"I have a black belt." That's a pretty powerful statement to make to someone – if they're thinking self-defense. But, I DO have a black belt – actually, I have more than one. By that last statement you now know that I'm talking about my wardrobe and not the ability to defend myself!

I wish I had a black belt in the Bible. When I think about a black belt I think of instant defense. Someone attacks you – you flip 'em or chop 'em or "whatever" without even giving it a second thought. If I had a black belt in Bible I would be able to draw my sword without thinking twice. I needed that ability this week. Found myself in a pretty difficult situation where I was betrayed. I didn't handle it real well.

Maybe this is God's way of answering a recent prayer. I asked Him to make me hungry. *I'm at Fuddruckers, but I'm talking Spiritually hungry.* God could have said, "Brenda, you need to be in my Word more." As a matter of fact, he has said that more than a time or two.

When I finished eating and studying, I went to the ladies room. I washed my hands and was about to put the paper towel in the trashcan when the door to one of the stalls opened. As I look at him and he looks at me, he says, "Oh, my!" I said, "I believe one of us is in the wrong room." I already knew who was where they should be because I always double check before going in – there's so many names for bathrooms – 'women's', 'ladies', 'lassies', etc! As he walks past me and opens the door, seeing what I already knew to be true, I told him I wouldn't tell. He said "thanks, but – it's okay for me to tell," because as I passed his table he was telling the others about the "really stupid thing" he had just done!

Perception is a funny thing. Yes, I felt "awkward" – but I didn't feel embarrassed or threatened. I was in the right room, and I was between him and the door. If he had been between the door and me I would have probably let out a blood curdling scream that would have brought every one in Fuddruckers into the bathroom. That's when I would have been very embarrassed.

Perception, like beauty, is in the eye of the beholder.

Wednesday, 3/19/97

I believe I've found the key to optimism! I never realized that we "wonder" in different tenses. For instance, I was just "wondering" where this last year went. The first year after Ron died was spent in surviving the great loss. But, I "wonder" what happened to the last year!

And then, in the next breath I was "wondering" where I'd be this time next year. At least past-tense-wondering has some facts behind it. It's kind of neat to read what I wrote a year or two ago. I'm always surprised to see how much I'd forgotten about the year.

It's interesting to see all the things I've forgotten. All of them aren't ho-hum type of things either. Zipper dying – Muffin dying. Then, there's the betrayal this month. But, other than those three things, nothing else of the sad nature jumps into my memory. I can sit for the same amount of time and remember many good things that have happened in that same period of time. Most of those things aren't the "biggies" either.

So, optimism seems to be dwelling on the good and forgetting the bad. I know – it's not quite that simple – but, it can be! If I sat here long enough I could remember more bad things. Or, if I read my journal those entries could bring up some negative things I chose not to write about.

I think it's a "dwelling" issue. If I chose to, I could dwell on the hard part of any situation. But if I acknowledge that I've been hurt and deal with it, I can, for the most part, put it in a box and shove it into a closet of my memory.

So, optimism, like being happy, can sometimes be a choice. It's snowing today – on the last day of winter. Last year it snowed on the first day of spring. It's been so beautiful to watch since it's been too warm to stick to the streets.

We have dress rehearsal for the play tomorrow night. *The End of the World* is playing – a perfect example of that memory thing. I could really sit here and conjure up some tears – here, on the eve of tomorrow – but I think I'll go back to work. (Sometimes it's good not to have time to stay lost in my memories too long.)

Thursday, 3/20/97
Two Years Today

Time – it really is on my side! There's a song about that and, it's true. I've come back to the same McDonalds again – the one I came to that morning and again last year. I was trying to define how I was feeling as I drove here this morning. The only word I could find was – numb.

Numbness is a funny thing. To become numb you first have to sustain a pretty severe blow. Think about it – after the shock of finding Ron, I became numb. How about the dentist? He's probably the best example. You go in, sit down and what does he do? He gives you a shot. He calls it an "injection" to distract you from the fact that it's a shot. Why does he do this? To "numb" you – from what? Pain. But – when he comes at me with that ten inch-long, one-inch thick needle (well, it may as well be), I really have to question if he's telling me the truth when he says the pain of the drill is a lot worse than the "tiny" prick of this wee-little needle. It's that perspective thing again – depends on which side of the needle you're on!

But, I've never been willing to find out if he's being honest with me or not. I take him at his word. So, I'm numb – but, that's okay. This too shall pass.

I look out the window and there is a little boy with his dad. There's also a puddle of water. You can pretty well predict what he does. Yep, he steps into it. Dad gently puts his hand on his son's shoulder and says something to him. They must have had this conversation before because he'd step into the puddle gently, making only a small splash.

Just as that Dad put his hand on his son's shoulder and spoke to him gently guiding him, my heavenly Father has kept His hand on my shoulder as He has guided me these last two years. I've been as a child

– listening, learning, asking questions, obeying (well, most of the time anyway). It's so awesome how God has made moms and dads in His own likeness. And, I can kind of see His reason for parents this morning. Children need a visible influence to guide them, to keep them in line and growing properly. As we grow we learn (hopefully) to rely less on them and more on God. I've certainly learned to lean on God more and more. As my Father, He knows when I really need a physical hug and He supplies my need. What an awesome God we serve!

We have dress rehearsal for the Passion Play tonight. Performance begins tomorrow night. Again, Gods' timing is impeccable on this, the second anniversary of Ron's death, I get to participate in the reenactment of the very act that gave Ron an eternity full of joy beyond measure or imagination!

To God

Thank You so much for another year of life – of happiness. You continue to teach me and guide me and love me. Lord, how do people get by without Your eternal love? Life is so much easier to bear when You're present and in control!

Thank You so much for another year of blessings. You continue to bless my life in so many other ways! Thank You so much for another year of patient teaching! You've taught me several vital lessons! Thank You for another year of provision. When I thought about lowering, or even dropping my missions giving, Your Spirit promised I had nothing to worry about if I'd only trust You. You have abundantly supplied way beyond what I increased!

And, thank You for another year of memories. You've let me remember things from my past with Ron. You've allowed new, wonderful memories to be stored up for the future, and You've helped me forget a lot of destructive memories! Thank You so much!

To Time

As I wrote earlier – you really are on my side. I'm not sure you're as "important" as Grief, but thank you for being a teacher anyway! You've slowed when I needed to stop and reflect – or feel – or rest. And, it seems like just yesterday I was writing another group of letters. Thanks for teaching me the real need to live in the present. It's okay to look back and even plan for tomorrow, but I need to "live" in the here-and-now.

To All My Friends

I'll never forget something Mom said as she was facing her own death and so many would come, or do something for her. She had commented on someone else she knew. This person was a loaner – didn't reach out and was often negative when others did. Mom worried about her. She was afraid when it came time for her to die, she'd be all alone. It didn't work out quite as bad as Mom had envisioned, but it was close.

I've been blessed by so many of you who have stood beside me and helped. While I've often felt lonely without Ron, I've never felt alone. Those of you at church, as well as at work who still ask and care deserve a very special blessing from the Lord. I pray that He will return your kindness many times over. Thank you!

To Lisa and Allen

I loved telling people that I had a daughter this year – and, without one labor pain! Lisa, you are so very special to me. I've enjoyed getting to know you and your family. Your parents are very special people to me! You have grown so much in the Lord. You're wise beyond your spiritual years.

And, Allen, you have grown too. I know you're making a lot of progress and that you truly love the Lord ... and, you love Lisa! I'm so proud of you! I know that your dad knows about Lisa, but I wish we could talk to each other about you two!

I know that life as man and wife isn't always a breeze – or fun – or romantic. Just please remember your commitment to God and things will always work out.

You all continue to make me feel very special. Thank you! (Have I mentioned lately that I can't wait to be a Grandma?!!)

To Steve

I really do appreciate you moving back home with me. You're rather easy to live with. I don't understand, and I feel bad for parents who can't stand their kids living at home. I'm so blessed and so proud that, when they share their horror stories I turn and share my blessings of having children who are supporting and helpful.

Thank you for the advice you give me and for following with the reminder that you're offering an opinion as a son. It would be so easy to slip into a position where I'm depending on you too much. But, we had discussed this up front. I really appreciate your help.

I'm so proud of you. You're really moving ahead in your job. The sky is the limit for you. Remember your father's work ethic and you'll succeed. God bless you!

Sunday, 5/4/97

AMS has brought me to Topeka, Kansas, to work for a couple of weeks. We're putting in some long days! Today they decided to give us a break and prepare us a nice picnic. I was able to find a church to worship in before the picnic started. It's so great to be able to go anywhere and find brothers and sisters in Christ! After the picnic they asked me to stay another week. The work is intense, but the people are great!

I was asked how I'm able to maintain such a positive attitude when others are getting so tired and cranky. God is SO awesome! He gives strength when mine is gone; hope when there is no visible sign of sunshine and peace in the midst of turmoil!

I've really found loneliness – here in Topeka. My "running" buddy went home for graduation this weekend. I've missed her. I'm on the third floor of the hotel. It's neat to open my living room curtains and see the capital building. The bedroom window gives a glance of other tall and lit up buildings. I lay in bed last night and looked out the window and – I felt the loneliness…the missing-of-Ron pain of long ago. How I wanted the ability to call him. Maybe I still would have been in Topeka, lying in this bed alone, but, just to know that I could call him if I wanted would have given such comfort.

Tuesday, 5/6/97

Saw a dead squirrel today at lunch – here in Topeka. Maybe it's missing Ron so much these last three weeks, but the death of that squirrel got me to thinking. There certainly wasn't a soul to be dealt with, but lying there in the street, that squirrel did have a life that had been snuffed out. As I drove by, I wondered how the driver who hit him reacted. Reminds me of a time that I was driving down an Interstate and saw a pigeon in the middle of my lane. He was alive and he made no attempt at dodging me. Dodging him would have caused an accident. I was so upset as I looked into his eyes right before impact. I looked in my rear view mirror. The pigeon was thrown into the air amid a great shower of his feathers. If I hadn't been so upset, the site would have made me laugh (I did laugh later when I was telling someone about it), but, life – even a squirrel's or a pigeon's ought to be thought of a lot more. Maybe if we, as a society cared about them, we'd care about each other and quit killing one another!

Part Two

Thanks For The Dance, Billy

I've said many times that the love Billy and I share is made perfect by having lost Ron. In having someone as wonderful as he was, and losing him like I did, it gave me an incredible appreciation for Billy when God brought him into my life.

We both know that his cancer can return at any time, but we find it hard to believe that God would bring us together just to tear us apart before we'd had at least twenty years together.

Chapter Nineteen

September, 1997~ June, 2001

Joy Unimaginable ~ An Update From 2001

It's been a while since I've journaled. Life changes seem to bring out the need in me to write. This one is a good one tho (I'm so excited!) ~ I've met someone very special. I can't wait for you to meet him. His name is Billy and - oh, I'm going to get ahead of myself. Go with me as I begin again.

September, 1997
Life has a way of working things out. In September of 1997, I was helping to register people for the Bible Institute at Capital. This man and woman came in together. I thought they were married, but they turned out to be brother and sister. That's the first memory I have of meeting Billy and his sister, Paula.

Cathy (the lady who had cried with me a time or two after Ron died) was usually with them, so I thought that she and Billy were dating.

May, 1998
Several months later: It was at the Bible Institute around the first of May, 1998, that I had gone downstairs to get some coffee and found a stack of pamphlets on "How To Know Who To Marry." I laughed and picked up a stack. I went back upstairs and began handing them to the singles.

Paula and Cathy were sitting at a table. I handed one to Cathy.

She gave it back and said, "No thanks! I will never marry again!" *I thought, "Wow...maybe there's a chance..."*

Then, I handed one to Paula. She said no thanks – that after her husband had died, she was sure she could never find anyone else to come close to him. I said, "I can understand that. That's how I felt for a long time after Ron died, but I really hope that God has someone for my future. I think I'm ready to love again." I didn't know it, but Billy had walked up behind me and Paula tells me now that Billy's eyes got really big!

May 18, 1998

It was a week or so later that Billy brought me a bag of Bordeaux cookies to the Bible Institute. He told me they were his favorite. We got to talking about favorite things and found out we liked many of the same things – like Pepperoni Pizza! We had talked before, but that night was like seeing him for the first time.

The next Monday was Memorial Day, so we didn't have class. Billy had sent me copies of the Christmas Play and Passion Play that he had video taped for the church. He had put another video together for Pastor Jay to show on Wednesday evening. After class he asked if I'd like to go to McDonalds with him and Paula and come back after Pastor Jay's last class to see the video.

It was very nice getting to know them. Paula had lost her husband several years before to cancer so she and I talked about MB and Ron a lot. *However, I was VERY aware of Billy's presence!*

We went back to the church and saw the video. It was of the children in the church with the background music of Ray Boltz' song "Thank You." That's one of my favorite songs about giving to the Lord.

June 8, 1998

The next Monday night I was secretly hoping to "visit McD's" again after class. That night, instead of cookies, Billy brought me a box of Russell Stover candy. *(Was this a message he was sending?!)*

Billy works a night shift and hadn't slept since Sunday afternoon, so he was tired. Except for the candy, we didn't talk much. He disappeared pretty quick after class. I was so disappointed. I prayed for him on the way home – that he would arrive safely since he lives an hour from church.

Before going to bed I knelt and prayed. God knew that I was falling in love with Billy. There's not much we can hide from Him, is there? I didn't know it, but the next thing I asked Him for (and the way He answered) was going to be one of the most significant points of proof to me over the next week or so that God was in total control of my life.

I explained that I didn't want to go on some kind of emotional roller coaster ride with Billy. It is then that I asked my Lord – my Father – to let this relationship go forward or end as He wished, but to let it be a quick answer.

Receiving a great peace that He was in control I slipped into bed and fell fast asleep. Less than an hour later, Steve came into the room with the phone to tell me Billy was on the line. We talked for a minute or two and he said, "Brenda, I joke around a lot, but right now I am so nervous!" I believe I asked him why and he said, "Brenda, I'm attracted to you." I told him I thought that was really great! He asked me if I would go out with him for a Coke to talk. I said yes, I would like that very much – he said he was relieved! *Billy told me later that he had looked at me across the parking lot and wanted so badly to come and talk to me, but he just didn't know what to say. He went home and called Paula and told her he wanted to call me, but wasn't sure he should…she told him to call! He then called her back and said that he was going to marry me…she told him to hold on just a minute! She told him not to even tell me that he loved me for one year!!!*

I don't remember ever being so excited and scared at the same time! This was the first "date" I'd been on in thirty years! So many emotions – I didn't sleep much that night.

Billy and I talked several times that week. He asked me out to lunch after church on Sunday. He'd told me that their other sister, Mary Jane was in town. When I got out of Sunday School I put my things down on the pew and stood to go to the choir. In my prayers that morning, I asked God for something to show me that things were going according to His plan. As I stood and turned, I looked into Billy's eyes. I felt such love for him that I thought my heart would stand still! He gave me a hug and told me that he and Paula were going to the deaf service with Mary Jane and that he'd meet me in the lobby after service.

Church was great and when Pastor gave the altar call, I went forward and laid everything about Billy and me on the altar to God. His Spirit asked if I was willing to go back to God being my husband and to walk away from Billy. I cried out that I couldn't imagine my future without Billy in it. How can this be? We haven't even had our first date! His Spirit said that wasn't the question – would I be willing to give Billy up? After a short pause, I said yes – that for a relationship to develop it had to be in God's perfect will for both of us. I asked my Father one final favor – to let Billy set the pace for our relationship. That no matter if it was to go forward, or to end that it would be unmistakably clear and that God would give a quick answer.

I went back to my seat and, with closed eyes, raised my hands to such an awesome God! Just about then I felt Billy's arm go around my waist. Our eyes met as he gave me a hug. Suddenly, I felt so protected again. It's one thing to know that God is protecting me, but to have Billy's arms holding me – if only for a brief moment – gave a physical reassurance that can't be explained. But it sure was nice!

We went to Arty's for a wonderful dinner. Billy opened the car door for me, he held my hand as we walked and, as we sat at the table holding hands, we looked into each other's eyes. Billy later told me that this was the moment he knew once and for all that we had a lasting relationship ahead.

You know, it's so easy to believe (maybe not "understand" but to believe) that Ron died suddenly. Why do we find it so incredible – impossible even, to believe that God can bring true, totally sold out love just as quickly?

But, we're human. We wonder. We question, especially if we bring past experiences into the picture. We had a wonderful lunch. I don't remember a lot of the conversation, but I do remember the bonding that took place. I remember being drawn to Billy in such a way that it seemed I'd known him forever. I wish I could explain it, but the words just aren't coming. It's almost too personal – too intimate to put into words. Perhaps it's something that is to be shared (and kept) between Billy and me alone. I do know one thing – I committed myself to him that day.

I gave Billy a card at the Bible Institute the next night. He asked if he could read it then. The front of the card said:

"I need to tell you something about myself
before our relationship can go any further.

I'm the kind of person who feels very deeply,
and, when I give my heart, I give it completely. I've never learned
how to love "just a little"
– So, as you can guess,
I've been hurt more than once.
However, I feel a strange and wonderful closeness
between us, as if, in this brief time, I can already
trust you, wholeheartedly. And that's why I
need to ask one simple question…
(inside)
If I fall for you,
will you catch me?"

As I walked away I heard – from across the room, "Yes!" I turned
and looked into his eyes and he said softly, "Yes, I'll catch you."
We sat for a long time after class and talked. He told me then that
he'd told his sons that I was going to be his bride. He asked if that
upset me. I told him, no. *Could he sense that I had already committed
myself to him? Is it possible that he understood that he held my very life –
my entire future in his hands?* I can't remember now if we saw each
other Tuesday night or not. I don't believe we did. (We live one and a
half hours from each other.)

When I came back from lunch on Wednesday there was a bou-
quet of balloons on my desk. The card said,

"Could I have this dance
for the rest of your life?
I love you, Brenda.
Billy"

That was so wonderful! All the "girls" were thrilled (and
impressed!) – most of the guys were ready to put a contract out on
him! (And, to answer your question – I said yes!)

Later, when I told him how wonderful and special he made me
feel, he reminded me that I had asked for the balloons. I know it
seemed we'd known each other forever, but I also knew I'd never used
the word "balloon" in his presence. He took me back to a journal
entry in my book:

Monday, 5/6/96

I know what it's like to be lost in a black hole. The oxygen keeps pumping into your lungs - so, life continues. You wish it would stop so you could. There's no way out of it. Somehow you ended up in this hole. It wasn't anything you did - or didn't do - it's not your fault. There's no one else with you - it's so lonely!

There's hope that someday someone will join you. That's selfish because for them to join you they'll probably have to go through the same trauma you've been through. Still, you don't want to be alone forever. You realize suddenly that this must be how someone waiting for an organ transplant feels. Hope - guilt - lonely. So many emotions.

Some day it will be better. Could someone please send a balloon with a message telling me when?! If only I knew I could look forward to it - I could plan for my future. In the interim I'll hang here in oblivion - in this black hole. (There must be something useful I can do while I wait).

I also realized what holds this black hole together - an entity called "Empty."

Billy told me he'd thought about sending one balloon, but he wanted to make the message perfectly clear that the pain was over! I teased him that, by saying, "Could I have this dance for the rest of **your** life," he was giving me permission to die first! (*You know how to respond to the one we love with, "No, I have to die first – I could never live without you!?"*) That was the response I expected, but what I got was, "You caught that, huh?" He told me that he never wanted me to feel the depth of the Grief that I had felt over losing Ron again. He said that it was his prayer when it came time for the Lord to call one of us Home that He would take me to be with Him first. Billy said that he would be the one to stay behind and grieve this time. *He wasn't misquoting Ann's song by mistake!*

Unless you have loved and lost, whether through death, as I had - or through divorce, as Billy had, you can't begin to understand the depth of sacrifice in those words! That's the kind of guy Billy is. He says he's "just a regular guy," but he's so much more! God has given him a creative gift to not only feel love, but to express it abundantly far above even my imagination!

I love it when he tells me that he promises to love me and cherish me and honor me and protect me (that part really makes me tingle) forever and ever!

Over the next week we met almost every night and we talked so many times on the phone that it's a shame we don't own stock in our long distance companies!

Paula had been very concerned about the rapid progression of our relationship. We shared very special letters between us. She loves her brother very, very deeply.

June, 2001

It's now June of 2001 and, to make a long story short, Billy and I have been married for over two and a half years. God has truly blessed me again. We both really appreciate what we have together. We look forward to retiring in October of this year. Billy has worked for Exxon for almost thirty years.

I went to work at the church as Pastor Reynolds' Adminstrative Assistant at the end of 1998. That has been a dream (and prayer) come true. I've prayed for years to be able to work for the Lord in full-time service. To think that He's blessed me to work for Pastor Reynolds as the last position I would have has been a blessing.

Billy and I truly know what it's like to love and lose and there's not a day that goes by we don't thank God for what He's given us. I stated at some point that having Ron and losing him would some day make a new love richer and fuller…and, so it has!

You know, time does have a way of healing the wounds of the heart. The best way to accomplish that is to let the Lord comfort and guide along the way. It's so hard to believe that Ron's been gone for over six years. I remember feeling that time would never move on. And now, the days are flying by. *It helps to work for a "driven" man like Pastor Reynolds! I get to work and turn around and the day is gone! I love it tho.*

Billy is a cancer survivor. He was diagnosed with Melanoma over seven years ago. With stage five being the worst, his was a stage four with lymph node involvement. In the last couple of years, he's lost two friends who were stage three so we know that God has him here for a reason. And, we know how precious time is. That's why we're retiring as soon as he turns fifty-five. We look forward to spending our days together in this journey called life. Whether we have months left together, or many years, we never take each other for granted.

I know that you may be entering the journey of Grief, but hang on...God's with you (if you know Him) and He won't let go. I pray that, in sharing my journey with me, yours will be made a bit easier. I mean it when I say that I'm here to help others who have found themselves on the road to recovery through a loss of their own. I've found by many comments about my first printing that it doesn't have to be a spouse that you've lost to feel as helpless as I did in losing Ron. For me, that was the ultimate loss...for you, it may be a parent or a child or a close friend. I've lost the need to "qualify" the depth of pain, somehow comparing it to someone else's. Life does go on and I'm so glad that it does. We never know what lies ahead in tomorrow. One thing we can all rest assured in is God's love and His protection. He wants His best for all of His children. He has sure blessed me beyond my wildest imagination! He took everything good in Ron, added anything I could have imagined asking for and then threw in a bonus or two of His own...and, He called him "Billy."

There's a part of me that can't wait until it's time for me to go and be with the Lord. It's my prayer that I can have Paul's testimony in II Timothy 4:6-8, *"For I am now ready to be offered, and the time of my departure is at hand. I have fought a good fight, I have finished my course, I have kept the faith: Henceforth there is laid up for me a crown of righteousness, which the Lord, the righteous judge, shall give me at that day: and not to me only, but unto all them also that love his appearing."*

For me, it all goes back to the one word FAITH. As Ron's mother said to me as we stood beside his casket for the last time; when I said I didn't know how I was going to make it, she said to me, "Brenda, you have a very strong faith in God. That's what's going to get you through." And, so it did. You know, a lot of people have "faith"... just remember that your faith is only as good as the Object of that faith!

I believe it was Pastor Reynolds who gave us this acrostic...I pray that this will always be my testimony:

Forsaking
All,
I
Trust
Him

Chapter Twenty

10/2/2001 ~ 10/9/2001

Ignorance Is Bliss

Tuesday, 10/2/01 ~ WE ARE RETIRED!
Billy's last day of work was yesterday. Today was a scheduled day off for him. My last day was today. There are such mixed emotions as we look to the future!

One main thing on my mind as I approach retirement is finally having the time to develop a closer walk with God. My heart wants to spend quality time in prayer. I just never seem to "make it." Maybe that's where I'll always live, in the Land of Wanting A Closer Walk. I hope it is. I pray that my spirit is always filled, but never full of God's presence and the desire for an even closer walk with Him. On this, the day we retire, I pray to grow closer and deeper to the Lord. Amen!!

Wednesday, 10/3/01

Today is:
Billy's 55th Birthday,
our 3rd Wedding Anniversary and,
our first day of retirement

We're going to Harper's Ferry for a couple of days, right after the dentist. Billy broke a tooth last night. We've got a reservation for a wonderful bed and breakfast with a view of the tri-state area from the balcony.

It's going to take a while for the reality of being retired to set in. We no longer have to get up at any certain time!!!

Our B&B is wonderful! The Last Resort is an apartment attached to the main house of this nice family. She had a sign on the door recognizing our three special reasons to celebrate today.

Billy's in a lot of pain with his tooth. (He couldn't get into the dentist office this morning.) We've decided to go home tomorrow morning.

We walked around the town today for a couple of hours. Not much happening this time of year. Many of the shops are closed. Billy really enjoys shopping in towns like this. I do too…I don't know when I've been happier! I love him so much. I am so blessed and I'm looking forward to the next twenty years (or however much time God chooses to give us).

We want to start shopping for a Yorkie tomorrow too. Can't wait to see the puppy that God has for us. We've been praying for Him to bring us the perfect pet ~ after all, this is a long commitment we're making.

Friday, 10/5/01

We brought Susie home today. She weighs one and a half pounds and she's precious. She slept all the way home! What a joy to have her. She is so tiny! She shouldn't gain more than another pound or so.

Saturday, 10/6/01

Billy's retirement dinner was today. It was so nice! We went to Artie's (where Billy and I had our first date).

Paula signed Alpha and Omega for Billy. She has been blessed to be able to minister in that way so beautifully.

Billy chose a beautiful Grandfather's clock for his retirement gift. He'd gotten a set of Waterford Crystal lamps for his thirty year gift (very generous gifts)!

Sunday, 10/7/01

My devotion today is on Job and how righteous a man he is. He definitely has to be the all time champion of suffering! And this morning, I feel a very small amount of identity with him. In God's wisdom, He called Ron home one day. Then, after a time (like He did with Job), He gave me Billy. I know the application is small, but it still fits. Bottom line is to always trust that God knows what He's saying and doing.

Monday, 10/8/01

This particular devotion came to mean a lot over the next few months. Today's devotion is on Job from Isaiah 38:5. It spoke of how God knows so much more than we what is best for us. He did with King Hezekiah when He told him to prepare to turn over his kingdom because God was calling him home. Hezekiah asked God for more time. God gave him fifteen additional years. During this time, Mannaseh was born. He was the most evil king ever to rule over Judah. He even passed his own son through the fire in a sacrificial attempt to please his god.

Tuesday, 10/9/01

Today's devotion is on God's sufficient Grace. I've been to where God is all I had to lean on and found that total trust in Him is all I need! The night I found Ron dead is when I've never felt more alone in my life. People told me I had two grown sons to lean on, and, lean on them I did! Yet, it's not the same. Never even came close! But, I put my trust and faith in God that night and He never failed me!

Chapter Twenty One

10/13 ~ 10/31/2001

Our Lives Are Forever Changed

Saturday, 10/13/01

I don't want to do this again. I don't want to write another book (it's too painful). Yet, as my mouth says the words, my hand reaches for the pen and I begin to write. I begin to write from the depths of indescribable pain, yet from the joy and peace that only God can bring.

I have no secrets from my Lord. He knows my every thought and He opened a brand new jug to begin collecting the tears from my now broken heart. I long to go back twenty four hours to the time my mind didn't know the things it now knows, to the time when my concern for Billy was his arthritis and his lethargy of the past week. I didn't understand why all he felt like doing was watching TV.

I'm too tired to continue *(or maybe my mind can't bear to write about what has happened).*

I was just joking. It was such an innocent question. It was supposed to be funny. How many times have I heard Pastor Reynolds tell us that our lives can be changed with just one phone call or one knock on the door and that we need to be ready and founded in

207

our Lord to handle these events? Billy and I retired just ten days ago. There is a surprise retirement party for him tonight at Capital, but things have changed now.

Just after midnight we were eating popcorn, watching TV. Billy raised his arm and began to wave it over his head. I said, "Little boy in the brown chair, what can I do for you?" He said that he was having a pain in his chest, going into his arm and neck. He was sweating too.

We thought he was having a heart attack, and how we wish it had been. That would have been "fixable." We have lived with the reality that Billy's cancer could return at any time. We now face the reality that it has and we know that Melanoma is one of the deadliest cancers once the lymph nodes are involved, as his were. The cancer has spread throughout the body and lies dormant for years. When it does return, it returns with a vengeance. People ask about treatment. There isn't any curative treatment. Billy has a tumor in both lungs and all the nodes in his chest are enlarged. The doctor has given him from "weeks to less than six months" to live.

Sunday, 10/14/01

The surprise party last night was turned into an incredible prayer service for Billy and me. We're very thankful for that! It was too late to contact everyone to stop the party from going ahead. Paula said there were many tears. Everyone is so shocked and saddened by the news. It was very hard on her to be there. (Paula told me much later that the party was also going to include a surprise for me ~ Pastor had added some things as a going-away to my leaving as his secretary.)

The CT scan of Billy's head is normal. He's had an echocardiogram (normal) and tomorrow he's having a CT scan of the abdomen and pelvis. The last test will be a total body bone scan.

O Lord, please keep my focus on You! Now, more than ever before in my life! Billy and I are facing a battle and we want to face it victoriously. We can only do that through and in You! We need

Your wisdom on decisions to be made. Please quiet our spirits when needed. Please help us to stay focused on the main thing!

That's why I made the banner for Billy today: "Keep The Main Thing The Main Thing. Keep Your Focus." It's hanging in his hospital room (more for me than for Billy).

They moved Billy from the cardiac floor to the oncology floor today. We know in our hearts what's wrong. Yet, there was something "permanent," almost "final" about being moved to the *cancer* floor. (What is it about certain words that invoke the emotions?)

Monday, 10/15/01

They did the biopsy today. We should know the results tomorrow. Sometimes my mind goes into the "what-if" land of make-believe. "What if" it's all a big mistake? "What if" they got someone else's x-rays mixed up with Billy's?

We've had about a million visitors! Everyone is so good to us. And, God has even supplied us with some humor!

We were eating dinner when a nurse came in and said that Billy had been discharged. I asked about the bone scan scheduled for tomorrow. She said that it had been rescheduled for the 26th. I asked how we could wait that long. She said that "…it really isn't "that" important."

I guess the stress had gotten to me because I screamed at her that maybe it wasn't "that" important to her, but that my husband has been diagnosed terminal and it was very important to me!! We left the hospital at 8:30 p.m.

We stopped by the CVS pharmacy near the hospital to get Billy's prescriptions filled. The clerk came back to tell me that they don't stock the Morphine. I asked why not…being so close to the hospital? She said, "Because it's a drug!" To which I replied, "Well, I'm not standing on a street corner!!!"

Wednesday, 10/17/01

It's 3:20 p.m. We've waited all day for the promised results from the biopsy. We're starting to get miffed. The report has been ready to send to the doctor since last night, but can't be until it's signed off on. It's so frustrating! We've been promised a call by the end of the day. Billy came home late Monday night, but still has a bone scan to go through on the 26th. The pain is controlled by a time released dose of morphine. There are two other pain meds to take care of his headaches and for break-through pain when needed.

Our attitude is positive. We're focusing on the positive things God has given us instead of "Oh, poor us." *We just wish the doctor would call. It seems so cruel to keep people on the edge of their seats at a time like this!!*

Turns out that the report was ready to be signed, but the pathologist hadn't signed it. I finally called and asked to speak to her. She said that she had ruled out the tumors being a new site so she'd have to figure out where the original site was.

I asked her if it's not likely to be his Melanoma. She said, "He's a Melanoma survivor?" I couldn't believe that she was working on a report and hadn't read his chart! She said it made sense because it looks like Melanoma. It'll take another twenty-four hours to grow the culture, but she's sure that's it.

Thursday, 10/17/01

God knew I needed the devotion today on Job, and the fact that God knew what He was doing, and that He's the only truly trustworthy One we can lean on. It speaks of how the Lord will reveal His character in ways we can't imagine. It promises that I will see God more clearly through the dark times.

We heard the final verdict this afternoon. Billy's melanoma is back. The doctor has given him from "weeks to no more than six months" to live. It depends on how fast the tumors grow. It's been a rough week. Even though we knew in our hearts, there's still something about hearing it from the doctor that brings Reality into focus.

The world stops tonight. As I look forward, I see no future for me. My future has been "our" future for so long now. I don't know where to go from here. *I later realized that my Grief began at that point. "We" no longer were united with one future. Billy had stepped off into a new path leading to heaven. I stepped into whatever the future holds for me without him.*

Victor came tonight to work on a wedding video with Billy. When he came in, his eyes were red and swollen. They'd had a family meeting and he told everyone about the results of Billy's tests. Billy was on the phone. I was standing in the family room. Victor came over...we both cried.

Friday, 10/19/01

Billy had a great day today! He's been himself. He has had very little pain. Jimmy and Kathleen came to visit. Pat and Chuck brought us dinner. We got a couple of gifts and a video of Justin and Tyler today. They are growing so fast!

Sunday, 10/21/01

We went to Dave and Wendy's for Quinn's birthday party yesterday. Kenny, Diana, and Patrick were there. Billy wants to see everyone as much as he can. And, they want to see him.

I watch and listen to Billy as he talks and witnesses to those around him. He talks so boldly. Yet gently. God is being glorified in many ways, and my heart is breaking. I long for a future with Billy – a long future. I love him so much. I pray that I'll be able to give him what he needs. I know that God will take care of me as I need His strength.

Monday, 10/22/01

We saw Dr. Essig this afternoon. Billy's decided not to try any treatments. There really aren't any effective treatments for reoccurring melanoma. I support his decision. Everything in me wants him to live, but I believe the most unselfish thing I can do is to let him do this his way.

I pray that I never get hardened to what God has for me. I really need to seek His will and His way a lot more though.

Wednesday, 10/24/01

We signed up with Hospice today. Cathy got a lot of Billy's meds straightened out. She reassured us about things like pain control and told us what to expect as the cancer grows.

It is my prayer that Billy and I will remember to praise God through these next few months. As hard as things are right now, we are trying to keep our focus on God and His blessings.

Thursday, 10/25/01

I went to Capital to work on the tithe records today. Billy went out with Pastor Dunn for a while. Earl is coming to work on the deck. *(We got a Yorkie on October 5th. Susie is less than two pounds so we had to renovate the deck to keep her from falling through.)* Pastor Reynolds came to visit tonight.

It's hard sometimes to look through the storm to see the rainbow. The Christian life is a twenty-four/seven way of life. I love to see (or hear) about God working in a way it can only be credited to Him.

People are giving credit to Billy and me for how we're "handling things." THAT, my friend is God at work with His "peace that passeth all understanding!"

Friday, 10/26/01

Billy had a bone scan at the hospital today. Johnny and Doris were here for a visit so they went with us. Kenny, Diana, and Patrick also came. We enjoyed the visits so much. There is such a renewal of a bond with everyone. Kenny assured me that if I ever need anything or if I ever have any trouble with anyone that he's there to help me. I feel so protected!

Billy's pain intensified greatly tonight. I had to call Hospice around midnight. They raised his pain meds by fifty percent. He slept good for the rest of the night.

I get spiritually drained sometimes. Right now it's hard for me to find time to pray and do an in-depth Bible study. I don't know why. Seems that being retired would offer a lot of time for these things. We are adjusting to a new way of life right now. But, I need to watch to be sure I don't grow cold.

Saturday, 10/27/01

The bone scan showed "non-malignant" masses in Billy's left jaw, shoulders, and left knee. A "metastatic appearing" mass in his left ninth rib. We'll get a better read on Monday from Dr. Essig.

One of Billy's co-workers from Exxon came for a visit. Victor and Billy finished the video tonight. Glenda, Jessica, Courtney, and Summer visited for a while. The girls were unsure about coming. They didn't know what to say. We talked and I assured them the pain is under control and that I'm going to keep him at home. They wanted to know what I'm going to do. I assured them that even if I move from Fredericksburg (as Billy and I have discussed), I want to stay in their lives. They were so happy to hear that! Makes me feel loved!

Sunday, 10/28/01

Billy woke at 4:00 a.m. coughing real bad and having a great deal of difficulty breathing. Hospice okayed cutting the waiting time on the break-through meds to every hour, and they've ordered oxygen to be brought in.

Paula came to Fredericksburg to go to church with us today. She and I surprised Billy by signing "Amazing Grace" for him. Amanda, a seven year old girl in the church, signed the Pledge of Allegiance for Billy too. He was very blessed.

Paula brought meatballs for lunch. Lisa and Allen brought the boys after church. We really enjoyed the day!!

Chapter Twenty Two

11/1 ~ 11/30/2001

I Am So Blessed
To Be Here

Thursday, 11/1/01

Darlene came today. She shared a lot with us about how she's never seen a Christian die a difficult death - it's always been peaceful. She went over a paper with us telling about the signs that death is near.

Susie continues to be a joy to us. She loves to steal Darlene's pens when she leaves them lying on the sofa!

Billy tires so easily. His retirement funds were dispersed today (the stock comes later).

Sunday, 11/4/01

We had a real good night. Billy only got up one time because of pain. He was up two or three more times, but that's okay. It's hard to believe sometimes that Billy is really dying. Our minds sometimes go to the future We talk...about my future, and about his future in heaven. We are enjoying Susie so much. She's a real delight!

Victor and Glenda went with us to Choice this afternoon to hear the Griffith family sing. Then, we went out for dessert. Billy had a rough evening.

Monday, 11/5/01

Last night was pretty bad. Billy's breathing was very labored. He woke in a lot of pain. It's spreading too. He talked about death a lot last night. It helps us both to discuss these things. It helps me to know what Billy thinks about what I should do after he's gone. He finds comfort in helping to guide me - reminding me not to make hasty decisions.

Friday, 11/9/01

Tonight was great for Billy! That's good, because the last few days have been rough. We continue to raise his pain meds. He becomes drugged until he gets used to the increases.

Our church family at New Life is so supportive! Pastor Dunn comes often to see Billy. It means a lot to him that Pastor "loves" him so much!

Saturday, 11/10/01

Paula came today. Victor videotaped her and Billy talking about their lives. It was great. Billy is drugged. He's not bouncing back this time. He talks out of his head sometimes. I find that I'm doing a lot of grieving for Billy now. Maybe it will be easier later. I read a joke in Readers Digest last night about a man and wife waking up and having something funny happen. My heart ached to have one more morning when Billy and I would wake up – retired and nothing special planned for the day. Retired – with a future together for an unknown time…without cancer dominating our present and about to end our future.

Memories are precious. Billy and I are trying to make some memories now. I'm going to miss him. God, in His wisdom has already been directing my thoughts to the future to help me deal with the present. It helps so much…it's all about balance.

Billy told me tonight that he feels his time is getting shorter. He even prayed, as we knelt, before going to bed and asked God to bring him on home - he's tired and he's ready.

Sunday, 11/11/01

I can't imagine what the future has in store fore me as I struggle to hold onto what's near and dear to me. I have to believe that God has it in His loving hands. The most precious "thing" I hold dear on this earth is Billy. Yet, I have to be willing to let him go. How else can I survive? It's hard enough to let him go without doing it kicking and screaming.

Tuesday, 11/13/01

Billy continues to decline. Last night was a pretty sleepless night. Billy was up constantly. I could get bummed on a day like today when I'm so tired - on a day like today when I know that I'm going to lose Billy. But, even today, God's love and His grace and mercy shine through. Today I'm tired. Today I grieve. But, not like the world grieves. I hold onto the hope I have for a bright tomorrow.

Wednesday, 11/14/01

We had a great day today! Billy was "his old self." I finally worked through a lot of emotions and have concluded that I need to stop living in the world of the "dying" and start to live again. My joy is being robbed. Billy is still here with me. He still holds me just about every night as we drift off to sleep.

God is faithful. He always has been. He always will be. He has to be! He's GOD!!!

Saturday, 11/17/01

Pastor Reynolds called last night and asked Billy and me to come to the Time To Build Thanksgiving Banquet. He was showing the video that Billy did for the campaign and wanted to honor Billy. It was very hard on Billy to go, but we were so glad we did.

Allen, Lisa and the boys, Steve and Lesley, Paula, Dad, and Karla, all came down today for a Thanksgiving dinner that Lisa brought. The guys did a lot of work around the house for us. It was a great day!

Sunday, 11/18/01

I have been so busy caring for Billy over the last month that I've hardly prayed and haven't done any Bible study. For the last few days I felt Billy pulling away from me. Last night it hit me. I needed to get into God's word. So, I stopped, came to the bedroom and read the first chapter of John. It was wonderful! And, when I finished, I went downstairs and woke Billy to come to bed. He was like he'd always been ~ tender and loving. We serve a jealous God. He is understanding when illness takes us away for a while, but then, He'll say, "Enough is enough! Come back to your first Love for a refreshing." I'm so glad He's like that!

Wednesday, 11/21/01

I talked to Dr. Essig today. He feels that Billy is holding his own. His immune system has kicked in. It seems that when he was on oxygen a couple of weeks ago that the tumors had shut off the path of oxygen through the lungs. While he was on oxygen the lungs were busy rerouting the air passages. Once they had done that, he didn't need the oxygen any more. God really created an incredible thing when He made our bodies. So, it looks more like the six-month time frame unless his immune system shuts down.

Thursday ~ Thanksgiving Day, 11/22/01

We went to Paula's today. All five brothers and sisters were there. It was a great dinner. Billy slept all the way home and most of the day. He is taking between 660-720 mgs of morphine a day, plus 900 mgs of Neurontin to block nerve pain.

What would we be doing now without our church family and our family? God has been so good to us. Marriage is good too. I am so blessed to be with Billy – to help him in this transition. Walking with God is vital too! He is the greatest Friend we could ever have!!!

Chapter Twenty Three

12/1 ~ 12/31/2001

I Find A New Focus

Sunday, 12/2/01

Paula, Billy, and I went to Mary Jane's yesterday, and came back today. We enjoyed it, but the trip was hard on Billy. *Will this be the last trip we take together?* We wish Mary Jane could be closer to us. It's been good seeing her.

Wednesday, 12/5/01

The devotion today said to hold fast to what is good or the world will take it away. Amen! Time is so very precious. It's going by so fast with Billy and me. For a few weeks I let satan rob me of my joy in just being with Billy. I have been so focused on losing him that I've forgotten to enjoy the time we still have. I began last week living one day at a time. We are enjoying our time together once again.

Friday, 12/7/01

Billy has had a fantastic ten days or so. He had become so lethargic that he asked for something to pick him up. They gave him 5mg of Ritalin and it worked wonders. He barely napped during the day. We have shopped and worked around the house together. It has been great!

But this week shows Billy wanting to sleep more. He fights it, but he wants to sleep. And, the pain is increasing once again. They raised his time released dose to 360 mg. twice daily. The pain was so bad last night that he had over four doses of the breakthrough medication before we could get it under control. He had a total of 1,180 mgs of morphine yesterday. The nurse last night said the disease is definitely spreading. Billy had already discussed that yesterday. It's no surprise. We know what's happening as reality strikes once again. *He really is dying.*

My devotion today was on not hardening my heart and to pay attention to what God wants me to do with my life. I need to cultivate my heart so that I can hear God. I pray that I never become hardened to His Word. I don't believe I ever could, but I know that I need to cultivate a deeper walk with Him. That's my prayer…just a closer walk with Thee!!

Sunday, 12/9/01

Billy was pretty out of it this morning. They raised his pain medication to 520 mg twice daily and the breakthrough to every half hour. We got a hospital bed because he probably won't be able to do the stairs much longer.

There's a scripture (II Corinthians 12:10) where Paul points out that it's when he's weak, that it's then that he's strong. That's where I am today. Billy's been in a lot of pain since Thursday. It's getting so much worse. He had 1200 mg of morphine yesterday. There is no way I could handle this without God's Spirit. No way!

Monday, 12/10/01

Billy's breakthrough morphine was quadrupled today ~ from 60 mg to 240 every hour as needed. Yet, he functions! We've been told that if your body needs it, you can't get addicted. I guess that's true. Billy "wants" to sleep, but he won't. Again, Darlene told me that I need to prepare (as much as I can) for Billy to die suddenly. His heart and his lungs are now showing a great strain on him. Billy told Jimmy tonight that his time is getting real short. Swallowing is getting more and more difficult.

Wednesday, 12/12/01

Billy told me this morning that he's sorry he has to leave me. He said that God is going to use me to be a speaker like I've envisioned for so long. One thing is for sure…when God strengthens you ~ you grow! And, that's a good thing.

I continue with the desire to get ever closer to the Lord ~ to spend more time with Him. Is God "growing" me through Billy's illness? If so, for what purpose? *Hum…*

Saturday, 12/15/01

They added another medication Thursday for bone pain. Billy and I went to Capital today for the Christmas play. We got to bed at 3:00 a.m. The nurse came out before we left, to check him over to be sure he could make the trip. We went to visit Jimmy and Kathleen afterwards. We were so tired when we got home!

Sunday, 12/16/01

Last night I was napping on the sofa. Billy came over and sat down at my feet and began to rub my legs. He gently said, "O, my Brenda, it's so hard to say good-bye to you, but both of us have to do it, and we will, when God's ready."

I'm so tired today. This is a hard journey to be on right now. What would I do now if my life weren't built on solid ground? There are times when I can't imagine my future any longer. And, there are times when I feel a sense of excitement on entering the unknown.

That has to be from God, because my future has fallen apart in the last two months. My "future" has (or had) Billy and me in it…travelling, doing the video business. Just being together. If I didn't have Christ as my Foundation, I wouldn't be able to deal with this at all.

Monday, 12/17/01

Today ends the journal that I had been keeping for a year. The devotion was on departing gifts. It tells me that my life affects those I come into contact with…whether I want it to or not. It tells me that

I should desire to leave a spiritual blessing to everyone around me. I write...

Needless to say, the most significant event of this past year has been the return of Billy's cancer. I don't need to scan the pages to figure that out, but this devotion today sums it all up so well. I pray (as I did when Ron died) that I will glorify God in all I do through this journey with Billy. He is failing fast (taking over 3200 mgs of morphine a day now).

Billy continues to do what this devotion says to do - to impart gifts to those around him. He advised me on Saturday that in those times I'm alone and lonely to remember that I'm not alone - that I should "be alone" with God. I know that I'm facing an incredible pain soon, but I also know that God will never leave me to face it alone!

Tuesday, 12/18/01

I took Billy to the hospital today for outpatient surgery to insert a port into his arm. It goes into his heart and will be used to administer Dilaudid intravenously. The Morphine just isn't working any longer. Billy realizes that he'll have this in his arm until he dies. The medication is carried, along with the pump, in a fanny-pak. They tell him that he can no longer take a shower. Another thing that cancer robs him of. Yet, he adjusts quickly in accepting what cannot be changed.

Monday, 12/24/01

Christmas Eve. It just doesn't seem like Christmas. Maybe because we have seen only one play. (This is the first time in years that I haven't been in one.) We haven't even been to church very often lately. But, more realistically, I'm sure that it's because of Billy being so sick. He is SO incredible! Darleen says that he's probably within a couple of weeks of dying. So, here we sit, side by side; Billy sleeping, me working on things. I'm so alone and so lonely. I quickly remember what he said to me about being alone. Yet, that doesn't seem to help now.

My mind goes back - back to when Billy and I had a future. Back to when we were finally beginning to have a past together. Three years had given us time to remember things that we had done together instead of with someone else.

My heart breaks in two. It hurts to even think about a couple of weeks ago when we would take walks together at night. Billy sits and he sleeps, drawn in more and more to unconsciousness. He wakens, spends ten to fifteen minutes eating or being out on the deck and he returns to his chair to sleep. He dreams. I know that he does, because he speaks in sign language…a language that I can't understand.

Tuesday, 12/25/01 ~ Christmas

It's been a hard two months…so many feelings and emotions. There has been laughter amid the tears, joy amid the sorrow. And, there has been peace amid the turmoil.

What do you do when the plans that you've worked toward for years are suddenly changed forever? How does your heart make sense out of the incredible pain that comes with the diagnosis of terminal cancer? We've known that Billy's cancer could (even probably would) return some day. But, "some day" is one of those illusive words that are supposed to remain so. They aren't supposed to become tangible.

Billy and I had looked forward to retirement, working the video business part time, travelling, spending time with each other, and getting to know all our grandchildren better. Billy's arthritis was getting pretty bad though. We were going to have to find a better treatment for him.

It's been an interesting couple of months. I'm so thankful that we got Hospice involved right away. How wonderful they are! So very caring and compassionate.

Billy is incredible. He said that it was a shock to hear he had less than six months to live, but he accepted it from the beginning. We both feel that God's timing is perfect. We are so thankful that we're retired so we can be together.

Billy just fell coming up the steps into the kitchen. He missed the top step and fell into the cabinet.

I really treasure the time we have together. We're trying to make every moment count.

Wednesday, 12/26/01

Billy is okay. He tore a couple of chunks out of his forehead. Last night was rough. Billy didn't sleep at all. He was very confused. It hurts him so much to be like this. We went out and ran a couple of errands today. He sat in the car most of the time. His energy is pretty well gone.

Victor came over with Summer tonight. We went into the studio for a while. It hurt to see Billy sitting at his computer knowing that the video for Ethan was the last one he will ever do.

Why does loving, (and losing) have to hurt so much?! Tonight I feel that losing suddenly (like Ron) is easier than watching Billy suffer so much. It's not so much the physical pain - it's seeing Billy losing so much ability to do everyday things. It hurts to see him hurt - to see him sad sometimes.

Friday, 12/28/01

It's a "typical" day. We sit in the family room. The TV is on…Billy sleeps and I play games on my Palm and I write.

Uncle Johnny and Aunt Doris came for a short visit this morning. It was nice seeing them, but hard to see them say goodbye to Billy. We never know when this will be the last "good-bye."

Saturday, 12/29/01

Last night was one of the worst nights that we've had. From 12:30 a.m. on, Billy was up…he was so confused. He fell again, hurting his arm. It's so hard not to sleep, but much worse is seeing him suffer, and wondering what comes next. I don't understand how I keep going. I haven't slept. Yet, I'm awake. I have a cold too. I just wonder how long I can keep this up. I don't want to let Billy down. I want to support him in the best possible way.

Victor and Jessica came over this afternoon. He assured us that he will help me sell the studio when the time comes. That has taken such a load off my mind, and a great one off Billy's!

I don't understand this "will to live" thing. If Billy's body is shutting down, how can this "will" override it? Just doesn't make sense. There's the honest part of me that is thrilled for the time I have with him. Yet, the practical side knows that he's suffering.

Life…death…love…grieving…such involved words ~ with incredible emotions!

Monday, 12/ 31/01

Our faith in God is really strong. Without that, I'm not sure how we'd make it. I remember that shortly after they told us that Billy's heart was okay and that the diagnosis didn't look good (we both knew what they meant), Billy prayed and asked God to give him strength. He felt the Lord telling him that He was bringing him Home. That, coupled with the devotion on Hezekiah that I had read five days before, made it impossible for us to ask God for a healing.

We believe that both of these things were given to us to help us accept this from the beginning. Rest assured, we would like for God to heal him, but we just don't feel led to ask for a healing. There have been many tears and many chances to witness. For some reason, people listen more to a dying man. There have been many memories to laugh about. The support that we are receiving is amazing. So many prayers ~ and that's what is getting us through.

Everyone is amazed that Billy made it through Thanksgiving and Christmas. As we face the New Year, we feel once again that we are nearing the end of his life. We've shared so many things together over these last couple of months. I'm so thankful for the time we have together. Billy has made every attempt to "be alive" as long as he's drawing a breath. "They" see this as a fight to live. Billy sees it as appreciating every moment God gives him and he wants to be a witness for the Lord for as long as he can. Everything is becoming harder now and taking more out of him. I really don't believe that he'll be with us much longer. Whatever this journey brings in the future, I know that I can face tomorrow because Jesus lives. I love that song! He got me through Ron's death and He'll pull me through this journey of Grief again.

I am so thankful for the folks with Hospice. I already knew that Hospice is an incredible organization, but I just didn't know how wonderful they are. We are especially thankful for Darlene, Billy's "regular" nurse.

Chapter Twenty Four

1/1 ~ 1/31/2002

It's 2002 and I Still Have My Billy!

Tuesday, 1/1/02

We had a lot of company today! Billy and I were kissing the New Year in. I had to wake him ten seconds before, but at least we saw it in together! Paula, Jimmy and Kathleen came early. Allen came with flowers and then Aunt Jewell and Uncle Wayne came.

Billy and I had a very nice candlelight dinner in front of the fireplace. It was a wonderful memory in the making!

Thursday, 1/3/02

Pastor Kevin came to visit "Uncle Billy" today. Pastor Kevin's dad and Billy were friends when they were growing up in Alexandria. We were all going to church at Capital for a long time before we connected! Since then, it's been "Nephew Kevin" and "Uncle Billy."

Friday, 1/4/02

I really enjoyed keeping a journal of devotions last year. I wanted to continue in 2002. Life isn't just a one-year journey. It's an ongoing, year after year, day by day event. 2002 comes in with my

Billy still by my side. We don't know how much longer he has, but we do know that his time is short.

This is truly going to be another memorable year in my personal journey of life. I don't look forward to the pain that's coming, but I do embrace my future with a certain "excitement." No matter what else I can say about what I'm feeling, I can truly say that "Because He Lives, I can face tomorrow"...because Jesus lives, I know all will be well!

We all face trials in our lives. Even though some are worse than others, my pain is not negated by that fact. So many have said it's not fair for me to be losing my second husband. They're missing the point that I've been so very blessed to have had two husbands ~ two very wonderful, precious husbands.

I know that I'm hurting and will be hurting very badly when Billy passes away, but I also know that God will see me through.

Saturday, 1/5/02

Paula came this morning. I ran some errands. She and Billy had a great talk. Pastor Reynolds came this afternoon. It was good seeing him again.

Billy didn't sleep at all today. He is extremely short winded. He enjoys people's visits and wants to be a good host when they're here, but it takes a lot out of him.

Monday, 1/7/02

Billy slept until 12:30 yesterday afternoon. He got up for a short time and went back to bed. He went through several "what-if" situations regarding his death last night. When we finished these different possibilities, he slipped away again into his own world where Exxon is important and working is a way of life.

Thursday, 1/10/02

Billy went outside tonight for a while. I went to check on him. He was on the lower part of the deck, leaned up against the rail. He was having a great deal of difficulty breathing. I got him inside and gave him his oxygen line.

He told me that he felt like he was dying and doubted that he'd be alive in the morning.

Friday, 1/11/02

Billy's breathing is so much worse. He can't be alone for a minute now. He called Paula and asked her to come down. He must not be well to ask her to close the office. Jimmy and Kathleen came down too. We are really enjoying their visits. They come at least once a week. We all wonder why we wait until someone is ill to get together more.

Darlene came again this afternoon and raised one of Billy's meds to help him relax. She told him to wear his oxygen all the time now.

Saturday, 1/12/02

Paula, Jimmy, and Kathleen came this morning. Billy never did get up while they were here. They came up and told him hi… talked to him, but he wanted to sleep.

For him not to want to get up with Paula, spoke volumes to me. Later, Victor, Dad, Allen, and Lisa came. Allen helped Billy down the stairs for a while.

Sunday, 1/13/02

Billy slept all night. He's been restless this morning. For over forty-five minutes, he kept trying to get out of bed. He finally beat me and turned to fall on his knees. He began praying in sign language.

When he finished, I asked him what he told God. He looked at me and said, "Tell God nothing!!!" I said I was sorry and said, "What did you ask God?" He said, "To bring me home now."

He got into bed and slept for three hours. What a man! Billy knew that he wanted to pray. He couldn't communicate that to me, but he wouldn't stop until he got on his knees! We kneel at night before going to bed and that's how he wanted to pray this morning…wow!

Monday, 1/14/02

Last night and today have been very bad. Billy no longer listens to instructions. He keeps trying to go downstairs, and yet doesn't have the strength to stand up alone.

He was up all night and was very confused. Lisa came at 11:00 last night and spent the night. I had to call Victor to come and help me with him.

We decided to put Billy in the Hospice area of the hospital. The doctor thinks he's only got a couple of days left. As he was being wheeled down the hall when we got to the hospital, he looked up at me and said, "I don't want to die here." It broke my heart!

Even in the midst of being so confused, not only does his walk with his Lord remain foremost in his heart, so does his sense of humor.

I was with him in the ambulance. Lisa was following behind. Billy is sitting up on the gurney, waving to her and tells me, "Hey, Brenda, watch this!" He immediately drops his head on his shoulder and drops his hands off his gurney. I began laughing and the nurse says, "MR. BROWN, don't do that!!!"

Tuesday, 1/15/02

With increased oxygen, Billy is feeling better. They also found that the steroid he was on had turned toxic. Within hours, he is much improved and the doctor has changed his prognosis!

Monday, 1/21/02

Paula came today (Martin Luther King's birthday). Billy called Deni & BJ to tell them how he appreciated the support they've given Paula. He really blessed their hearts!!

Darlene said that Billy's left lung is no longer returning air and his right lung is so bad, she can no longer hear any wheezing. He was shoveling snow last week! Darlene is amazed that he hasn't had a massive heart attack!

Billy and I have enjoyed our love growing day by day. Love seems to be like a muscle. The more you exercise it, the more it grows, the stronger it gets. Seems like it can't get much better! We have looked for ways to make our love grow, and there is always something that comes up.

Wednesday, 1/23/02

We found out today that Billy's Aunt Helen has a brain tumor, tumors on her lungs, and lymph node involvement. She and Uncle Allen had recently retired. Life was good...hum...

I asked God today what He wants for my future. I pray that the vision He gave me fifteen or twenty years ago will finally come to be. I want to be a speaker for ladies' groups. We'll see. I need only to be available. God will take care of the rest.

Friday, January 25, 2002

Guess I need to reach for God's hand more during this journey we're on. My days sometimes get so busy that I don't make time for God. Of all times in my life, I need to be closer to God now to see me through losing Billy. I believe it's all about priorities. I need to make time with God the most important thing I do each moment.

Saturday, 1/26/02

Today was a very special day. Paula has helped Billy with getting me a birthday present. Billy told her that he wanted to give it to me today...just in case he doesn't make it til next week. *Does he really feel that he's that close to death?*

He gave me a beautiful leather swing coat. It's an incredible gift. Paula went through a lot to find one! They also ordered a cake for me. A lot of people came by today so it came in handy!

James and Melissa came with their girls. James has written a song for Billy. It is so good! Billy has asked him to sing it at his funeral. How wonderful for James to do that for Billy. Imagine having a song written just for you!

Sunday, 1/27/02

All of Billy's brothers and sisters, and many others came to visit the last two days. (B.J. and Deni came after church. It was good seeing them again!) Billy was down yesterday with all the activity. He said it feels like everyone is going to get on the boat and he's being left behind.

My focus changed last week. I've been dealing with the "how" and "when" of Billy's impending death for so long that I've been living with death. My focus got realigned to where I'm now enjoying every moment I have with him.

Monday, 1/28/02

Sometimes like now, I feel that God is far from me. I know that He's not, but I just can't "feel" His presence. Reminds me of a saying… "When you can't see God's hand, trust His heart." Yes, I know that He's with me. Still, there are times (like now) when I pray, "Lord, please make Your presence known to me today." And I rest, assured that He will!

Pastor Dunn came to visit. Renate came to see us too. She was one of the videographers at our wedding. She had never seen the video so we went up to the studio to see the hi-lite. Usually, Billy will go on and show a couple more things that he put together for our wedding video. But, I noticed that as soon as the hi-lite finished, he shut the system down.

After Renate left, he told me that it really bothered him to watch the video of our wedding. He said the memories are just too painful for him. He doesn't want to go back in there again.

Except to help me review the system components so I can sell the studio later, Billy never did go back in the studio. That part of his life was now over. Cancer robs him of that too. I really hate this cancer growing inside my husband's body!

Aunt Helen had her surgery today. We are praying that she will be okay. Billy says he feels like they have a common bond now that no one else close to him can share.

Tuesday, 1/29/02

I get so tired sometimes with the prognosis of Billy's

cancer...one day he's dying. Next day, I'm told he won't make it til such-n-such, on and on...and, each time he rallies and fools us all. There is so much emotion when you think "it's" finally happening, and his coming back from it means we're going to have to go there again.

But, for whatever reason, God's got us here and He will help us deal with the emotions. It's just so hard. *But, I'm so happy each time I get my Billy back (if only for a day or so)!*

From my devotion today: "God graciously directs our paths. The One who placed you on the path is the One who steadies your steps upon it. You will not stumble while on your knees...it's time to pray!"

Lisa brought Justin and Tyler for a visit today. They are so much fun. When Justin saw Billy's oxygen line, he tried to take it off of him. He said, "Off, Granddaddy." He just knew that it didn't look right! Jimmy, Kathleen, and Johnny came for a visit too. It's so wonderful to see how many people care enough to drive all the way here to see Billy!

Wednesday, 1/30/02

Billy hadn't eaten, but a bite or two for six days. He got up at 1:00 a.m. this morning and ate three pieces of pizza, a piece of cake and drank a coke.

Sometimes, I feel that I'm some kind of a horrible person when I get on the yo-yo with "Billy's going soon" and "now he's not." Yet, I know each time it looks like his death is near, I lose him all over again. I prepare myself.

It's only when I get my thoughts off me and focus on Billy and caring for him (and loving him) that I can enjoy being with him and not worry about the future.

Thursday, 1/31/02

Billy was reading about the Doctrine of Angels in the *Wilmington's Guide to the Bible*. He was reading a story by Billy Graham. Pastor Dunn called. Billy told him he was reading and relaxing…to come on by for a while.

Pastor Dunn decided to stop by a store and buy a book for Billy. It was *Angels: God's Secret Agents* by Billy Graham! He had no idea what Billy was reading!

Billy considers that a hug from God, just to let him know that He's still here!!

Chapter Twenty Five

2/1 ~ 2/28/2002

Am I Ready To Lose Him?
Yes...No...

Friday, 2/1/02

Tuesday and Wednesday were beautiful days. It's been in the 70's and 80's - incredible for January! We stayed outside on the deck. I sorted through some drawers and boxes on Tuesday.

It got up to 80 today, but it's cloudy and very windy. We have been here on the deck all day. The roar of the wind through the trees has been thunderous at times. The clouds rush by us overhead, driven by the wind.

We've been reading books on death and dying, books about heaven, the *Wilmington's Guide to the Bible*, and the Bible itself!

We called Barbara this morning. She had planned on calling us today because we've been on her mind all morning. Her prayer for us today was that God would give us the desires of our hearts, and she gave us Lamentations 3:22-23. It talks about God's faithfulness. *"It is of the LORD's mercies that we are not consumed, because his compassions fail not. They are new every morning: great is thy faithfulness."*

I believe that God has given Billy and I today to build a vital memory to help me in the future. There is such peace and joy here today. "Joy" is almost too strong a word... "contentment" – that's the word!

The weather couldn't be more beautiful. There are birds singing, squirrels running through the trees. Susie sleeps in my lap with the wind blowing her hair, making writing difficult.

As I read the New Testament in the Wilmington's Guide, I read something that reminds me of Billy telling me to be alone with God when I get lonely, and it occurs to me that the first time I come home without him, that I won't be alone. God will be here waiting for me. I share this thought with Billy and tears fill my eyes once again as I finally find comfort, knowing that God will see me through the Grief once again.

We've been through a lot the last three and one half months. We've come a long way (as they say). Billy was concerned about me in the beginning...afraid I'd manage the money wrong. So, I've gone through some thought processes with him, hoping to calm his concerns, and I believe I have. I've asked his advice on future decisions. He's helped me a great deal. Even though he knows he's going to heaven (a place far better than here), he feels left out of everyone else's life. Fact is, life does go on for everyone else and it's quite natural to (on a very small level) want to think of everyone else ceasing to exist because we do.

Most who have been care-givers, if honest, would admit it gets hard to see the one you love so much slip away so slowly...*I pause – wanting to put the pen down...it seems to be too painful to go here right now.*

Saturday, 2/2/02

Billy has had a couple of days of growing pain. Today, it escalated considerably. He's gone from 18 mg of Dilaudid an hour to 25 and his boluses from 9 mg to 20 mg every ten minutes as needed. He didn't eat today.

Paula, Jimmy and Kathleen, Pastor and Debbie Dunn, Billy, Sherry and the kids all came to visit. Billy Jr. comes often to visit his dad. They talk...share...laugh together. Billy treasures those visits!

My faith is so strong right now. It's all I have right now! It's all I had on March 20, 1995. And, it's all I need! God is so very faithful. He will never leave me. He can't, He's God!!!

As the devotion said today, "Sorrow looks back. Worry looks around. Faith looks up." AMEN!!!

Sunday, 2/3/02

My birthday. It's been a good day. Billy gave me the beautiful leather swing coat last week, Paula gave me gloves to match. Janet gave me a candle and New Life a wonderful plant. Glenda came by with a bag including some Oil of Olay bath soap with a puff (so very soft). Lisa topped it all off with a doll that plays "Amazing Grace."

Monday evening, 2/4/02

Billy developed a new pain in his back last Thursday. It got so bad, that by last night, we had more than doubled his Dilaudid. It finally eased off a bit. Today has been a quiet day.

Tuesday, 2/5/02

Billy's up to 52 mg an hour with 36 mg boluses every ten minutes. His appetite is nil. Ate a small bit of pizza tonight and said he doesn't want to eat again. He asked me to pray for him today. I read scripture to him tonight. He has a new pain in his lower back now. Darlene convinced him to rest in bed since sitting up is only aggravating it. He said every time a nurse comes, he loses something else.

Wednesday, 2/6/02

I got to the point last night that I did when I cared for Mom when she was nearing the end of her life. I feel okay now. I got my focus off me again and back on caring for Billy.

Paula is so tired and bummed. She's about to lose her life-long best-buddy. She comes here every Saturday and Sunday to visit and to let me get out of the house to run errands. I don't hang out anywhere. I want to be with Billy. He's my life!

Is it horrible of me to say that I look forward to when I can sleep all night again? Someday, some far off day, I will sleep again. Won't I?

Saturday, 2/9/02

Billy heard the testimony of Chief Buddy Farris, an officer who was struck by a car on a traffic stop outside of Richmond, Virginia. They took him to the morgue to find out that he wasn't dead! It's a great story about him being at heaven's doors.

I happened to remember this tape and was able to find it immediately. I called him and he wants to talk to Billy. He'll even try to get here to visit him.

Paula, Billy, and I listened to the tape again. It helped Billy to realize that even the strongest Christians fear certain aspects of death when confronted by it. Remember, it's not being dead that's the problem…it's getting dead!

Tuesday, 2/12/02

The devotion today asks if I have surrendered to God's will for my life? I answer, "Yes…no." It's one of those questions like, "Are you ready for Billy to die?" "Yes…no." How can I be ready for him to die? If we lived to be a hundred years old, would I be "ready" to lose him?

"Yes" – to see him go to heaven…

"No" – I don't want to lose him.

And so it is with losing him now. Surrender to God's will? Of course I do, even though it hurts..

Thursday, 2/14/02

Billy fell last night and then couldn't hold his medicine down. We got to bed about 11:30. He got up at 4:30 and ate a lot of peanut butter crackers and then got incredibly dizzy and weak. He had chest pains. It took over an hour to get him back up stairs to bed. It was very scary. Darlene said Billy experienced an arrhythmia of his heart (a very irregular heartbeat). I couldn't find a pulse during that time.

I love Billy so very much! I'm so very thankful that I'm able to be with him during this time in his life. Again and again, he wonders out loud where he'd be now without me. I'm so thankful that he'll never have to know the answer to that. I will be with him for as long as he draws a breath. Sure, it's hard sometimes. I get tired. I hurt for him and for me. Most of all, I am incredibly blessed to be his wife.

Friday, 2/15/02

Three days ago my prayers changed from a general, "help me through this, Lord" to a more defined "help me today, Lord. Give me the grace and mercy for today."

It has helped a great deal, but, at the same time, there's a sadness. A sadness that I can't think about now. *Maybe "tomorrow," but not now.*

Saturday, 2/16/02

Billy got up at 4:30 a.m. and fell again. His neck is hurting really bad. He was afraid he'd broken it.

Monday, 2/18/02

From the book, *Grace for the Moment,*

As you stand, observing God's workshop, let me pose a few questions. If he is able to place the stars in their sockets and suspend the sky like a curtain, do you think it is remotely possible that God is able to guide your life? If your God is mighty enough to ignite the sun, could it be that he is mighty enough to light your path? If he cares enough about the planet Saturn to give it rings or Venus to make it sparkle, is there an outside chance that he cares enough about you to meet your needs?

I needed that today. Thank you Lord!

Wednesday, 2/20/02

There is no other way to tackle my problems except with God's courage. "Brenda" has already collapsed many times over the last four months. It's God who keeps picking me up and handing me my crutches. I believe their names are Grace and Mercy. God cheers me on. He encourages me and makes me believe in HIM all over again.

Saturday, 2/23/02

Our next door neighbor Bud, died today. He had a heart attack while out with a friend. Bud and Grace are both seventy-six and they've been married for fifty-five years. Grace is so devastated! She wonders how she is going to handle it?! And, Billy is very upset. Bud came over yesterday when we were on the deck. They gave each other a big hug when he left.

Tuesday, 2/26/02

Billy is making a lot of neurological changes. He's developed a new pain in the back of his head by his ear. He is weak, almost falls, drops things. We were up every hour last night. It hurts to see him get worse.

Chapter Twenty Six

3/1 ~3/19/2002

Memories of Billy

Saturday, 3/2/02

Paula came today It's so good to see her each week! Christine, Billy's former supervisor, heard about his cancer. She came today, and she cried when she left.

I had a run in with a clerk in Wal-Mart. I almost cried as I realized my reaction to her was the pain in my heart over losing my Billy. It's almost unbearable! I explained it to her, and asked her to forgive me. We both almost cried.

Lord, how on this earth am I going to withstand the pain of losing Billy? How?!!

Sunday, 3/3/02

I find rewards in little things; a hug from my grandchild, a special word from my husband, a card from a friend.

So many tell me how wonderful it is that I'm "standing by Billy." Where else on this earth would I be? I'm his wife and that, my friend, makes me special!!

I've been working on a Creative Memories album of our lives. It includes pictures from our childhood. It has really been a blessing to work on this while I sit with Billy. He enjoys seeing the pages as I complete them.

I sent an email asking people to share their memories of Billy. Here are some that have come in:

"When I think of Billy - I think humor, funny, hilarious yet a sweet heart. I remember most the fun times at Bible Institute - I so looked forward to Monday nights with him and Paula and the wild antics between them. I laughed at his jokes and comments so hard so many times that it brought tears to my eyes. He always brightened my day, no matter how rough it had been."

–Becky

"The first word that comes to mind when I think of my uncle Billy is love. I remember him coming to our house when I was a kid and he was just so sweet to us. He'd pick us up and tease us and it was the greatest feeling. Many times children do not feel that they are really "seen" - well, Billy saw us and made sure that we knew it. That has never, ever been forgotten and never will be.

The second word, just for fun, is "crazy." His sense of humor is through the roof - absolutely fearless. I remember all the jokes he'd play on my mom and I remember her getting him back one time. She can't tell the knee-slam-to-the-sink story without laughing herself silly. Mama, you gotta tell Brenda if you haven't already.

I love you guys so much. Strength, Peace, Love, Light."

–Jo

"The first thing I think of when Billy crosses my mind is how CRAZY his sense of humor is (and a real PRANKSTER)... I was his victim many times. I've spent my life trying to "repay" him for the "fast ones" he's pulled on me... too many to list...

I remember two incidents vividly... Once, before we hit puberty..he was in the bathroom for a verrry long time, primping I suppose, combing that red hair of his... I don't remember what he did to me to prompt me to "pay him back" but anyway... I positioned myself at the bathroom door, on my knees... picture this... I had my thumbs and index fingers simultaneously pulling the corners of my eyes down and my lips pulled up... a really ugly face I did make... and waited and waited and waited...Finally he opened the door, saw me and screamed like a girl. I just about wet my pants laughing so hard... Ahhh, sweet revenge!!!

The second time, we were all growed up! (but not at heart.) He used to spend a nite or two at my house in Springfield... this was in the early 70's... He was pulling the night shifts, driving the Exxon tanker... and instead of going home to F'burg and heading right back to work, he would crash at my house. Well... this one time, he asked me if he could use the master bedroom bathroom to wash up and shave, whatever... Again, I don't know what he did to me that made me want to pay him back, but I can guarantee he did SOMETHING!!!! So... he was in there shaving....I snuck into the bedroom and as loud as I could... I yelled BOO!!!! His right leg shot up, he jumped, grunted really loud and banged the dickens out of his right knee on the bottom of the bathroom sink. I thought I would bust my ribs laughing and I think he limped for a couple of hours.

I never could "break" him of pulling pranks on me...but the "paybacks" were so much fun!!!! I still laugh when I think about those times..."

–Paula

"I wanted to get recorded in the "Book of Billy." Simply... "Billy Graham!""

–Roy   (*Roy admired how Billy would share his faith. He nick-named him Billy Graham.*)

"I can't come up with one word that describes Billy. There are too many. I can't tell you how he and you have impacted my life and Chuck's also. I fell in love with Billy as soon as I got to know him. But, of course you understand that, can't you? Ha! He is one of the most caring people I know and the two of you fit together like honey and bees."

–Pat & Chuck

"My first impression of Billy, it was GENUINE."
–Janet

"I began to love Billy before I ever met him, when you shared with me about the balloons that he had delivered to you at work and his message about saving the dance for him.

Secondly, when I did meet him in June of 1999, I was impressed with his generosity. Here he was turning over his prize, "*the ghost*" (our car) to three women he did not know, only one of which he had heard of through his wonderful wife.

Thirdly, I loved him with a deep and very special love for the fantastic storybook way he loved my special friend. To see the two of them together and see her happier than I had ever known her to be (and Brenda has always been a happy optimist) was so precious to me.

Billy, more than anything, because of conversations with you, because of the way you have dealt with this illness (as told by your loving spouse to me). I am motivated by you to be more in love with the Saviour. You are an example, your wife is an example and has been for so long in my life. I am thankful that God chose to have mine and Brenda's path cross - hence yours as well.

My friend, keep on going toward the light. Soon you will leave all darkness behind and you know that Brenda will be with you in a short time. Actually in eternity one is no longer bound by time, so to you it will seem but the blink of an eye. All of us who know and love her will be here to love her, to serve her and to do whatever we can as she continues her journey toward the light."
–Jan

"It's hard for me to chose only one word to describe Billy. I think of him as kind, loving, caring, sincere, fun (a joker), a GREAT HUGGER (his hugs always make me feel sooooo good), he always smells wonderful, and his beard is so soft!

I just love being around him because he strengthens me and makes me more faithful. He makes me feel like I matter to him.

What more can I say - I love him!!!"
—Deni

"Billy is sincere. I never heard him say anything that he did not sincerely believe. I can say he was a true blessing to me in helping me get through the final year of the Bible Institute."
—Cathy

"I feel a better person having known him."
—Renate

Wednesday, 3/6/02

Mina came tonight to see Billy. She really focused on his bolting and got on the phone with the doctor on call. Billy has been throwing up for two days - he's in pain - he's weak. They took him off two meds and put him on three new ones. The bolting stopped within a couple of hours!

He wants me by his side all the time. I can't even go down long enough to put something in the microwave. I love him so much and I want to be with him!

Paula and I were talking tonight. It's one of those things you say and before you know it, your life has changed. I said that I felt like packing Billy and I up and moving in with her. Long story short, she's calling Northern Virginia Hospice tomorrow to see if it's possible. I could use some help and we'd be on one level. It makes good sense.

Thursday, 3/7/02

Billy's been in bad shape. We've begun the process to move to Paula's on Saturday. Billy is very excited! In the middle of a million phone calls, we're dealing with the final distribution of Billy's stock with Exxon. We always have a lot of balls in the air at once!!!

Friday, 3/8/02

Billy woke at 5:00 a.m. and wanted to dance. We danced to

our favorite two songs. How wonderful (very romantic)! Thanks for the memory, Billy. Thank You, Lord for answered prayer!

Saturday, 3/9/02

We moved to Paula's today. Allen and Lisa came to help out. It all went very well. Our neighbors all cried. They know that Billy won't be coming home again. Billy is so heaven-minded that he left the home he's had for twenty-six years and never looked back. He just doesn't have earthly things on his mind these days.

Tuesday, 3/12/02

Billy's nurse came yesterday. The case worker signed him up Sunday with the local Hospice. If you had ten doctors, you'd have ten treatments, I guess! They've begun changing his medicine already. They had their team meeting today and everyone agrees that we need to change him from Dilaudid to Methadone. That would get him off the I.V. which would thrill him!

To do this, we need to check him into the Hospice facility in Arlington. They found a bed was opened so we checked him in. I'm staying with him. I can sleep right by him on a roll-away. He's in a ward with three others.

Wednesday, 3/13/02

Billy looks to me to answer the questions the doctors ask. He slept all night except when they woke him to give him medicine. I slept pretty good myself, knowing that Billy was being cared for.

Friday, 3/15/02

Good morning, Lord! What a beautiful day. This whole winter has been incredible. Thank You!! Lord, thank You for dying for me. Thank You for the life You've given to me. You gave me wonderful parents, friends, family, Ron, Billy. Thank You for everything! I stand amazed at how You have blessed me throughout my entire life.

Lord, as I sit by Billy's bed in the Hospice Center, I yearn for us to return to a "normal" life of no cancer. Seems to my mind that You could have used him for many more years. He always glorified You with the videography work he did. Yet, your ways are much wiser than mine. I'm not going to spend precious time worrying about that. Life is too short to spend it in "What-If" land. I'll just praise You for what we have today.

Saturday, 3/16/02

What joy a hug and a kiss from a grandchild can bring! Lisa and Allen brought Justin and Tyler to see Granddaddy. They are so cute and so full of life!

Billy seems to be better; at least in his breathing. He sleeps more and more as the methadone is increased. He's supposed to adjust. (I pray that he does.) He has a minimum of "weeks" left. The doctor here says that he's no where near death. And, he promises that we're going to get Billy "functional" again and not so sedated. I'm thrilled to have him with me if he's not in pain. I don't want him hurting just to keep him with me.

We're settled in at Paula's. It really feels like home. When I went to Fredericksburg this week, the house seemed so empty. The life was gone from it. Knowing that Billy is not coming home again kind of settles that. I'm praying about going on and putting the house on the market soon. I've pretty well decided that I don't want to stay there. I'm not sure where I'll end up, but I know that I don't want to stay there alone. I'll keep praying and waiting on God. I don't want to act on emotions. And, I don't want to burden Billy with my thoughts. He's already said that he would feel better knowing that I'd be moving closer to Paula, Steve, and Allen.

Sunday, 3/17/02

In just three days, it will be seven years since Ron died. Seven years. How in the world has it been so long? It's so hard to believe.

I went and got Steve, Lesley, and Susie this afternoon and brought them to the center. Steve hasn't been feeling well enough to drive so they were glad to see Billy. Susie about went crazy when

I put her in the bed with Billy! He was so happy to see her. The nurses told me that I can keep her here, but I declined! They encourage pets to stay with patients.

I'm tired tonight. I'm tired of me and of this need to know the future. I lie here in Hospice among the one who died today, the one beside us who is so near death, the lady who's afraid to live, and my precious, precious Billy. He is in so much pain. It's being managed, but he's got to be in incredible pain to take so much to control it.

And then there's the ten-year-old girl down the hall who lost her mom today; the wife of the marine who's not in such good shape herself; the daughter who will now care for mom, and…me. What about me? Where am I in all this? I wonder how I've done it for the last five months. Can there be anything worse than to watch the strong, vibrant man I married be so torn apart from this horrible cancer that grows inside him? Daily, it consumes more and more of my Billy and the man he's always been. Yet, there are traces of him there. They come out in so many ways. My love for him grows daily. And, when I think about losing him, I stop short of going there. I just can't go there yet. I don't need to go there yet.

More than anything, I want to be able to love Billy each and every day without the fear (or dread – or knowledge) of losing him. I can't begin to remember what life was like before October 13th. From a chair in our family room to a rollaway bed beside my husband in a Hospice facility.

It's not just how I got here, it's why? And, where do I go from here? I wonder what it's like to be a child again. I looked into Summer's big beautiful brown eyes today and I wonder what it's like not to live with "death" over me, and I wonder how I can turn Death into a friend – a teacher, like Grief. How do I learn from this experience, something that I can turn into good? I know that all of these questions are answered and summed up in one word - FAITH. It's my faith in God that has gotten me here and through this new journey, and it's Faith that will lead me into tomorrow and all it has to offer. Be it good or bad, Faith will see me through once again.

And remember, Faith is only good as the Object of that Faith. My Faith is built on nothing less than Jesus Christ – AMEN!!!

Tuesday, 3/19/02

Billy is off Dilaudid and on the Methadone. He's very drugged right now as he adjusts to the new medication. He's getting 300 mg every eight hours. We're hoping to go home Thursday.

Billy was so happy to be able to get into the shower this morning! It took every ounce of strength for him to finish and get back to bed, but it was such a wonderful feeling for him.

Chapter Twenty Seven

3/20 ~3/26/2002

Billy's Home

Wednesday, 3/20/02

I was helping Billy with our morning routine this morning. He suddenly asked me, "What's it like to die?!" *There was an excitement in his voice - an excited urgency to know.* I said, "We don't know for sure, but I can imagine that when you take your last breath, that Jesus will be there with His hand out and He'll say, 'Well done thou good and faithful servant! Now, get on in here, Billy Brown!!'"

Billy said, "That's great! Then what?!!" I said, "Then, you turn around and there's your mom and dad and me and Paula and everyone you love!" He said, "That is SO cool!"

I asked him why he was thinking about heaven right then. He said, "Because I'm going to die soon. I know I am."

Billy had always been kind of nervous about what the actual dying would be like. But this time, there was not an ounce of worry or fear. There was an absolute excitement!! That is such a blessing to me, to know that he wasn't at all scared.

Billy has declined overnight. I don't understand, but maybe the doctor can explain it more. The "strange" thing is that today is the seventh anniversary of Ron's death and the first day of Spring. It's raining. (*Does the sky know that it's a sad day?*)

Billy and I went outside once today. He really didn't respond very much from late afternoon on. He continues to decline. The doctor really feels that he must have thrown a blood clot or something.

I just wish that Billy was awake enough to respond to me. When Paula came in, she kissed him and he puckered his lips up at her! It was precious! Everyone agrees that it's a physical decline and not the meds.

We had a lot of visitors today. Victor called and Paula put the phone to Billy's ear. He couldn't respond verbally, but we could tell that he could understand what Victor was saying. About five minutes later, Billy became coherent. He wanted to know what had happened to him. He looked at me and said, "I love you, Baby!" Then, he was gone again.

Today is the seven year anniversary of Ron's death. How ironic it would be if Billy went to be with the Lord today. It's so weird to think about Billy dying at the same time I see the anniversary date of the first love of my life. *Lord, how much pain can I take?*

Thursday, 3/21/02

Billy no longer responds to anyone or anything, not even pain. His temperature rises. They're sure that he has pneumonia. The doctor said that he could respond to the antibiotic, but doesn't really believe he will. She said that we're going to lose him soon.

Friday, 3/22/02

Last night before I went to bed, I talked to Billy for a long time. I told him again how much I love him and I told him that I know how much he loves me and that he probably was trying to tell me, but just can't. I told him that I'd be okay as we've discussed before. And, I said, "Thanks for the dance, baby."

I went to sleep ~ eighteen inches from him. At 2:45, the nurse woke me to tell me that he was gone. I wanted to be with him, but God knew that and would have allowed it if it had been in His plan.

Our prayers have been answered. We have prayed that Billy would slip into a coma and die in his sleep. A nurse was with one of the other patients and heard him take the final "deep breath." It was very peaceful.

What happened? We were supposed to go home yesterday! I'm so sad. I just can't believe that he's gone. I'm so thankful for all the memories and for being here with him. I may not have been holding his hand, but I was with him and I believe that he knew that.

I drive down Rte. 66 on my way to Paula's. I reach Pastor Dunn. Those who have said to call "if anything happens," I can't reach. Billy Jr. has the phone off the hook. (I find out later that Kenny left his cell phone at home.)

Saturday, 3/23/02

People are so wonderful and kind. They all want to help. I'm going to Fredericksburg today to print the funeral bulletins. Billy had planned his funeral. It's going to be a real celebration!

Paula's at the florist. I'm "alone." When I even try to think about Billy not coming back (or that he's not alive), I get very "logical." Deep, deep inside my chest I feel the lump and hold it down. I just don't want to go there yet. I slept well, but felt really drugged when I woke up.

Sunday, 3/24/02

Church at New Life was great! It's the first time I've been in our new building. Everyone is so wonderful.

Grief ~ Time ~ Cancer ~ they have been teachers to me. As I begin this journey once again, I wonder what will become of me. Where will I be a year from now?

Paula, Mary Jane, Kathleen, and I went to the Passion Play at Capital tonight. Pastor Reynolds dedicated it to Billy. When he explained that Billy had video taped the plays for the last several years and that he had passed away, there was a collective gasp across the sanctuary.

What a blessing the play was! This was the first year since they started doing the Passion Play seven years ago that I wasn't in it myself.

Monday, 3/25/02

We went to view Billy's body before they took him to the church for the viewing. It went better than I'd thought. The viewing was wonderful. The Statler Brothers CDs played. A hundred and seventy one people came. What a blessing!

Tuesday, 3/26/02

The funeral was a blessing too. It was raining today. I was going out to the car to get something a couple of hours before it began and ended up falling. I've hurt my wrist, but it will be okay.

Everyone tells me that the funeral was the most uplifting and joyful one they've ever been to. That's what Billy wanted.

Billy's grave is just nine spots up from Ron's and mine. I had decided that I wanted to honor him today too. As we left Billy's grave, we stopped back by Ron's. I shared that if it hadn't been for him (and losing him), I could never have completely appreciated what God gave me in Billy.

Chapter Twenty Eight

3/27 ~ 3/31/2002

A Heavy Sigh and Those First Few Steps

Wednesday, 3/27/02

As I sit in Paula's living room, I feel the loneliness…just finished having a really good cry. I cannot believe you are gone, Billy. We were supposed to come home last Thursday. It just doesn't seem real.

It's that brick-wall thing. We've been running in high gear since Friday and now it's all done. Picking up the pieces begins now. I feel so very numb today. I'm not sure I have the energy to carry on. But, I know that life is going to go on, one day at a time - and, so it must.

I really miss you, Billy. It seems that our three and a half years together were so short. I'm so numb. I love you so much, Billy. I'm glad that you're not suffering any more tho. I'll love you forever!

Thursday, 3/28/02

Ice cubes made me cry today. I got some out for my milk at breakfast and remembered how Billy had to have ice water (with plenty of ice) by his side for the last month. Coming home last night was so hard.

I went to church. That was good. I went to see Grace afterwards. She's so lost. I'm so lost.

When we got the hospital bed, I had them put our bed in the shed. I didn't think about the mattress soaking up the fumes from the lawn mower. It's ruined. Billy Jr. was going to take the bedroom set later so I went ahead and got a new bedroom set. I wasn't planning on doing it so soon, but that's okay.

Friday, 3/29/02

It was an empty wall today that brought the tears. Since I had to empty the furniture for Billy to pick up, I went ahead and bagged up Billy's clothes and gave them away.

I walked by the wall in the laundry room where Billy kept his coats. I ended up in the floor crying really hard. It upsets Susie to see me cry.

I asked God for a hug. Five minutes later, the doorbell rang. The UPS man had an Easter box for Grandma Brown. It was from Lisa, Allen, and the twins. God is SO awesome!

Anniversary #1 ~ one week today...

Saturday, 3/30/02

The last two days have been so bad. Yesterday was the one week date. I guess that had something to do with it.

The furniture was delivered today. It's so hard to go into the studio and see where Billy worked for hours on end, producing so many incredible videos.

The pain and loneliness I feel is so very deep and unrelenting. I don't feel the same as when I lost Ron. It's just as deep and yet, different. Guess that makes sense (on some level) that if the love was different, so would the Grief be.

There's such an incredible feeling of loss. It's almost like childbirth the second time around. The first time is scary, but you don't know what's happening. Then, the next time it's more severe and you know what's coming.

We knew for five and a half months that Billy was going to die at some point. But it happened so suddenly and so totally. He was "gone" before we knew it. There wasn't any warning. Tuesday, he was fine. I'd give anything to go back and savor every moment. I'm so glad that I had the conversation with Billy before going to bed the night he died.

My heart is so hurt. I'm so sad ~ so lonely ~ so empty.

Sunday, 3/31/02 ~ Easter Day

Joy cometh in the morning! I'm so thankful for the resurrection of our Lord. I now have two husbands living there for all eternity. They are home at last!

Church was great this morning. I went to Allen and Lisa's for dinner. I stopped by Dave and Wendy's on the way to see Paula and pick up my mail.

The last few days have been very hard. I arranged for the house to go on the market in two weeks. That's going to hurt (everything hurts)! But, I want to move so I'll do what I can to accomplish that. I leave it to God. I trust Him that He'll stop me if He wants me to stay here.

It's Easter morning. It's a time to count the blessings:

- The five and a half months we had.
- The beauty of the weather this winter.
- The hours we spent talking, reading, sitting outside together.
- The birds in the air ~ the wind in the trees.
- The walks we took.
- Watching the rain while we sat on the tailgate of the truck in the garage (talking, remembering, wondering).
- Billy got to shower again after getting to the Hospice facility.
- He had a day of walking around without the I.V. in his arm.
- Steve and Lesley brought Susie to see Billy the Sunday before he died.
- Billy got to see Justin, Tyler, and Summer (and parents) at the Hospice facility the Sunday before he died.

Chapter Twenty Nine

4/1 ~ 4/30/2002

Starting Over - Again

Monday, 4/1/02

I wish I could describe the pain I feel. I miss Billy so much. Everywhere I look, everything I do, everything I eat screams of his memory.

I was cleaning the office tonight and found the following email. It was sent by Billy from home to me at the church on December 5th. The strange thing is that I left the position at the church in October! Billy didn't know Word so he must have sent it by email, printed it out and stuck it in that stack of papers ~ knowing that I'd find it some day when I was filing. That's something he would do. Here's the email:

Subject Line: My Love

I love you more than life.
See you in Heaven
Forever yours
Billy

Thursday, 4/4/02

Dear Lord, "Good morning, Lord! Will I see You today?" Billy used to say that when we woke in the morning and he'd look at Your picture on the wall by our bed. Now he lives with You and I am forever grateful! I am also heart broken that he's not here with me.

Thank You for going to Calvary, Lord. That was not an easy assignment! Yet, You willingly kept Your focus and mind set on that day.

Friday, 4/5/02 ~ 12:26 a.m.

Dear Lord, Please stop this pain in my heart. Please don't let it hurt so bad! Yes, I remember Your Spirit asking me (when Billy and I began getting serious) if I was willing to love him if Your sole purpose was to have me care for him as his cancer returned to take his life. I said yes, and I'm so thankful. I wouldn't change a thing.

I guess it's normal not to want the pain though. Yesterday when I "saw" the cabinet in the garage, I was reminded that we were going to clean the garage after we retired. God, I'm so sorry, but for the first time, I feel like asking, "Why, why so soon?" And, I guess (if I'm to be honest), I do ask You that question, but I still trust Your timing. I still know that I'll never know this side of heaven the answers to the questions that my heart cries out in pain to ask. And, as I reread this last paragraph, I know that the questions cause pain.

So I will (with Your help) get back to being thankful for what You've given me. I'm just so lonely, so very lonely. Help me, God. Please help me!

Later ~ 7:30 a.m.

Thank You, Lord, for drying my tears. Thank You for all You do for me, day by day. Lord, give me a hunger for more of Your Word. Like Billy told me, when I feel lonely, let me remember what he said and lean on You.

You really are all I want for the rest of my life. You have blessed me with two wonderful men. I want to spend the rest of my life glorifying You and passing on the word of Your grace and mercy and (most of all) Your love!!

As I begin my day, Lord, I ask that You watch over my family. Thank You for all the calls I've received. Thank You, Lord. Thank You!

Later still...

I'm better this morning. I know that God's going to get me

through, but somehow, I thought that a lot of Grief work had been done over the last six months. It has been. The shock, the "accepting" that I was going to lose Billy. All that HAS been worked through. It's the EMPTY feelings and the MISSING him that I couldn't possibly have worked through "in advance." And, that's the tuff part. Not being able to feel myself wrapped in his arms once again, or a shared sunset or beautiful day - all the neat "everyday" stuff.

Saturday, April 6, 2002

Prayer is a cry of faith! God answered my prayer for a hug last week. I feel so blessed and so special when God sends me a hug.

Allen and Lisa are coming to help me today. I want to get the stuff out of the attic and see if I can mow the grass. I'm not sure that I can pull the starter.

The loneliness is almost unbearable. There is just such a void in my heart where Billy used to live. I am constantly amazed that I have to hurt so bad. And, I wonder how long I'll hurt. It's amazing how very strong another's presence is in our lives. Then, when they're gone, the void is just tremendous.

When Mom died, I felt a real sense of relief (of getting my life back). I cared for her for five months, like I did for Billy. But, with Billy, I don't feel this sense of relief. For some reason, I never felt that caring for him was a burden. I got tired, of course, but I was glad to care for him. With Mom, I had a husband and son in high school so being separated from them was hard, even though I wouldn't have been anywhere else, but taking care of her.

I still don't understand how this can hurt so bad. It seems like it would be easier this time; knowing what it's like and having the last five and a half months to say goodbye. But, you know what? I think God let's us forget the deepest feelings of Grief. Maybe, because, just like in childbirth, if we remembered the pain, would we be so willing to do it again? Maybe - maybe not. Anyway, I know that I'll survive and someday I'll even be happy that I did. Right now, I'd be glad to just go on home with Billy and Ron. *I wonder what they're saying about me!!!*

Sunday, 4/7/02

Today was a wonderful day! I woke up with a joy in my heart.

Church at New Life was very soothing. (It was our first day with Sunday School classes.)

I went to Steve's for lunch with him and Lesley. Then, I went to Paula's to go to church and spend the night. I have several errands to do tomorrow in this area.

Monday, 4/8/02

I woke this morning from a dream about Billy and me sitting at Paula's table. I reached out for his hand. My elbow slipped off the chair. We laughed and our hands met. I said to him, "It is so good to have you back, if only for a moment!"

Billy was his old self (before cancer). I could actually remember what it had been like. I could remember those feelings after I woke up. Thank You, Lord!

Later in the afternoon...

I'm back home and cleaning things out again. That puts me back in the land of "Reality" where Billy used to live and work and make my world spin. I found his baptism certificate and other things that sent me back to the floor, doubled over in pain.

Later in the evening...

God gave me another hug soon after I cried out to Him. Pat (from Louisiana) called to get my address. She wants to send me a book to read. She said that she didn't know why she picked up the phone and called instead of emailing. (I explained it.)

Thursday, 4/11/02

I went to Paula's tonight. We went out to eat and went shopping. I had taken Billy's wedding band, along with the angel pendant he gave me for Christmas last year, and had the pendant mounted inside his ring. We went to pick it up tonight. I put it on the chain I wear around my neck.

Friday, 4/12/02

I wonder where the tears of my heart live. Doesn't seem to take much for them to appear. All I have to do is say something about missing Billy or share a special memory of him and there they are, on a moment's notice ready to fall from my eyes. Many times I hold them back. Which brings up another question or two. How do I have that power and why do I exercise it? Why would I want to hold back? It seems that the tears hold the pain because when I really let them flow is when I really really hurt. THAT'S IT!!! The pain lives in my tears. However, the healing lives there too, because crying helps. I know it does. That makes sense. To be cured of other kinds of pain sometimes takes surgery. The procedure and the recovery hurt, but then you're okay. Crying hurts - but then I'll be okay Someday I'll be okay. "Some" day.

Saturday, 4/13/02

I am so empty without Billy. I know that I am incredibly blessed with a wonderful family, terrific friends, two church bodies. But, Billy and I shared all that. Without him, just about everything has lost meaning and purpose. As I write through my tears I don't want to feel like this. I want to be joyful in the Lord and glorify Him, but I just can't get through this pain. I know that I have never hurt like this. (I couldn't have and survived.)

Everything I see, do, eat, or live screams of life with Billy. When he left and went to heaven, he took my heart, and I don't know how to go on "happily." I know that it's too soon to expect to be happy, but I also know that I've got a long time for this journey of Grief and I just don't want to face it again. Sometimes I wish I could slip into some kind of coma or maybe have a "nervous break-down" and slip from Reality. *I did hit my head today on Paula's car. God, that could certainly bring on a coma or something, couldn't it?*

I'm watching Touched By An Angel. Andrew is by the bedside of her son with her. He tells her that, "God wants you to give your broken heart and spirit to Him and He will restore it all to you. God loves you."

Oh, God, help me to survive again. You remind me (again) that You asked me if I was willing to be used like this. To face this pain again if Your purpose in bringing us together was that I'd care for Billy as he died from his returning cancer. I know that I hesitated before answering. It wasn't a rash answer that I gave You. Maybe I couldn't remember the pain of the loss of Ron at that point, but I could remember the joy I was then sharing with Billy. I knew that we had a future (however long) of happiness together. And, I was willing to risk the pain to enjoy the glory.

So, why do I cry out to You now, not really wanting to go back on the deal, but wanting to escape the pain? I never did figure out what the purpose of hurting so bad is.

It's all about faith, I believe. Faith that You are in control gets me through and it relieves a lot of worry.

Monday, 4/15/02

I've spent the day working in the office, going through all the videos from beginning to end. It's a project Billy and I were going to do *when we retired*. Oh, how I wish we could have done that. We did go through a lot and gave many away, copied others. But, we didn't scan each tape.

I've watched so much of Billy's life go before me today. A life before me, before us. There are many skits (most by Billy, Billy Jr., and Victor). I laughed out loud so many times today.

I long for another twenty years with Billy. To see him so healthy and know how his end would come leaves me feeling so very cheated tonight. I know that I haven't been cheated. Quite the contrary! We lived more and closer in the almost four years we had than many couples live in twenty years together. For that, I am eternally thankful.

Still, I go downstairs, into the family room, or out to the garage and I feel more alone than I've ever felt in my life. I don't remember ever feeling so lonely. I remember what Billy said about being alone with God when I feel lonely. And, oh, Billy, I try. I try so hard to let God fill the void, but I just can't feel the emptiness in my heart filling yet. Your absence fills my heart. And, I know that as long as that is there, I can't begin to live again.

Wednesday, 4/17/02

Alone – in the dark. Literally. I was pouring my heart out to You, Lord, on the computer and the lights went out. The entire neighborhood is black (really black)! Called the electric company - can't get a live person on the line to find out what the problem is, but the phone's so smart that it's reported the outage, using the phone number. Technology - isn't it grand?! Actually, I'd like to speak to a person to find out when they expect to have the lights back on!

Lord, I already felt alone in the world tonight. The blackness that now envelopes me only magnifies those feelings. When I left church tonight, I cried all the way home. I felt Billy's absence stronger than ever before. I missed him so badly. I remember when he was alive and well. I remember us going to church, hand in hand, walking in and greeting everyone, holding hands whenever anyone prayed to You. I remember the hugs and the jokes and the searching of Your Word together in church.

I wonder if I really want You to bring me home too. Do I hurt that bad, to where I just can't take it? *Is this Your Spirit asking my heart these questions?* Honestly God, I don't believe that's what I want. I know I have a lot to live for. I have a lot to do.

I also know that the lights will come on again when the problem is fixed. I know that the pain won't always be this dark. It's just that I don't like the discomfort of the lights being out and I certainly don't like the pain of the Grief being so strong.

Just that suddenly, the lights are back on. So, God, why doesn't Grief work like that?!

Thursday, 4/18/02

I went to Maryland today. Lisa and I went house shopping with the boys. We had a lot of fun. I found one I really like, but can't put a contract on it until this one sells. I'm glad that God's in control of this too or I'd be crazy!

It was good seeing them. I look forward to being around them more. I stayed for dinner to avoid rush hour, but it was still a bear! There's no such thing as good traffic anymore!

Friday, 4/19/02

Debbie and I were supposed to look at houses in Virginia today, but she got sick so I came back home. A couple of agents came with clients and another lady has already called about coming tomorrow. I hope it sells this weekend. I really have a need to get settled.

I went to BJ's today. I got a rib-eye. I cried while I was there. It was so painful to be there without Billy. He was the cook. He was the one who told me what to buy today and how to prepare it. Only problem is, I never watched him cut the steak into serving sized portions. I butchered it! *No pun intended!* Will the pain ever be gone from everything I do?! I didn't realize how much eating would hurt. For over three years, Billy cooked for me. He loved cooking for me. Even if he was going to work at night, he'd have my steak and baked potato in the refrigerator (always with a love note written on top). I am very thankful that I have the experience in Grief to know these memories won't always hurt so bad. I know that some day the memories will be good and bring great joy and comfort.

Aunt Julie (Ron's aunt in New York) is very sick. She only has one lung and has pneumonia. They aren't expecting her to live very long. I have such incredible memories of her and Uncle Jerry. *See, those memories bring me comfort tonight. Thank You, Lord!*

Saturday, 4/20/02

Good morning, Lord! It's a beautiful day. Thank You! Thank You for all the blessings. Today is the seven year, one month anniversary date of Ron's death. How can it be so long?

And, I remember one month ago today. It would be the last day that Billy would be even slightly responsive to us. It was raining that day but we went outside one time. It was the day that he was so excited as we discussed what it would be like to die and go to heaven. My mind wonders for a moment but, it's too painful to continue.

Tuesday, 4/23/02

Aunt Julie died a couple of days ago. I came to New York for the viewing with Allen, Lisa, and the boys. We left last night at 10:15 and got into NY at 2:45 this morning. We're going home tonight so I can take Steve to Johns Hopkins tomorrow to see a specialist.

The wall seems to be up today. I miss having Billy with me. How I wish he was here to hold my hand. Oh, Lord, to hear him call me "Puddin Pop" one more time (*the tears come and stop short of beginning their descent*). I wonder what happens to the stopped tears. Are they held in reserve to fall later, in front of the new tears, or do they replace future tears? Seems like sometimes they multiply like rabbits. (I believe they must intensify too.)

I also realize that I'm fast approaching the time when I will be the next generation of *"the elderly."* Is this how it was for Mom & Dad or for grams and grandma? Did they sit and watch the children and babies and wonder what it would be like to turn back the clock, to be young again, married and raising the children? Or, were they like I am? I am very glad to sit and watch and even to participate by collecting a wet kiss or two ever once in a while? Were they glad to be "retired" and non-constricted by the 9 to 5 (or 7 to whenever with Pastor Reynolds) timeframes?

Seems that there are tradeoffs everywhere and with every situation that life offers. It's called taking the good with the bad, I guess. It's times of Grief and pain that makes it hard to remember the good-ole-days. Someone today mentioned that I have so many good memories of Billy. I agreed, but added that those memories hurt a lot right now. She was surprised by my response. It really makes sense if you think about it. The memory of Billy calling me "Puddin Pop" makes me long to hear those words from him again.

The Lord has brought a couple of those memories to my mind recently. I was in the grocery one night, on the way home from work when, over the loud speaker, I hear, "I love you, Brenda. You're my life!" Billy had seen the van in the parking lot as he passed by and came in. He asked a clerk if he could borrow her mic. She looked at him and said, "Sure." That was so very romantic!

And, it was just like Billy when he could tell someone on the phone had asked how he was doing, for him to cry out in a pitiful voice, "I'm dying!!!" (Scared people sometimes.)

Pastor Dunn told me yesterday that my joy will be returned in the future - that the present is but a vapor, but what seems impossible to explain is that time for me is at a stand still. I'm frozen in today. Today, where Billy's absence is magnified. Today, where the pain and tears are but a thought or a touch or a fragrance away. I know it will be many "todays" before I'll be whole again and able to enjoy the joy without the pain. Oh, but I will. I will be whole again…*someday.*

Friday, 4/26/02

It's so bright that it overshadows the stars and clouds and everything else out tonight. The moon was an awesome sight tonight as I headed down Rte. 95 towards Fredericksburg. I don't know when I've ever seen such a glorious moon. There was one star off to the left in my peripheral vision, but just slightly visible. Everything else was overshadowed by the brilliance of the moon.

Today has been a wonderful day (yet, a sad day). I sold the house this morning - the house that Billy owned for twenty-two years before I came along - the house that we loved being in together.

People would ask if I had a "problem" moving into a house that Billy had shared with Christie. I never had any qualms in that area. When we were here together, we were in our home. And, after we were married, we redecorated much of the house to make it "ours." Billy always said that I made it a "home" with my special touches. No, there were no problems in that area - 9 Yosemite Lane has been our home.

But today I sold it and that makes me sad. As I sat signing the papers I realized that I would once again be sitting across the settlement table from a man and wife and I'd be alone.

The moon tonight was so brilliant that it seemed to be there just for me to show me that God is incredibly in control and that He's holding my hand all the way and there's not a step that I have taken, am taking, or ever will take alone.

Saturday, 4/27/02

I put a contract on a townhouse in Laurel, Maryland, today. It's the perfect home for me. With the seller's market in Maryland, there's no guarantee that the offer will be accepted, but my faith is in God, not in the housing market.

Sunday, 4/28/02

My dear Billy,

Hi there! How's heaven? I can only imagine what you must be doing right now. I guess it must be normal to wonder (to imagine) and to even wish I was with you. But, for some reason, God's chosen to leave me behind again.

Billy, so much has happened since you left on March 22nd. I guess you know that I fell two hours before your funeral service. My hand and ankle still hurt. Guess I'd better see an orthopedist this week. It's really easy to ignore physical pain when the emotional pain is so horrific.

For some reason, I actually expected the pain to be easier this time. After all, I've been here before and we had almost six months together to prepare. But, it's impossible to prepare to lose the love of your life. Our talks about what it would be like didn't even touch reality. How could they?!! Everything important to me seems to be changed. Maybe "dulled" would be a better description.

Going to church is so difficult without you. I can't bear the emptiness beside me. Remember how you'd hold my hand, how you'd be looking at the references in the Bible as Pastor would preach? Remember how you would put your arm around my waist while we sang? Oh, Billy, the emptiness in the chair is matched only by the emptiness in my heart.

I haven't been able to go into the family room for more than to run the vacuum or to open and shut the curtains. Your shoes still sit by your chair. (Did we take those with us to Paula's? We must have. I just can't remember.)

Dear Billy, my heart is breaking. I am so very empty without you. How in this world will I ever find the joy to go on and make sense out of my life? All I can do is cry when I think of a future without you. While I'm glad to have found the perfect home for my future, there isn't a lot of joy in my heart. I know that I would never be moving if you were still here with me. I wouldn't have done anything I've done if you were still here.

Did I really do okay in taking care of you? I know that we talked so much about everything, but I feel bad that I ever discussed my future with you. I'm afraid that maybe I hurt you. Did it ever feel like I was wanting to "get on with my life?" I know we discussed it, but did it really feel like that to you? Did I hurt you? And, if I did, I know that we even discussed that and now it really doesn't matter to you. You are far beyond those feelings. So, why do I let dumb ole satan torment me with such thoughts?

I'd give anything for more time with you. Time when you weren't in pain and hurting. I wouldn't wish that on you (even in my most desperate moments). Remember us figuring that God wouldn't bring us together just to tear us apart after a few years? It didn't make sense, did it? You know what? It still doesn't make sense to me. But, I know that it's my pain talking. For you, I am truly happy. You will never hurt again, Billy. You won't go any deafer and you won't get any worse with your arthritis. But, for me, I won't have you cook me breakfast or steak. (I just remembered that you never got to cook that Rock Lobster Thermedore for me.) Billy, we'll never laugh together, go on that cruise together, enjoy retirement, make love together again. Oh, Billy, I'd give anything if you could help me right now. Your words about being alone with God when I'm lonely have one thing missing. We didn't discuss the semantics of how to do that. I'm trying. I'm really trying, Billy.

Monday, 4/29/02

I remember standing on the deck with Billy. I would wonder to myself if I would feel safe on the deck at night after he was gone. We're in a safe neighborhood. (Why did I write "we're" when it's "I'm" now?) Yet, it's that false security thing.

I can say that I have chosen not to get caught up in the trap of fear. Tonight that was really brought to a test. I was cleaning up the kitchen. I heard the squeak of a ball that Susie had been playing with earlier in the day. I turned to pick it up to throw it. She was five feet from me and the ball was no where in sight. It scared me. I knew I'd heard the ball squeak. And, I knew all the doors were locked. So, I reminded myself that I wasn't going to live in fear and went back to work. As I finished, I decided to find the ball. I turned to leave the kitchen and saw the ball against the counter under the dishwasher. Susie must have "thrown" it under there, causing it to squeak when it hit.

Chapter Thirty

5/1 ~ 5/18/2002

They ask, "Are you okay?"
I answer, "Yes...No"

Tuesday, 5/1/02

I realized tonight that I no longer want to cry when I close the blinds at night. Billy always closed them at sundown. He definitely wanted the blinds in my office closed. It used to make me cry ~ I seem to miss him more at night. It's becoming routine now. Yet, as I write about it, I seem to want to cry again.

I'm going to Maryland tomorrow to eat lunch with Allen, Lisa, and the boys. I'm going to measure things one more time and then go to the annual HOA meeting. My life is so busy. Some day I need to start packing!!!

Thursday, 5/2/02

Laughter is necessary for life, I believe. I wonder sometimes why there's no recorded time of Jesus falling down laughing hysterically. Billy used to imagine the disciples sitting around a campfire and Peter would say something silly. Jesus would then hit him on the head with a pebble and tell him to quit being such a twit! Peter, rubbing his head would tell Jesus that wasn't nice!

Billy made me laugh. He used to sit and watch Paula and me joking around. He said he'd never seen anyone make Paula laugh like I do. *I haven't made Paula laugh lately...we do cry sometimes tho.*

Saturday, 5/4/02

We had a yard sale at the church today. That was fun. As we were putting things out, there it was - Billy's pink shirt. Adam had put the things he couldn't use in the bags for the yard sale. I picked the shirt up and held it. With tears coming out of my eyes once again, I told the ladies I was sorry - that I wanted to keep it.

In my devotion this morning, I found out that Mananesah was in Jesus' blood line! (He's the wicked king in my devotion five days before Billy's diagnosis.)

Friday, 5/10/02

Lisa made an appointment for a week from Monday to have her wisdom teeth pulled. I told her that I'd come and help out. She pointed out how busy I am. I explained that that's one of the benefits of retirement. If something comes up, I can postpone Monday til Tuesday!

I really do enjoy not having to work a regular job for now. I hope that I'll be okay just doing the video duplications and work into speaking engagements. I'm looking forward to speaking at the Single's Conference at Capital in June.

Susie just jumped off the bed growling at someone or something (in her wee little head...*I hope...*). You'll never convince her that she can't whoop up on the best of them!

I went to Victor and Glenda's to take them a form they need to set up their business. As I walked up the sidewalk, a red and white truck drove by. My heart jumps with joy as I think, "Billy's here!!!" Then, the pangs of Reality strike so hard that it takes my breath away. The tears come and I hear Glenda's voice behind me. I turn to answer and she sees the tears. I explain what just happened and, I apologize for crying. Why???

Saturday, 5/11/02

I've tried to get someone to mow my grass and can't find anyone. So, I decided to go on and buy an electric lawnmower. (I can't pull the string on the gas powered one.) I manage to get the mower out of the truck and finally got it out of the box, but I can't get the handle on it!

Lisa called to see if I was at home. They wanted to come down to see me for Mother's Day since they'll be at church all day tomorrow. And, she wanted to know if the yard needed cutting. They're willing to drive a minimum of three hours to mow my grass! Allen and Lisa mowed, I played with Justin and Tyler. I'm going to Steve's tomorrow. He and Lesley are taking me out for lunch.

I really miss Billy. It's a longing for an old friend. As I write this, my stomach gets a knot in it as my heart races towards the memories. My natural defenses stop the heart dead in its tracks, just short of arriving at the point where the tears live and fall and make me sad.

That's where I've lived all week, just short of my feelings. Seems that I needed a break from the emotions. Yet, the current of sadness runs deep. The pain may be kept down for a while, but just like the agitator in a washing machine stirs things up, my memory goes back to a time before that night – a time where we were truly together forever - a time when Melanoma was just a possibility.

Paula remembers when M.B. died, she felt guilty for getting his life insurance because he had to die to get it. Lisa expressed those feelings today. She said they're happy to have me moving so close and then feels instantly sad and guilty because the only reason I'm moving is because Billy has died. *I never did like roller coaster rides!*

I talked to Billy, Jr. tonight. He's really hurting. My heart longs to fix it for him, but I know that I can't. Some of what he's hurting over can't be fixed by anyone other than the Lord. I need to pray more for him. I'm hoping to pick Jonathan and Sandy up after school one day this week. That's something Billy and I were going to do once a month, have an afternoon with them at McD's and Toys R Us. *Heavy sigh...*

Sunday, 5/12/02

When I was getting ready for church this morning, I had vivid memories of Billy and I getting ready to go to church together. That was such a special time when we'd get ready to worship together. How we looked forward to retirement and making that a regular thing to do. I remembered him and how he would comb his hair and spray it first and THEN put his shirt on, how he'd tuck his shirt in, get his lapel pin and put it on. Oh, I miss him so much. I'd literally give anything short of my salvation for just one more day with him. (*Who am I kidding? I want twenty or thirty more years with him!!!*)

Got to church...the music begins, and so do my tears. I just couldn't stop them. As I sang (or tried to), the tears continued to fall. When the worship team finished, Mandy came back and sat beside me. I really appreciated that. Then, the tribute to moms began by the men in the church. I wasn't crying alone any longer! They had all us women in tears.

Thursday, 5/16/02

I really enjoyed today. I picked Jonathan and Sandy up from school and took them out for a couple of hours. We went to Carl's for ice cream and Toys R Us for shopping. We talked and had fun. It's fun being with them. It's so important to spend time with our grandkids.

Saturday, 5/18/02

I walk out on the deck with Susie for a moment and the chill in the air that I feel is quickly vanished as I hear it coming - that familiar roar of the wind through the trees. And, I smile as I remember sitting on the deck with Billy that fall day when the leaves were gone from the trees and the weather was a lot warmer then than now. There is no sadness in not having him with me today - just a warm glow in my heart as I remember that day that I wrote about at the time and how it was making a memory for me for later when I would need such memories to make me smile. Thank You, Lord for making me smile today. And, Lord, thank You for Your assurance that one day I'll smile more than I cry. Thank You!

A Closing Note

I'm thankful for the last two entries. In reading this second section, it seemed to me to be very sad (naturally). Still, through the sadness, God always lifts me back up. It's almost as though I can see His hand stretched forth to mine to help me up from the floor every time Grief sends me there again.

I guess that's the one thing that I've held onto through both losses - that God would never leave me. Sometimes the head knowledge of this fact seems to be less than enough, but I know in my heart that it is.

Now, to answer those questions (not sure why some of them come up so soon after a loss, but they do). I'm in the process of moving closer to Allen and Lisa. That will happen the end of June. I'm looking forward to getting settled.

When I sold the studio equipment, I kept the duplication system and will be working to build a client base for those services. As a matter of fact, I have my first large client for July. I expect to be making copies the entire month. (Just after moving - not really good planning, is it?)

Beyond that, I hope to be able to speak to ladies' groups and retreats. I want to share the faith and the blessings that the Lord has given me. One of my favorite characters in the Bible is Barnabas. He was such an encourager for those whose lives he touched. I would like to be a "Brendabus" for those who are hurting. I pray that this book has been that for you. You don't even have to be in the middle of a major loss to benefit from a book like this. You can learn how to encourage those who are hurting around you.

And, now for the big question…yes, I've already been asked this after losing Billy ~ which, by the way, blows the theory after Ron died that the shock was so that they didn't know what else to say…we knew Billy was going to die for over five months. I guess it just comes from the natural wonderings of our minds. What's the question? "Will you remarry?" or, "God brought you Billy, He'll bring you another one."

My life has been made complete in Ron and Billy. When I lost Ron, marriage was all I'd known. To love (and to be loved) was vital to me, but I learned to live with God, as my focus, until Billy came along. I now know that I can make it with Him and Him alone. That's truly what my heart longs for. I've got a beautiful home, a wonderful family, and two fantastic church families to fill my life with. What more can I ask for?!!

Still, there are times when the loneliness is unbearable. I long to have Billy to travel with or to share those special sunsets or windy days with, but I know that God will either send me someone (after He changes my mind) or He will fill that need in me too. There certainly isn't anything my God can't do!!! And, in that fact, I remain confident.

September 6, 2002

It wasn't long after we got the diagnosis, that Billy asked Pastor Dunn to officiate at his funeral service. Our church was less than a year old so Billy was probably going to be the first member to die. (He also asked three of the pastors from Capital to participate.) Pastor Dunn began coming over and spending time with Billy talking about what he wanted his service to be like.

Billy told him the first thing he'd want people to know is that seven years before when he got the original diagnosis that he wasn't ready to die. He asked the Lord for more time to make a difference. Then, he decided to do what the doctor told him to do…to go on with his life.

Billy began getting his older relatives on video in their own video autobiographies. (He did this for my grandma and Ron's dad and sister too.) He did a lot of work in the field of videography. He did so much to help our church and others. So, the message he wanted was that we should all be thankful for the additional seven plus years that God gave him.

Billy wrote the following notes for Pastor Dunn to read during the service. I'd like to end my book with these words from Billy. Thank you for sharing my journey!!

My Dear Paula,

Every road is shorter, every load lighter…with you by my side. All these years you have been such an important part of my life. You have always been there for me whenever I needed you.

You were more than a brother could ever ask for. This, along with your compassion, caring, thoughtfulness, and your unlimited ability to the giving of yourself are the treasures that I hold ever so dear.

Thank you for being my Paula. Thank you for the honor of being your brother. God bless you, my sister. See you soon!

Love, Bill

Jimmy, Mary Jane, and Frank,

When God handed out brothers and sisters, He gave me the best!! One of the greatest gifts of my illness is that we have all drawn closer together. It is my prayer that each of you will draw closer to the Lord each passing day. Watch out for each other and stay in touch with each other. Family is so important!

Love from your favorite brother! Billy

Dear Kenny and Billy,

I think of you two and I am proud. A father couldn't be more proud. You have worked very hard ever since I could possibly remember.

As for being fathers yourselves, I've never seen a greater love than the one you have for your children. What a joy this is! Keep on keeping on, and keep the main thing the main thing.

"Train up a child in the way he should go: and when he is old, he will not depart from it." (Proverbs 22:6) Remember your heavenly Father!

Love, Dad

Dear Allen and Steve,

I couldn't be prouder of you two if you were my own sons. To two very fine sons whom I love dearly. I wish you the best of all things.

I know you will be there for your mom when she needs you. Keep in touch with her, and with the Lord's word always. I am very, very proud of you both!

Love, Billy

Dear Victor,

To my friend and brother-in-Christ. I have enjoyed working with you in the tree business and the video world. I remember so many times of laughter and fun on the tree jobs.

You and Brandon carry the flame of the Tree Removal Service into the future. (Just remember to teach him how to talk right and how to wear his cap!)

I love you, Victor! The Boss

My Brenda,

You have given me so much love, joy, and peace. Our time together was short, but it was beautiful! Soon we will be together forever!

Thank you for your special sense of humor. Your care and concern for others never ceases to amaze me! The Lord has given you so many gifts I couldn't begin to count them all! (Thank you, Lord, for giving me Brenda!)

My Brenda, your love for the Lord is held in my highest estimation of who you are in Him. I feel so much peace and joy when you praise Him "over and over," especially in the midst of trials.

Your willingness to leap out with me means so very much to me. Brenda, darling, I respect you so very much and I can't tell you how much your respect for me empowers me. You give me strength. You have always been there for me; just as you and I both know that God is always there for you. Because we mean so much to each other, I know there will be moments of loneliness for you! There are ways to escape this (some good, some bad), but I know you honey, and I take great comfort in knowing also, that when you feel lonely you will seek and find companionship in our friends, family, and most importantly, in our Savior!

Brenda Baby, you are the light of my life and I love you very much. Thank you for loving me and for loving God. One last thing, Honey. Jesus says to us in Matthew, chapter five, "Ye are the light of the world. A city that is set on an hill cannot be hid. Neither do men light a candle, and put it under a bushel, but on a candlestick; and it giveth light unto all that are in the house. Let your light so shine before men, that they may see your good works, and glorify your Father which is in heaven."

You have been my light, I have seen you shine. My desire is that you would continue to shine for our God, and that you would shine on others as you shined on me. I will see you soon.

Love forever, Billy

Appendix

A Little Insight On Survival

You probably noticed there aren't any initials behind my name, but I'll still state here that I'm not a professional in the medical, mental health, or theology fields.

I'm a Christian. Therefore, that's the context of my journal. Please answer a question to yourself. It's the most important leg of my survival and therefore the one thing I think is essential to surviving such a loss victoriously. If you were to die right now, would you go to Heaven? Unless you answered immediately, affirmatively, and with confidence, please read the track that follows. It was written by my Pastor, Steve Reynolds of Capital Baptist Church. It explains the way to salvation. For you, this is what I would consider to be the first step on this road of Grief — acceptance of Christ as your Lord and Savior. He doesn't promise a life without pain and suffering, but He did promise never to leave us or forsake us or to let us suffer than we can stand (although His idea of what I can handle and mine are worlds apart sometimes)!

Please know (even though it may be only intellectually at this

281

time) that you will get through this — that you will be happy again.
I'd give anything if I could give you a date so you could know for
sure, but I can't. You may (or may not) find happiness with someone
else in the far-far away future. That's between you and God. In the
beginning, I didn't find I had control over my emotions at all times
but many times I did make a conscious decision to be happy - or to
feel the sadness and pain for a while. Emotions are funny things. Just
know (in your mind) that you really will want to live again.

Whatever you do, keep (or get) close to the Lord - He's
wonderful! He's there and He cares. He knows what we're going
through here on earth. He grieves, He cries and He rejoices with us.

Journalize - I found this to be so valuable and I did it every
time an emotion or thought hit me that needed to be dealt with.
Even if you've never written before, you may want to try doing it
now. It helps so much to look back and see how far you've come
(or regressed.)

Reach out — To the Lord, family, and friends. I find it more
difficult to talk to family and friends the further away from Ron's
death I get. It's not their fault but mine — and, I'm not sure why
I don't. I know it helps a lot when I do.

I asked for guidance — but followed my heart as the Lord led
me. I wasn't "supposed" to move for one year (according to the
experts), but I bought a condo within the first two weeks of Ron's
death. It's one of the best decisions I've made.

I'll be praying that God will guide you on your journey. I have
every confidence that He will. He's "no respecter of persons." Take
care — may God bless you!

HOW TO KNOW FOR SURE
YOU ARE GOING TO HEAVEN
(Reprinted here by permission of Pastor Steve Reynolds)

You Can Know For Sure
When asked the question, "Are you going to heaven when you

die?" the vast majority of people say, "I'm not sure" or "I hope so."

Wouldn't it be wonderful if you could know for sure you were going to heaven when you died? Well you can. It is possible to have this confidence.

The Bible says,
"He that hath the Son hath life; and he that hath not the Son of God hath not life. These things have I written unto you that believe in the name of the Son of God; that ye may know that ye have eternal life." (I John 5:12-13).

In a world full of uncertainties, the Bible says you can have the assurance of heaven at death through the Lord Jesus Christ.

God has given us a plan whereby we can be saved and know it. Obedience to this plan can change you from being a (hope-so) person into a (know-so) Christian.

God's Plan of Salvation

Admit that you are a sinner and deserve hell.
"For all have sinned and come short of the glory of God" (Romans 3:23).

"For the wages of sin is death" (Hell) (Romans 6:23a).

Believe that Jesus Christ died on the cross for your sins and rose from the grave so that you could go to heaven.

"...the gift of God is eternal life through Jesus Christ our Lord" (Romans 6:23b).

"But God commendeth His love toward us, in that, while we were yet sinners, Christ died for us" (Romans 5:8).

"...if thou shalt confess with they mouth the Lord Jesus, and shalt believe in thine heart that God hath raised him from the dead, thou shalt be saved" (Romans 10:9).

Call upon the Lord through prayer for salvation.

> *"For whosoever shall call upon the name of the Lord shall be saved"* (Romans 10:13).

Receive Christ Today

"...now is the accepted time; behold, now is the day of salvation" (II Corinthians 6:2)
"But as many as received him, to them gave he power to become the sons of God, even to them that believe on his name" (John 1:12).

If you would like to receive Christ as your personal Lord and Savior, tell God in the following prayer:

"Dear God,
    I am a sinner. Because of my sin, I deserve to spend eternity in hell. I believe that Jesus died on the cross, was buried, and rose from the grave for my sins. I therefore, turn from my sins and put my faith in Jesus Christ to get me to heaven. Thank You for saving me today, and help me to serve You the rest of my life."
    You became a Christian the moment you received Christ. Don't trust your feelings for they will change. Take God at His Word and believe His promises. You can now say, "I have received Christ and on the authority of God's Word I am going to heaven when I die."

"But grow in grace, and in the knowledge of our Lord and Savior Jesus Christ..." (II Peter 3:18).

If you have received Jesus Christ as your Savior and Lord through reading this information, please write or call me at the address or phone number below so I can rejoice with you.
    I would like to send you a free booklet on how to live the Christian life.

Write or call:
Pastor Steve Reynolds
Capital Baptist Church
3435 Aston Street
Annandale, VA 22003
(703) 560-3109
Email: sreynolds@capitalbaptist.org